THEORY AND INTERPRETATION OF NARRATIVE

James Phelan, Peter J. Rabinowitz, and Robyn Warhol, Series Editors

The Vitality of Allegory

*Figural Narrative in
Modern and Contemporary Fiction*

GARY JOHNSON

 The Ohio State University Press • Columbus

For Emily, Chase, and Madeleine

Copyright © 2012 by The Ohio State University.
All rights reserved.

Library of Congress Cataloging-in-Publication Data

Johnson, Gary, 1966–
 The vitality of allegory : figural narrative in modern and contemporary fiction / Gary Johnson.
   p. cm.—(Theory and interpretation of narrative)
 ISBN 978-0-8142-1182-3 (cloth : alk. paper)—ISBN 978-0-8142-9281-5 (cd)
 1. Allegory. I. Title. II. Series: Theory and interpretation of narrative series.
 PN56.A5J64 2012
 809'.915—dc23
                                            2011040059
Paper (ISBN: 978-0-8142-5649-7)
Cover design by Larry Nozik.
Type set in Adobe Minion Pro.

Contents

Acknowledgments		ix
INTRODUCTION		1
CHAPTER 1	Strong Allegory: Shirley Jackson	33
CHAPTER 2	Weak Allegory: Kafka and a Carrot Named Coco	50
CHAPTER 3	Embedded Allegory	79
	Independent Embedded Allegory: Achebe and Kafka	82
	Dependent Embedded Allegory: Barth	99
	Interdependent Embedded Allegory: Barth and Coetzee	106
CHAPTER 4	Thematic Allegory: Roth	129
CHAPTER 5	Ironic Allegory: Dante and Mann	149
CHAPTER 6	The Presence of Allegory: Barth Revisited	182
CONCLUSION		193
Appendix	"Click" by John Barth	199
Works Cited		227
Index		235

Acknowledgments

THIS BOOK has evolved over more than a decade, so the list of people to whom I owe some debt of gratitude is long, too long, unfortunately, to fit in a reasonable acknowledgments section. There are, however, a number of individuals who have been especially helpful in advancing the work to this final stage, and I would like to thank them here.

Andrew Ade, Eric Iversen, and Christine Tulley, all friends and insightful readers, provided helpful feedback on the introductory material. Their comments, suggestions, and encouragement are greatly appreciated.

John McGowan, who was the first to recognize that a work that began as a theoretical approach to the concept of character probably had more potential as a book about allegory, remains for me the ideal reader. For fifteen years John has helped me to recognize both the import of my own ideas and how to shape them into a coherent form. His mentorship has influenced me profoundly.

During the summer of 2005, I had the good fortune to participate in a National Endowment for the Humanities Summer Seminar, "Narrative Theory: Rhetoric and Ethics in Fiction and Non-Fiction," in Columbus, Ohio. Six weeks of focused reading and discussion proved to be a wonderful forum in which to test my ideas and to receive critical feedback from insightful colleagues. I am indebted to each of my fellow participants and to the seminar's director, Jim Phelan.

Jim's involvement with my project predates the seminar by about five years, and it likely would never have made it to this point without him. Jim's own work on a rhetorical approach to narrative has had a clear influence on this book, but his kindness, his generosity, and his patience have been just as valuable to me and just as instrumental in the process of turning some very rough early ideas into a reasonable premise for a book. I take full responsibility for the imperfections in this book, but the fact that it exists as a book at all owes much to Jim.

Readers for The Ohio State University Press—including Peter Rabinowitz, coeditor of the series Theory and Interpretation of Narrative—provided insightful comments and helpful recommendations. As a result, the final draft is, I think, much improved over what I had originally submitted.

I am also grateful for an NEH Summer Stipend, which I received in 2006 and which afforded me time and funds to devote to this project. Of course, any views, findings, conclusions, or recommendations expressed in this book do not necessarily reflect those of the National Endowment for the Humanities.

Finally, I want to acknowledge and thank my wife, Emily, and my two children, Chase and Madeleine. They inspire me every day.

Earlier versions of several chapters appeared elsewhere in print, and I am grateful to those publishers for the permission to use that material here: "The Presence of Allegory: The Case of Philip Roth's *American Pastoral*," *Narrative* 12 (2004): 233–48; and "*Death in Venice* and the Aesthetic Correlative," *Journal of Modern Literature* 27 (2004): 83–96.

I am also grateful for permission from the University of Pittsburgh Press to reprint the Billy Collins poem "The Death of Allegory," which originally appeared in book form in *Questions about Angels* (Pittsburgh: University of Pittsburgh Press, 1999), 13–14.

"Click," from *The Book of Ten Nights* by John Barth (copyright © 2004 by John Barth) is reprinted by permission of Houghton Mifflin Harcourt Publishing Company. All rights reserved. I thank Houghton Mifflin for allowing me to reprint this story in the appendix.

Introduction

IN 1959 Edwin Honig wrote that "Opinion about allegory in literary histories is fairly unanimous: most agree that it is dead but disagree about the date of its demise" (5). Nearly forty years later Theresa Kelley pronounced similarly on the fate of allegory: scholarly objections to allegory, "which become commonplace in English culture by the late seventeenth century, mark the end of [it] as a viable symbolic mode" (1). Even E. D. Hirsch has recently advised that "Allegory . . . has more or less gone away" ("Transhistorical" 551). By far the most entertaining obituary for allegory comes from the poet Billy Collins in "The Death of Allegory":

> I am wondering what became of all those tall abstractions
> that used to pose, robed and statuesque, in paintings
> and parade about on the pages of the Renaissance
> displaying their capital letters like license plates.
>
> Truth cantering on a powerful horse,
> Chastity, eyes downcast, fluttering with veils.
> Each one was marble come to life, a thought in a coat,
> Courtesy bowing with one hand always extended,
>
> Villainy sharpening an instrument behind a wall,
> Reason with her crown and Constancy alert behind a helm.

> They are all retired now, consigned to a Florida for tropes.
> Justice is there standing by an open refrigerator.
>
> Valor lies in bed listening to the rain.
> Even Death has nothing to do but mend his cloak and hood,
> and all their props are locked away in a warehouse,
> hourglasses, globes, blindfolds and shackles.
>
> Even if you called them back, there are no places left
> for them to go, no Garden of Mirth or Bower of Bliss.
> The Valley of Forgiveness is lined with condominiums
> and chain saws are howling in the Forest of Despair.
>
> Here on the table near the window is a vase of peonies
> and next to it black binoculars and a money clip,
> exactly the kind of thing we now prefer,
> objects that sit quietly on a line in lower case,
>
> themselves and nothing more, a wheelbarrow,
> an empty mailbox, a razor blade resting in a glass ashtray.
> As for the others, the great ideas on horseback
> and the long-haired virtues in embroidered gowns,
>
> it looks as though they have traveled down
> that road you see on the final page of storybooks,
> the one that winds up a green hillside and disappears
> into an unseen valley where everyone must be fast asleep. (27–28)

These thoughtful and entertaining obituaries notwithstanding, critics have never quite managed to retire allegory—or any particular instance of it. While it is certainly true that a very particular kind of didactic-religious-personification composition from the Middle Ages and the Renaissance has mostly faded from the best-seller lists and from our collective critical consciousness, to say more globally that allegory is dead is manifestly untrue, and Honig, Kelley, Hirsch, Collins, and others of their leaning understand of course that they greatly exaggerate the rumors of allegory's death.[1] They do so, I think, partly for rhetorical effect—there is something impressive about

---

1. Collins even has a poem in the same collection that revives one of those "tall abstractions" parading around in capital letters. In "The Lesson" Collins writes of "... History / snoring heavily on the couch...." (6).

breathing life into an entity previously thought dead—and partly to underline a claim about the multiple meanings that inhere in the term "allegory"; it is perhaps dead if we only think of it as the kind of didactic composition peopled by upper-case abstractions, but not if we allow ourselves to reconceptualize, redefine, or rehabilitate it.

In short, allegory has not died, despite the passage of centuries since its popular zenith and despite the attempts of a number of influential critics (most notably Coleridge) to kill it. Certainly no contemporary writers whom the academy values pen allegories of Christian salvation along the lines of *The Pilgrim's Progress* or *The Divine Comedy*, but even so these earlier works survive and continue to make themselves heard in the grand conversation of literary history; in that sense they are as vital as ever. Yet allegory has also been kept alive because readers and critics apparently have too much at stake to let it fade completely away and because writers continue to find productive ways to incorporate allegorical elements into their fictions. We find ourselves tending to allegory—especially when it seems severely wounded—because allegory embodies something about the literary experience that we value highly. This, I think, is the only way to explain the constant lure of a much-maligned literary phenomenon.[2]

My aim in this book is to explore the ways in which allegory—or the ghosts of allegory—continue to haunt narrative fiction. Primarily, I intend to demonstrate that allegory can be present in a narrative to different degrees and in different ways and to argue that the presence of allegory can produce a variety of results within a fictional narrative.[3] I contend that many of the problems we face in dealing with allegory stem from the limits imposed by our common, conventional conception of the term and from our general insistence on applying the conventional designation "allegory" or "allegorical" only to entire works. As Edwin Honig claims in *Dark Conceit: The Making of Allegory*, "The form of an allegory must also be the form of the medium (prose or poetry, drama or novel) conveying it. But in whatever medium, it is a form that characterizes the allegory as a totally achieved literary creation" (14). This claim—and in particular its emphasis on totality—compels Honig to see allegory *only* as a genre. While we certainly do find entire works of fiction that are allegorical and that, taken together, might constitute a kind of genre, this does not exhaust the potential of allegory. My

---

2. I will explore the trope of the death of allegory more fully in chapter 1.
3. Ralph Flores makes a similar claim when he argues that since the late 1970s we have seen "a plethora of studies on allegory, and in the writings especially of Rosemond Tuve, Walter Benjamin and Paul de Man, allegory has been detected in surprising places and discovered to have uncanny powers of renewal. Or perhaps allegory did not really die but remained at play in texts—as the enigmatic textuality of texts" (4).

aim is to broaden our conception of allegory by acknowledging not only this kind of complete narrative work but also the many narratives that are not really allegories in Honig's holistic and generic sense but that have traces or hints of allegory in them.

The challenge I have set before myself is to devise a theoretical approach to allegory that will account for both the generic conception of allegory favored by the majority of critics and the fact that we often find evidence of allegory in literary texts that—taken as a whole—do not seem allegorical in the final analysis. I am convinced that the path to this theoretical solution I seek must take us back through allegory's rhetorical roots. So, I will begin there, move toward a novel generic conceptualization of allegory, and finally show how that conceptualization can also accommodate the presence of allegory in nonallegorical narratives.

I understand allegory as belonging to the extended family of tropes. Thus, allegory bears some resemblance to figures such as synecdoche, metonymy, simile, and metaphor. Each of these figures of speech asks readers to understand or to see one thing in the terms of another; they are all substitutive in nature. The classical rhetorician Quintilian was one of the earliest to insist on a close association between allegory and other tropes that rely on an implied or explicit comparison or substitution. For Quintilian, allegory in its most common form actually depends upon and consists of metaphor, which he considers by "far the most beautiful of tropes" (427):

> Allegory, which people translate *inversio,* presents one thing by its words and either (1) a different or (2) sometimes even a contrary thing by its sense. (1) The first type generally consists of a succession of Metaphors, as in
>
> O ship, new waves will take you back to sea:
> what are you doing? Be resolute, make harbour,
>
> and that whole passage of Horace in which he represents the state as a ship, the civil wars as waves and storms, and peace and concord as the harbour. (451)

If we view allegory from Quintilian's perspective, it amounts to something close to extended metaphor, and this is a view that has held considerable sway over the intervening centuries.

I contend, on the other hand, that we need to recognize a significant and qualitative distinction between metaphor and allegory. We can begin to reveal this distinction by first thinking about the resemblances between metaphor and the other tropes closely related to it: synecdoche, metonymy, and simile. As I claimed above, this group of figures of speech operates on the premise of substitution—take x for y, or see x in terms of y. Synecdoche and metonymy substitute one thing for another based on contiguity while simile and metaphor encourage substitutions based on comparison, or similarity. These latter two tropes require a different kind of interpretive work because they force the reader (or auditor) to recognize the common ground between the two terms or concepts being compared. For Quintilian, allegory is more or less an extension of metaphor.

But pronouncements about allegory are complicated by the fact that it has a dual nature, both aspects of which are captured by Quintilian's example. First, when we speak of allegory we might refer to an individual textual element—an allegorical *figure* such as Horace's ship. As Quintilian notes, however, this figure of speech—the state implicitly compared to a ship—is essentially a metaphor. And we can produce countless other examples of the same phenomenon. If we encounter a narrative, for instance, that describes a character who "has a cross to bear" we have what amounts to a metaphorical reference to Christ, though we might be tempted to call this an allegorical character. If there is no substantial difference between calling this figure a metaphor and calling it an allegory, then why do we need the term allegory at all? Why not simply call metaphors—whether they occur individually or in series—metaphors?

The answer to this question lies in what Quintilian's example implies happens when we get a series of this kind of coordinated metaphoric figuration in the context of a narrative. All of the metaphors that Quintilian uses as examples from Horace's poem—the state as a ship, "the civil wars as waves and storms, and peace and concord as the harbour"—work in concert to produce an effect that differs, certainly in degree but also perhaps in kind, from the effect of any single metaphor. Using the term "ship" to refer to the "state" on its own invites readers to understand the latter term through those aspects that it shares with the former (the ground for the comparison); this enterprise, viewed from the perspective of the author, amounts to a strategy for description. But when that author adds metaphoric plot elements (storms as civil wars) and metaphoric states of affairs (safe harbors as times of peace) we have moved from the realm of description to the realm of narrative, which is the second fundamental aspect of allegory. The series of metaphors that Quintilian cites, in other words, constitutes a figural narrative that enacts the transformation of some phenomenon, in this case an idea about governance.

Precisely how this kind of transformation occurs may not yet be clear, so a brief example might prove helpful. Consider the well-known parable of the fox and the grapes from Aesop: "A famished fox, seeing some bunches of grapes hanging from a vine in a tree, wanted to take some, but could not reach them. So he went away saying to himself: 'Those are unripe.'" There would likely be near-universal agreement that this kind of animal parable constitutes an allegorical narrative. However, a close examination of the parable reveals that it does not constitute a series of metaphors, as Quintilian would argue. If this were so, then the fox would have to be a metaphor for humankind, the grapes would be a metaphor for anything humans desire but cannot obtain, and the tree would be a metaphor for some obstacle that frustrates our attempts to get what we want. If we evaluate these instances of figural language on their own—outside of the context of the brief narrative in which they occur—they fail as metaphors; at best, they are paralogical metaphors, or metaphors with no substantial ground connecting the tenor and the vehicle. What, for example, is the intrinsic similarity between the fox and humans? Why not use a dog, or a goat, or a pig? It seems to me that the author could achieve essentially the same result with any number of different animals, a fact that argues against the claim that the fox is a metaphor for humankind.[4] And we could easily make similar arguments against calling the tree and the grapes metaphors. The fox, the grapes, and the tree do act as substitutes (and herein lies the rationale for calling allegory a kind of trope) for humans, desires, and obstacles, respectively, but I would not call those substitutions metaphorical ones. The substitutions in this parable do not depend on similarity; instead, they result from the author's need to realize his rhetorical purpose (to satirize humankind's remarkable ability to rationalize our failures) via a narrative. Thus, the tropes that he uses function as elements of a figural narrative, but they do not necessarily work well as individual figures of speech, nor do they need to.

If one remains committed to defining allegory through the concept of metaphor, then he or she might claim that the parable as a whole functions as a metaphor. In this scenario, the narrative acts as the vehicle and the author's rhetorical purpose acts as the implied tenor. Even this proposal—which seems plausible at first blush—strains the logic behind metaphor. There is no common ground between the narrative, strictly speaking, and Aesop's message; the similarities surface only after we have interpreted the

4. As a counterexample, consider a textbook case of the Homeric simile: Homer uses a lion as a metaphorical figure for Achilles, and to substitute a gopher for that lion would destroy the effect he seeks to produce. Similarly, one could argue that a fox does resemble a human more than does some other animal in terms of the capacity for rationalization, but I am not convinced by this. The ability to rationalize our decisions strikes me as distinctly human, and in that sense no other animal would work well metaphorically here.

story, only after we have decided what the message is. To say, therefore, that the story of the fox and the grapes is a metaphor for humanity's penchant for explaining away our shortcomings is tantamount to making the tautological claim that the author's meaning is a metaphor for his message. In reaching this point in the hermeneutic process, we have actually recognized but not articulated the fact that the figural elements in the parable are the result of the author's desire to narrativize his rhetorical purpose.

So, what we end up calling allegorical figures can be recognized as such only after we determine how they function in the context of a narrative. Sometimes a metaphor is just a metaphor, but sometimes it does become allegorical. We must also recognize the existence of a more ambiguous middle ground, an interpretive realm in which we might not be sure whether a figure is "merely" metaphorical or whether it is allegorical. Some examples of figuration—including the Christ reference I used above—immediately evoke such powerful and well-known narratives that we often jump to the conclusion that they must be intended as allegories. When a character becomes a Christ figure or a Satan figure, or when a garden appears Eden-like, the whole Christian narrative of humanity's Fall gets activated and we tend to read these figures as allegorical ones because we assume that the text in which they appear is a transformation of that prior cultural narrative into a new story. We might be wrong in jumping to this conclusion, but the fact that we do so often make the leap to the allegorical in cases such as these helps to illustrate my larger point that allegory, unlike metaphor, is a concept that we can apply only within the context of a narrative. Quintilian succinctly defines a trope as "a shift of a word or phrase from its proper meaning to another" (425), but allegories need more time and space to develop than what is afforded by a single word or phrase. Thus, I contend that allegories are figures of narrative more than they are figures of speech, taken in the traditional sense.[5] For this reason, among several others, I will be proposing a theory of allegory that is predicated on a rhetorical approach to narrative.

If allegory does belong to the family of tropes, then a rhetorically inflected approach to allegory must pay heed to the root meaning of the term "trope"—that is, "to turn." If we want to identify a genre of allegory, then this tropological foundation strikes me as a good starting point. Rather than by virtue of the more traditional generic markers such as form, technique, or

---

5. This distinction between figures of speech and figures of narrative is meant only to convey the idea that allegory tends to work on a larger scale than do most (other) figures of speech, which often are indeed confined to a single word or phrase. Figures of speech and figures of narrative both apply to "verbal" utterances, but I want to stress that allegory entails the kind of extension characteristic of narrative; when we find allegory, we find not just words, but also (at least) agents, events, and often narrators, not to mention authors who tell stories to achieve some rhetorical end.

subject matter, the individual texts that comprise the family of allegorical narratives resemble one another primarily through the distinguishing feature of the authors' intention to transform something (*turn* something) into something else. When we are dealing with allegory, the "something else" in this formulation is always a narrative that is highly figural. Aesop, to return to the example of the fox and the grapes, has as his ultimate aim the satirizing of humankind's penchant for rationalizing our failures; to achieve this purpose he transforms his observation about humans into a narrative that relies on figuration—things representing or standing for other things. Generalizing from this particular case, I suggest that we define allegory as that class of works that fulfills its rhetorical purpose (whatever that purpose might be) by means of the transformation of some phenomenon into a figural narrative. Paying close attention to the author's rhetorical purpose, which I maintain is the governing principle behind allegory, will allow us to account for both the whole-text type allegories on which critics such as Honig focus and the various textual manifestations of allegory on which I want to shed more light.

In the first section of this book, I deal with the kinds of texts that most readers most closely associate with allegory—those complete narratives that readers interpret, often confidently and relatively unproblematically, as entirely allegorical. I situate these texts on a continuum, ranging from what I call strong allegory (the subject of the next chapter) to weak allegory (chapter 2). I use the terms "strong" and "weak" in a value-free way; I do not intend to privilege the strong over the weak, or vice versa. Rather, as will become clear, these terms simply designate degrees of allegoricalness that we can measure, however roughly, on a narrative scale. Approaching allegory in this way will allow us to talk productively but not reductively about allegory while also allowing us to understand how some texts that are not clearly allegorical (that are not "strong" allegories, in other words) elicit very strong allegorical readings.

While developing the criteria by which to establish a continuum of allegorical narratives can help us to understand and appreciate entire works of fiction—those narratives that Honig calls "totally achieved literary creations"—we also need to be aware that allegory can be present in a narrative without being the defining aspect of it; indeed, allegorical narratives can be present in a larger work of fiction that is not itself an allegory. Thus, in the later sections of the book I move to a discussion of what I call "embedded allegory," subdividing this category into "independent," "dependent," and "interdependent" embedded allegory (chapter 3). Next, I examine further manifestations of allegory in narrative fiction. Chapter 4 addresses "thematic" allegory (a work that presents allegory as one of the themes of the narrative), and chapter 5 lays out a theory of "ironic" allegory (an allegorical narrative that the reader is not meant to take seriously, or to accept at face value).

I realize that such a taxonomic approach to allegory might make it appear as though I am implying that all instances of "allegory" will fit neatly into one of these categories or subcategories and that I can provide clear-cut criteria that we can use to classify these instances. I am not; many, if not most, examples of allegory offer some resistance to this process. I recognize, therefore, that the model I am proposing needs to provide some flexibility and that the borders between different kinds of allegory are somewhat amorphous. Moreover, several of what at first glance appear to be binary oppositions within my schema (most notably strong or weak and interdependent or non-interdependent) might actually work better if we think of them on a continuum rather than as categories with fixed and impermeable boundaries. Similarly, I readily acknowledge that many allegories will be combinations of the categories I have devised—weak independent embedded allegories or strong ironic allegories, for example.

The complexity that becomes apparent as we analyze contemporary instances of allegory will make clear the value of the heuristic I am developing, a heuristic designed not to forge Procrustean categories but rather to provide a flexible schema for recognizing and analyzing the varieties of allegory in what many assume to be an age that is inhospitable to allegory. My aim throughout this book is to provide what I think are good examples of the basic categories I have described above while at the same time acknowledging that some cases are less clear-cut than others. I find this more invigorating than threatening. In my penultimate chapter (chapter 6) I devote my full attention to a very complex story—"Click" by John Barth—that serves as a good test case in the sense that it does not fall neatly into any one area. As we will see, though, even such an evasive narrative will reveal the utility of the rhetorical approach to allegory that I am proposing.

To begin examining in more detail how allegory works, I want to return to my definition of allegory (*that class of works that fulfills its rhetorical purpose by means of the transformation of some phenomenon into a figural narrative*) in order to parse it; I explicate the key terms in the order in which they appear in my definition.

"Rhetorical Purpose"

This phrase denotes an author's intended effect(s). As I mentioned earlier, the author's rhetorical purpose is the governing force behind allegory. This question of authorial intention (and whether it is knowable or something that should be sought) is of course a central concern in the theorizing of literature, especially since the mid-twentieth century. I do not intend to add to the debate that surrounds that issue; instead, I take it as a given that authorial intention is a crucial component of allegory. I concede that we might never know definitively what an author wants to convey through his or her work, but a rhetorical approach to allegory operates under the premise that an author has hermeneutic intentions and necessitates that we make an effort to figure out what these are. This process is not complete guesswork; indeed, the author's intention becomes knowable through the details of the text and its construction. A text progresses in one way as opposed to another, and that fact provides readers with valuable hermeneutic information.

"Transformation" and "Phenomenon"

By "transformation," I mean a change in form, either from nonnarrative to narrative or, if the phenomenon transformed is itself a narrative, from that narrative into another. As a means of supporting this aspect of my definition of allegory I turn here to a rather unlikely source, the historiographer Hayden White. In *The Content of the Form*, White makes the provocative and somewhat contentious claim—at least for other historians—that all narrative works of history must be considered allegorical because the process of transforming literal events into a narrative requires "tropes and figures of thought" (48). We should avoid, White cautions, "mistaking a narrative account of real events for a literal account thereof. A narrative account is always a figurative account, an allegory" (50). While I would stop short of labeling all works of narrative history allegories, I do think that White has the right idea regarding how allegory works. It metamorphoses a real (possibly historical) phenomenon into a narrative structure. If we are to understand allegory, we must recognize it in these terms.

Arguing that allegory is a transformation emphasizes what I see as its "progressive" nature—something happens in allegory, and by that I mean something fundamentally different from what we mean when we say that something happens in a realistic narrative. In this latter instance, we refer to the incidents of the narrative, or the plot, when someone asks us what happens in the work; in the former, we refer to the kind of transformation that occurs as some "thing" is repackaged in a narrative structure. Thus, for example, if I ask someone what a novel such as Richard Ford's *Independence Day* is about, a response along the lines of "a man, struggling with middle age, the death of a child, and the dissolution of his marriage, takes a trip with his adolescent son" will generally suffice. I would be less satisfied, on the other hand, if someone were to tell me that Orwell's *Animal Farm* is about pigs in conflict. Although accurate in the most literal sense, this response fails to capture what most readers would consider the essence of Orwell's novel. Judith Butler's formulation of allegory as "a way of giving a narrative form to something which cannot be directly narrativized" perhaps overstates the case slightly (I will argue that the "something" can indeed be and often is narrativized directly); it does, however, capture the idea that in allegory some thing (that "thing" that a synopsis of the literal Orwell story misses) is transformed into a narrative and that that indirect way of achieving some rhetorical purpose has merit (369).

The phenomenon—the "something"—that is transformed in an allegory could be nearly anything—an idea, a historical event, a lesson or moral, a situation or predicament, or even a previous narrative.[6] The transformation of the phenomenon can be understood as occurring on four levels. In the first level, the phenomenon exists as the allegory's main object of "imitation." Aesop, in his fable of the fox and the grapes, wants to represent a particular human foible—our habit of rationalizing our failures, of devaluing those desires we are unable to attain; this is his phenomenon. At the second level, he constructs a literal narrative (the one with the fox and grapes) that illustrates the phenomenon and provides a bridge to the third level. In the third level, the reader infers the figural intent behind the literal narrative: the fox is a stand-in for any human and the grapes for something the human strongly desires. That inference, in turn, allows us to move to the fourth level, the recognition of Aesop's rhetorical purpose: using satire to goad his readers into recognizing this particular human failing and to reflect on it.

It is my contention that this quadripartite structure—including the object or phenomenon to be represented and transformed, a literal narrative that enacts the transformation, a secondary narrative that emerges from the figural interpretation of the literal narrative, and the author's intention—characterizes all allegorical narratives. To further illustrate how this struc-

---

6. I anticipate that this idea of the "phenomenon" will prove to be the most contentious component of my definition of allegory; it does, I concede, raise some legitimately thorny questions: Is the category "phenomenon" too broad to be of any real help? Does a reader have to know the phenomenon before reading the text in order to "get" the allegory? Does, therefore, allegory depend on an "elite" readership? Is a text (still) an allegory if it is misread or "underread"? Can a text be an allegory if the author did not have a particular phenomenon in mind when he or she composed the work? Recognizing that they present serious challenges, I will address these questions in the chapters that follow, and even more directly in the concluding chapter. At this point, though, we should note that many of the issues that lie behind these questions—meaning, intention, reception—pertain not just to my conception of allegory, but to the interpretation of most any narrative; indeed, these issues have animated hermeneutics for centuries. This takes us back to a basic tenet of my approach to allegory—that is, the recognition of its narrative nature.

ture functions and how the four levels intersect, we can look at Jean de La Fontaine's reworking of the fable of the fox and the grapes. In his version, La Fontaine makes a slight but significant addition to the opening lines:

> A starving fox—a Gascon, Normans claim,
> But Gascons say a Norman—saw a cluster
> Of luscious-looking grapes of purplish luster
> Dangling above him on a trellis frame. (205)

The rest of the story remains largely unchanged from Aesop's telling of it, but La Fontaine's decision to note that the fox's identity—as determined by its geographical and ancestral heritage—changes depending on who does the observing allows us to look freshly at this fable as an example of allegory.

The slight change that La Fontaine makes to the literal narrative of the fox and the grapes does not change the basic way that we read the parable; we recognize the same hermeneutic clues and perform the same interpretive maneuvers toward the same end of discovering his purpose. The observation of the human tendency to rationalize our failures also remains a constant in La Fontaine's version; however, the "name calling" element of the later variation of the story forces a reexamination of the particular phenomenon that the author seeks to narrativize. In addition to bringing to light a particular human tendency, La Fontaine adds another dimension to it: we see this tendency as an existential failing and understand that groups of people are more likely to notice and point out this failing in others than they are in themselves. In other words, La Fontaine shares Aesop's purpose of asking his audience to confront a human weakness, but he adds a wrinkle to that purpose by making it difficult for us to say that the weakness exists in others but not in ourselves. La Fontaine's observation about the human character might be summed up as "humans are quick to ascribe faults to others that they do not recognize in themselves." In a general sense, La Fontaine's rhetorical purpose is quite similar to Aesop's: to force readers to confront a human foible. The particular weakness, however, or the "phenomenon" represented, is slightly different in the two versions of the story.

"Figural"

The addition of the adjective "figural" is meant to designate the transformation of the phenomenon from level two to level three: we recognize that a literal narrative stands in for another, usually more general, narrative. In this sense, the figuration is implicit in the literal narrative, as it is imbued with the authorial purpose. When encountering an allegorical narrative, readers who remain with its literal components are underreading—they remain stuck at the second level of the allegorical transformation. Because allegory is figurative in nature, it bears some resemblance to metaphor, a trope that, as we have seen, some critics actually use to define it. In their *Handbook to Literature,* for example, Holman and Harmon contend, echoing Quintilian, that allegory "may be thought of as an elaborate metaphor in which the tenor is never expressed, although it is implied" (288). While it can be helpful to think of the real phenomenon or rhetorical purpose in my definition as a kind of "tenor," I do not think it is adequate to conceive of the figural narrative that emerges after the transformation as a "vehicle," because that conception does not account for the radical change in form—the narrativization—that is fundamental to allegory. Allegory does more than compare—whether implicitly or explicitly—two "things"; it changes, as I tried to show with my reading of Aesop's fable involving the fox and the grapes, one "thing" into something else.

Still, like metaphor, allegory is figurative or symbolic, and this serves to distinguish it from mimetic fiction. In mimetic narratives, real phenomena are frequently incorporated into a narrative structure—as themes or settings, for example—but this incorporation differs from the kind of transformation that I see operating in allegory. As Scholes and Kellogg note in their landmark study *The Nature of Narrative,* "Allegory is distinguished from other forms of fictional narrative by the illustrative character of its imagery" (109). This illustrative aspect of allegory necessitates a typological approach that often comes at the expense of mimetic representation. I would argue for a continuum, however, stretching from the most obviously allegorical to the most determinedly mimetic rather than trying to fix a clear line of demarcation between the two.

"Narrative"

Critics have long recognized a close association between allegory and narrative.[7] The congruence of allegory and narrative is obvious in cases of narrative allegories—allegorical stories or narratives, in other words. Gay Clifford, for example, claims that literary allegory "is distinguished by its reliance on structured narrative" (14). Speaking to the now well-rehearsed distinction between allegory and symbol, Clifford goes on to argue that "It would be

---

7. I use the term "narrative" here, but I do not want to limit the scope of my project to literary narrative exclusively. There are certainly narratives in other media (film, painting, sculpture, etc.) that could be allegorical.

ridiculous to say that symbolism is impossible without narrative: of allegory it would be true" (14). Narrative is essential for allegory because allegory entails "some form of controlled or directed process" (15), and narrative is the vehicle through which such a process is both represented and structured. The idea of process clearly invokes concepts connected to narrative, concepts such as plot and temporal progression. It is not surprising, then, that Clifford understands allegory as a "kinetic" mode.

But the connection between allegory and narrative runs even deeper than the coincidental convergence that we see in narrative allegories. Indeed, even Paul de Man, a theorist who focuses on allegorical signs within a work of fiction rather than on entire narratives, finds that allegory rests on a structure that is inherently narrative. Subsequent to an interpretation of one of Wordsworth's "Lucy" poems, de Man argues that the structure of allegory manifests itself "in the tendency of the language toward narrative" (*Blindness* 225). De Man's larger aim is to contrast irony and allegory, and he does so through the issue of temporality. Irony is synchronic, allegory diachronic. Even in a lyric poem, what de Man identifies as allegory entails duration, and duration in the context of a literary work implies narrative more than it does lyric, for example.[8]

As a side note, and with the understanding that I will return to de Man in more detail in chapter 2, I want to acknowledge here that in one important way I am following the direction set by de Man when he began the process of rehabilitating allegory in the 1960s by reemphasizing its rhetorical nature; however, de Man's use of "rhetoric" differs markedly from the idea of rhetoric as the "art of persuasion." De Man focuses much of his attention on what he calls the "allegorical sign," which he holds in opposition to the concept of "symbol." Temporality, as I showed above, distinguishes the two; whereas symbol functions synchronically, de Man argues, allegory operates diachronically:

> In the world of the symbol it would be possible for the image to coincide with the substance, since the substance and its representation do not differ in their being but only in their extension: they are part and whole of the same set of categories. Their relationship is one of simultaneity, which, in truth, is spatial in kind, and in which the intervention of time is merely a matter of contingency, whereas, in the world of allegory, time is the originary constitutive category. The relationship between allegorical sign and its meaning (*signifié*) is not decreed by dogma.... We have, instead, a rela-

---

8. Robert L. Caserio arrives at a different conclusion regarding de Man's ideas concerning narrative. See his "'A Pathos of Uncertain Agency': Paul de Man and Narrative."

tionship between signs in which the reference to their respective meanings has become of secondary importance. But this relationship between signs necessarily contains a constitutive temporal element; it remains necessary, if there is to be allegory, that the allegorical sign refer to another sign that precedes it. The meaning constituted by the allegorical sign can then consist only in the *repetition* (in the Kierkegaardian sense of the term) of a previous sign with which it can never coincide, since it is of the essence of this previous sign to be pure anteriority. (*Blindness* 207)

In keeping with his deconstructionist predilections, de Man clearly favors allegory because of its failure to have signifier and signified coincide. As Jim Hansen points out, in de Man's approach, ". . . in opposition to symbol, allegory consciously points to its own temporality and, in so doing, embarrasses its own claims to truth" (672). And it is of course precisely this kind of embarrassment that the deconstructionist seeks in and from a text. The value of de Man's approach lies in his recasting of allegory as a rhetorical figure; this move opens up significant possibilities for recognizing the variety of ways in which allegory can figure into a narrative text even if it does not finally define the generic or ontological status of that text. These kinds of texts will be the central concern of chapters 3–6.

In the first section of this book I intend to address the kinds of narrative texts that reveal the most obvious gap in de Man's rhetorical approach: its apparent lack of concern for complete narratives that not only contain "allegorical signs" but that seem to be—or even insist on being—allegories. Northrop Frye calls such works "actual" allegories, which we have, he explains, "when a poet explicitly indicates the relationship of his images to examples and precepts, and so tries to indicate how a commentary on him should proceed" (90). Because de Man focuses exclusively on texts that are not typically considered allegorical in this sense, it is unclear how such a narrative would fit into the de Manian schema. Readers of actual allegories, I contend, usually find that the allegorical signs succeed pretty well in representing something, no matter what a critic practicing what Hansen calls de Man's "relentless strain of deconstruction" might argue to the contrary (665).

Clearly, a refocusing of allegory through a narratological lens such as I am proposing requires, in addition to a definition of allegory, a clear articulation of what I mean by narrative. My approach to reading narrative—including allegorical narratives—borrows from the work of James Phelan, who proposes a rhetorically inflected version of narratology in a series of five works:

Worlds from Words, Reading People, Reading Plots, Narrative as Rhetoric, Living to Tell About It, and most recently, *Experiencing Fiction.* In each of these works, Phelan starts from the premise that "narrative itself can be fruitfully understood as a rhetorical act: somebody telling somebody else on some occasion and for some purpose(s) that something happened" (*Living* 19). As for analyzing and interpreting such a rhetorical act, Phelan "locates meaning in a feedback loop among authorial agency, textual phenomena (including intertextual relations), and reader-response. In other words," Phelan continues, "for the purposes of interpreting narratives, the conception assumes that texts are designed by authors in order to affect readers in particular ways, that those designs are conveyed through the language, techniques, structures, forms, and dialogic relations of texts as well as the genres and conventions readers use to understand them, and that reader responses are a function, guide, and test of how designs are created through textual and intertextual phenomena" (18).

I find two aspects of Phelan's approach to be particularly useful. One is his recognition of the multifaceted nature of narrative. This recognition allows him to transcend the textuality of narrative and to view narrative as an act whose primary manifestation is as a text. Such an approach necessitates the reintroduction of authorial intention (or "agency") and reader response, issues that can be easily overlooked in the textually oriented incarnation of narratology that had its origins in Russian Formalism and French Structuralism. The second point of Phelan's that I find helpful as I wrestle with allegory is the "feedback loop" as a heuristic for explaining the phenomenon of meaning in narrative. We can see the utility of this approach for my purposes by looking forward to the question that I will claim ultimately decides how critics have approached allegory; that is, to what entity should we turn in order to decide whether a narrative is or is not allegorical? I will posit three possible answers: 1) genetic issues, including the author, his or her intention, and the context of composition; 2) the text itself; and 3) readerly concerns. These coincide neatly with Phelan's tripartite hermeneutic feedback loop consisting of "authorial agency, textual phenomena (including intertextual relations), and reader-response" (18). Rather than aligning myself with any of the three broad allegorical camps I have described above, I am going to argue that each of these entities plays an important role in allegory and that we cannot reduce allegory to a single, primary cause or essential feature. I want to be faithful to what I see as the complexity and variety of actual instances of allegory by offering an approach to allegory that remains flexible. This flexibility can come from something like Phelan's feedback loop because it (the feedback-loop idea) locates meaning in a recursive relationship among a variety of crucial features of the narrative act.

Rather than identifying one particular feature of an allegorical narrative or its origins as the source of its ontological status, I will argue that allegory emerges from a complex interaction among authorial intention, the nature of the narrative text in question, the rhetorical situation that gave rise to that text, and the reader's response to it. This conception of allegory understands it as a kind of gestalt, and it differs significantly from the ways in which critics have traditionally treated this subfield of literary studies. To illustrate how a narrative-rhetorical approach offers a new perspective from which to view allegory, I would like to turn to an exemplary text, George Orwell's *Animal Farm*. I have chosen this novel because it is so widely known and so widely accepted as an allegory; beginning with such a text will relieve me of the task of "proving" that it is an allegory and allow me to focus instead on examining two issues that are central to my concerns in this book. The first of these is the question of how critics usually determine whether a text is allegorical, and the second is why we can achieve consensus about some texts, such as *Animal Farm*, but not about others. My hypothesis is that lingering questions about the allegorical status of some works of fiction point to problems with the usual means we employ to assign that status and that these are problems that a narrative-rhetorical approach can mitigate, if not eliminate completely.

Allegory and Genetic Concerns

A. Authorial Intention

Broadly speaking, we can classify the different conceptions of and approaches to allegory that we find in twentieth-century literary criticism according to how they answer one key question: to what entity should we turn in order to decide whether a narrative is or is not allegorical? Traditional conceptions of allegory give deference to the author; allegory is an intentional act. This remains the dominant idea for a number of contemporary critics and probably for a majority of contemporary readers; for people of this inclination, the intentions of the author are of paramount importance and are the compelling force behind the interpretive act.

If genetic considerations are the standard for judging allegoricalness, then the case for Orwell's *Animal Farm* would seem to be fairly clear-cut, even if authorial intention is the *only* piece of evidence we have. From his own writing on the subject of this novel, we know that Orwell felt that the Russians had perverted the socialist ideal and that he was "convinced that the destruction of the Soviet myth was essential if we wanted a revival of the Socialist movement" (405);[9] he apparently intended his narrative to be a means for achieving a larger political end. Indeed, in the preface to the Ukrainian edition of the novel, Orwell confesses that, following a trip to Spain,

> I thought of exposing the Soviet myth in a story that could be easily understood by almost everyone and which could be easily translated into other languages. However, the actual details of the story did not come to me for some time until one day (I was then living in a small village) I saw a little boy, perhaps ten years old, driving a huge cart-horse along a narrow path, whipping it whenever it tried to turn. It struck me that if only such animals became aware of their strength we should have no power over them, and that men exploit animals in much the same way as the rich exploit the proletariat.
>
> I proceeded to analyze Marx's theory from the animals' point of view. To them it was clear that the concept of a class struggle between humans was pure illusion, since whenever it was necessary to exploit animals, all humans united against them: the true struggle is between animals and humans. From this point of departure, it was not difficult to elaborate the story. (405–6)

Such an explicit pronouncement from the author concerning both the genesis of his work and his aims in writing it cannot be dismissed lightly and must surely influence the ways in which readers engage the narrative. This pronouncement, in other words, provides the basis for an interpretive hypothesis that the reader can then test against the details of Orwell's text. If Orwell claims that he intends his story to expose the reality of Soviet-style socialism, then it behooves his readers, on some level (an ethical one, I would argue), to read it in such a way that they take that claim seriously and as if it were made in good faith, at least until other evidence emerges that might call into question Orwell's professed intention.[10]

---

9. This quotation, and those that follow from Orwell, are from his own preface to the Ukrainian edition of Animal Farm. It is reprinted in *The Collected Essays, Journalism, and Letters of George Orwell*.

10. Readers of Edmund Spenser's *The Faerie Queene* face a similar dynamic. In a letter to Sir Walter Raleigh, Spenser writes: "Sir knowing how doubtfully all Allegories may be construed, and this booke of mine, which I have entituled the *Faery Queene*, being a continued Allegory, or darke conceit, I have thought good as well for avoyding of gealous opinions and misconstructions, as also for your better light in reading therof, (being by you so commanded,) to discover unto you the general intention and meaning, which in the whole course thereof I have fashioned, without expressing of any particular purposes or by-accidents therein occa-

In making this kind of prefatory pronouncement, Orwell arouses in his readers certain expectations concerning the kind of narrative they are going to encounter. Although I have resisted adopting an exclusively generic approach to allegory, the concept of genre is nevertheless relevant to our discussion. Rather than thinking of genre as a kind of literature, we need to understand it, following E. D. Hirsch, as "a type of meaning" (*Validity* 72).[11] Although Hirsch largely restricts his discussion of genre to a section of his book devoted to explaining verbal meaning, what he says has definite implications for our discussion of the interpretation of narrative. This is especially true in the case of allegorical narratives because the author of an allegory writes with a specific purpose in mind and with the intention of transforming some phenomenon that the reader is meant to recognize. For Hirsch, the concept of genre is central to the successful realization of such a purpose, and it applies more to the interpreter than to the speaker of the text because, as he explains, "the details of meaning that an interpreter understands are powerfully determined and constituted by his meaning expectations. And these expectations arise from the interpreter's conception of the type of meaning that is being expressed" (72). Generic expectations, then, are expectations concerning what type of meaning a speaker (or an author) intends, and such expectations are often critical in the process of interpretation. Rather than trying to argue for allegory in all of its various manifestations as a genre with commonly identifiable characteristics, we might more profitably argue that some authors, including Orwell in the case of *Animal Farm*, intend their works to mean something identifiable on a figurative level. In other words, Orwell's preface prepares us to respond to a narrative that meets my definition of allegory: the fulfillment of a rhetorical purpose by means of the transformation of some phenomenon into a figural narrative. The phenomenon, as Orwell makes clear, is the Soviet implementation (or perversion) of Marxist theory, and the fabulist story, of course, is the figural narrative. Once the reader knows that this is what the author

---

sioned" (1). As is the case with Orwell, we do not ultimately have to accept this pronouncement as the defining one concerning the text in question, but we do have to take it seriously.

11. In his later work, *The Aims of Interpretation*, Hirsch puts forward a fairly persuasive argument against a model of interpretation that relies heavily on applying the concept of genre to literature entirely or to some subset of it. Critics who pursue this angle, according to Hirsch, "assume that literature as a whole or some sub-genre of it has a definable essence or telos which can govern the formulation of criteria. But we may be permitted to be skeptical so long as that essence is not satisfactorily defined. According to Aristotle, the essence of any class is that system of characteristics which are shared by all its members, and which are not shared by things outside the class. Thus, a true class requires a set of distinguishing features that are inclusive within the class and exclusive outside it; it requires a *differentia specifica*. That, according to Aristotle, is the key to definition and to essence. But, in fact, nobody has ever so defined literature or any important genre within it" (120–21). This applies to allegory.

has in mind, the act of mapping correspondences between narrative and the historical phenomenon (Napoleon the pig = Stalin, for example) becomes a fairly straightforward process. This is the work that needs to be done if one is to "get" the allegory.

The question of Orwell's intentions raises an important issue regarding the interpretation and evaluation of a work of literature: aesthetic merit. In fact, we can attribute directly to this issue a significant portion of the "death wish" that some critics have harbored for allegory. If we hold Orwell to the standards that have dominated literary studies over the past two centuries and that have been at least partly responsible for the negative connotations that allegory has carried during that time, then we might incline toward a negative evaluation of *Animal Farm* as an aesthetic object—as a fictional narrative, some might argue, it is too contrived and its meaning is too obvious. Moreover, as his preface makes clear, Orwell's primary intention might have been to produce political results ("exposing the Soviet myth in a story that could be easily understood by almost everyone and which could be easily translated into other languages"), an aim that some might see as being at cross purposes with more "purely" aesthetic objectives. And, indeed, many critics have focused almost exclusively on the political aspect of *Animal Farm*. Witness the perspective of Richard Rorty:

> Orwell was successful because he wrote exactly the right [book] at exactly the right time. His description of a particular historical contingency was, it turned out, just what was required to make a difference to the future of liberal politics. He broke the power of what Nabokov enjoyed calling "Bolshevik propaganda" over the minds of liberal intellectuals in England and America. He thereby put us twenty years ahead of our French opposite numbers. They had to wait for *The Gulag Archipelago* before they stopped thinking that liberal hope required the conviction that things behind the Iron Curtain would necessarily get better, and stopped thinking that solidarity against the capitalists required ignoring what the Communist oligarchs were doing. Whereas Nabokov sensitised his readers to the permanent possibility of small-scale cruelties produced by the private pursuit of bliss, Orwell sensitised his to a set of excuses for cruelty which had been put into circulation by a particular group—the use of the rhetoric of "human equality" by intellectuals who had allied themselves with a spectacularly successful criminal gang. ("The Last Intellectual" 141)

This evaluation of the novel does not privilege complexity or ambiguity or even beauty as much as it does clarity of vision and descriptive efficacy. Orwell provided a new way of seeing a particular historical situation, and his intention was to make this as clear as possible.

But should the political and didactic aims of Orwell's novel—even if those aims are undeniably met—automatically engender a harsh aesthetic judgment? Or, perhaps we simply and necessarily have a lower standard of aesthetic merit for works whose genesis is political and whose intentions appear to be didactic? A rhetorically oriented approach to allegory can help us with these seemingly intractable issues by providing a more solid ground from which to offer an aesthetic judgment. Rather than beginning with some ineffable standard of aesthetic merit to which a particular work either mysteriously (and sometimes inexplicably) rises or fails to, the rhetorical critic starts by asking what an author's purpose in writing that work might have been. Phelan explains that "our question is whether the work under consideration is a high-quality example of how to achieve [some] purpose whatever that purpose happens to be" (*Experiencing* 142). Once we have made a hermeneutical determination concerning the author's purpose, Phelan continues, "we can then proceed to judge the quality of the work within the terms appropriate to that kind" (142). Proceeding in this manner allows the critic to value *Animal Farm* as a work of art that aims for very specific ends and that achieves those ends in a way that speaks to the author's mastery of his aesthetic craft. Orwell, in other words, does not have to write *Madame Bovary* in order to produce a novel that has artistic merit, because he was aiming for a different target than was Flaubert.[12]

B. Historical Context and the Author

If we expand the range of genetic criticism beyond the author's (explicitly stated) intentions and look as well at the historical circumstances in which Orwell wrote and at his own biography, some readers might conclude that Orwell's work was bound to be allegorical, whether or not he consciously intended it to be. Fredric Jameson, in his work on postcolonial literary theory, adopts this kind of position regarding allegory. In "Third-World Lit-

---

12. Simply recognizing the need to include the author's purpose in any consideration of aesthetic value, however, does not eliminate the subjective aspect of this kind of judgment. Thus, we are unlikely ever to arrive at some universal standard of aesthetic merit. For a thorough treatment of this issue, and an interesting case of applied aesthetic judgment, see chapter 6 of Phelan's *Experiencing Fiction*. Here Phelan describes four levels of aesthetic judgments, with the fourth allowing for the comparison of whole works even if they have different aims. Phelan comes to the conclusion that we will not find any elusive universal standards on which to base our judgments, but he does not find that this makes comparative evaluations impossible. They will, in all likelihood, be subjective, but this does not mean that they will be completely idiosyncratic.

erature in the Era of Multinational Capitalism," Jameson makes the sweeping claim that "All third-world texts are necessarily . . . allegorical" (69). This is so, Jameson maintains, because the historical, political, and material context of third-world literature always makes the private story of an individual (generally the stuff of novels) a statement about the collective whole. Thus, when Jameson uses the term allegory he intends it in a particular way; he believes that all third-world texts must be read as "national allegories" because these works, "even those which are seemingly private and invested with a properly libidinal dynamic—necessarily project a political dimension in the form of national allegory: *the story of the private individual destiny is always an allegory of the embattled situation of the public third-world culture and society*" (69, emphasis in original). Jameson contrasts the situation of the third-world text with that of the first-world text. In the case of the latter, we Western readers have the "luxury" of accepting the private realm described in literary texts as simply and exclusively private. This "view from the top," as Jameson describes it,

> is epistemologically crippling, and reduces its subjects to the illusions of a host of fragmented subjectivities, to the poverty of individual experience of isolated monads, to dying individual bodies without collective pasts or futures bereft of any possibility of grasping the social totality. This placeless individuality, this structural idealism which affords us the luxury of the Sartrean blink, offers a welcome escape from the "nightmare of history," but at the same time it condemns our culture to psychologism and the "projections" of private subjectivity. All of this is denied to third-world culture, which must be situational and materialist despite itself. And it is this, finally, which must account for the allegorical nature of third-world culture, where the telling of the individual story and the individual experience cannot but ultimately involve the whole laborious telling of the experience of the collectivity itself. (85–86)

In this passage Jameson significantly attaches the adjective "allegorical" not to "text," "story," or "literature," but rather to "culture" itself. Thus, we must recognize that in his view, the determining force behind allegory is culture and its historical and materialist situation.[13]

13. For a trenchant critique of Jameson's position on national allegory, see Aijaz Ahmad's *In Theory: Class, Nations, Literatures.* Ahmad's arguments against Jameson include the assertions that Jameson simply ignores many third-world texts that are not allegories and that Jameson makes out all third-world writers to be inherently nationalistic. For more on the debate that ensued as a result of the work of Jameson and Ahmad, among others, see *On Jameson: From Postmodernism to Globalization,* edited by Caren Irr and Ian Buchanan. The essays "National

At first glance, this conviction that allegory can arise—perhaps even unbidden by a specific author—out of a particular historical situation might not seem to apply directly to Orwell. I think it does, however, for two reasons. First, in his famous essay "Shooting an Elephant," Orwell's thesis echoes what Jameson says, albeit from the perspective of the colonizer rather than the colonized. Orwell writes of his experience as a police officer in Burma during the time of British rule, and he makes it clear that everything he did and everything the native Burmese did reflected the political and historical realities of the context. The impetus for the essay, Orwell recalls, was "a tiny incident in itself" (*Collected* 2), but he comes to see it as revealing of "the real nature of imperialism—the real motives for which despotic governments act" (2). At issue in this case was what to do about an elephant that was "ravaging the bazaar" of a small Burmese village. Orwell, in his capacity as a security officer, was summoned to do something about the situation. With his rifle in hand, Orwell confronted the elephant before a crowd of more than two thousand interested Burmese. While he never intended to harm the elephant, Orwell comments that his position as an officer of the imperialist power and his possession of "the magical rifle" made it so that he would have little choice in the matter. "And suddenly," he writes,

> I realized that I should have to shoot the elephant after all. The people expected it of me and I had got to do it; I could feel their two thousand wills pressing me forward irresistibly. And it was at this moment, as I stood there with the rifle in my hands, that I first grasped the hollowness, the futility of the white man's dominion of the East. Here was I, the white man with his gun, standing in front of the unarmed native crowd—seemingly the leading actor of the piece; but in reality I was only an absurd puppet pushed to and fro by the will of those yellow faces behind. I perceived in this moment that when the white man turns tyrant it is his own freedom that he destroys. He becomes a sort of hollow, posing dummy, the conventionalized figure of a sahib. . . . He wears a mask and his face grows to fit it. (5)

Orwell feels deeply his position here, apparently having internalized the larger political struggle in which he plays only a minor role. Moreover, Orwell's acute consciousness of the plight of the native people and his developing sense of the insidious folly of the British imperial project predispose him to recognize the allegorical potential of this "tiny incident" with the elephant.

Using Orwell's expository essay as background material, we might rea-

---

Allegory Today: A Return to Jameson," by Ian Buchanan, and "Who's Afraid of National Allegory? Jameson, Literary Criticism, Globalization," by Imre Szeman, are of particular interest.

sonably draw some conclusions about how Orwell views himself and his position in the world. In particular, we can say with some confidence that Orwell was the kind of person for whom certain historical contexts were also "rhetorical situations." When I refer to the rhetorical situation, I do not mean simply the setting of the narrative proper, but rather the context of its actual composition. Following Lloyd Bitzer, we shall define the rhetorical situation as "a complex of persons, events, objects, and relations presenting an actual or potential exigence which can be completely or partially removed if discourse, introduced into the situation, can so constrain human decision or action as to bring about significant modification of the exigence" (386). Clarifying his terminology, Bitzer explains that an "exigence" constitutes "an imperfection marked by urgency; it is a defect, an obstacle, something waiting to be done, a thing which is other than it should be" (386). "Shooting an Elephant" is essentially an essay describing Orwell's epiphany concerning the true nature of colonialism and its impact on both the colonizer and the colonized; this is the exigence that his work seeks to unmask. Such exposure of the exigence might, we can hope, lead to an eventual change in the situation.

Turning back to the fictional *Animal Farm*, the reader will certainly recognize a similar rhetorical dynamic: a writer recognizes a situation that is "other than it should be" and he sets to writing about it in such a way to effect some change. As Rorty argues, rhetorical acts—or "redescriptions"—that "change our minds on political situations . . . are the sort of thing which only writers with very special talents, writing at just the right moment in just the right way, are able to bring off" (143). Rorty makes a good case that Orwell is one of the writers with these special talents, and I would contend that his ability to translate historical contexts into rhetorical situations is chief among them. When we view the author of *Animal Farm* in this way the allegorical nature of the novel seems, if not predetermined, then at least unsurprising. The combination of Orwell's personal predilections and the historical moment in which he lived and wrote is a powerful indicator of how we should read this narrative.[14]

Allegory and Textual Phenomena

A second view of allegory—a formalist one—shifts the focus from the authorial and genetic issues I discussed above to the text itself. Morton Bloomfield

---

14. While clearly "fictional" in an important sense of that word, Orwell's narrative, as Rorty's analysis makes clear, comes close to being a work of history, a narrative constructed around "real" historical actors and a series of "actual" historical events. This is why Rorty's claim that *Animal Farm* amounts to a "redescription" makes sense.

gives voice to one version of this approach when he writes that "The only stable element in a literary work is its words, which, if we know the language in which it is written, have a meaning. The significance of that meaning is what may be called allegory. The problem of interpretation is the problem of allegory" (301). Bloomfield sounds very much like the critics who emphasize the reader's role in constructing allegory, but the emphasis on language and the implication that the arrangement of words in a text results in a meaning that the reader can uncover give Bloomfield's pronouncement a decidedly more formalist air. Orwell would seem to give some credence to this view when he claims that *Animal Farm* should be able to voice its own meaning.

We might take a single word from Orwell's novel to illustrate what Bloomfield calls the significance of the meaning of the novel's language. Indeed, the first word actually spoken by Old Major—"Comrades" (7)—goes a long way toward introducing the overarching theme of the work, situating it historically, and identifying the nature and identity of the characters because it is a term so inextricably and resonantly associated with the communist movement. As this example demonstrates, the most basic and fundamental of all textual phenomena—the words that comprise the novel—do in fact play a significant role in the transformation of Orwell's rhetorical purpose into the narrative. And in some ways, the careful choice of language (as the term "comrades" reveals) can make the "problem" of interpretation that Bloomfield identifies far less problematic than it could otherwise be.[15]

When we endeavor to interpret *Animal Farm*, however, we are dealing not only with issues of language per se—issues of the meaning of words and the significance of those meanings, that is—but also with certain aspects of narrative, which also constitute "textual phenomena." Take character as just one example. The personified animals in this work point readers rather unambiguously toward an allegorical interpretation. When the pig called Old Major addresses his fellow farm animals to tell them about his "strange dream" and the nature of the life of a farm animal (7), sophisticated readers recognize the obvious allegorical possibilities, or what Wayne Booth would call the "invitation" of allegory (*A Rhetoric of Irony* 25). Clearly, we are not meant to rest on the literal level of the narrative, as these fabulous characters offer the reader an invitation to respond to the text differently than we might respond to a more mimetically oriented narrative. Thus, the very nature of the characters has a significance that is at least as meaningful as the nature of

---

15. I do not mean to put undue emphasis on this single word; indeed, for a writer such as Walt Whitman "comrades" simply means "fellow men." But, given the historical moment in which Orwell worked, this word does carry considerable and special weight. As a general point, I want it to illustrate the importance of this kind of textual phenomenon to the allegorical enterprise.

the language that Orwell uses. In addition to language and character, other textual phenomena that can contribute to the allegorical nature of a narrative include plot, point of view, and themes. I will address these more fully in the following chapters.

Allegory and Readerly Concerns

As reader-response critics are quick to point out, every text needs a reader if it is not to remain forever inert. The reader of a work of fiction, according to both these critics and rhetorical critics, encounters not only the textual phenomena that I addressed above but also the whole range of genetic considerations with which I opened this section. And the ethical reader—the very one who feels some obligation to give due credence to an author's claims about his or her own work—has divided loyalties. While there is an obligation that attends genetic considerations, the reader must also be true to him or herself as a reader and maintain room for doubt. In other words, good readers will not simply take an author at his or her word concerning intentions and meanings, for the possibility always exists that a particular work of fiction will belie any authorial pronouncements about it. Despite what Jameson says about the power of context to impose "allegoricity" on a fictional narrative, we should be skeptical of such a sweeping claim. For these reasons, a number of critics—especially those with formalist leanings—have adopted the stance that allegory is primarily, if not wholly, a function of reading and that authorial intention and the context of composition have little or no role to play in deciding whether a work of fiction is, finally, allegorical or not.

Emphasizing the reader's role in constructing allegory has a long history, going back at least to neo-Platonic Christian interpreters of Homer.[16] Dante, one of the most influential early theorists of allegory, also conferred considerable power on the reader, power to uncover the truth that was often hidden behind the "beautiful lie" of a fictional work's surface-level meaning.[17] For Dante, validation of literature itself was at stake, and he needed a way to justify expending time and energy producing and reading "mere" fiction. His solution was similar to that hit upon by the Christian exegetes

---

16. See Robert Lamberton's *Homer the Theologian* for an insightful history of allegorical reading.

17. Dante's most sustained discussion of allegory comes in Book II, chapter 1 of the *Convivio [The Banquet]*. Allegory is also the topic of the *Epistle to Can Grande*, but scholars cannot definitively attribute this work to Dante.

of classical texts: to use allegoresis as a tool to get at the moral and spiritual truths hidden beneath the literal level of literature. In this way readers can allow themselves to continue to enjoy and value works that might not at first seem reconcilable with a particular religious faith.

We can see, then, that allegory develops along two different tracks, a compositional track and a hermeneutic one. This split has been the source of some confusion, and critics often fall on one side of the divide or the other, depending on their critical inclinations. In the twentieth century, theorists such as Hirsch focused on the compositional side while others emphasized the reader and his or her role in interpreting a text. For this second group of critics, allegory is an interpretive enterprise rather than a genetic one. Maureen Quilligan, for example, remarks that "[Critics] have had to remind us that all literature is, in essence, allegorical, if only because all literature has readers, and readers, as is their wont, think about what the work 'really' means . . ." (15). Striking a similar chord, Northrop Frye famously notes that "all commentary is allegorical interpretation, an attaching of ideas to the structure of poetic imagery. The instant that any critic permits himself to make a genuine comment about a poem . . . he has begun to allegorize" (89). Sayre Greenfield echoes this sentiment in *The Ends of Allegory*, in which he argues that "Allegory is always . . . a way of interpretation" (52). From this angle, it seems to be the reader who bears the responsibility of realizing literary allegory. Moreover, and perhaps more significantly, there would appear to be nothing—including the author's original intentions—that could stop a particular reader from construing any particular work as an allegory of something else.[18]

In practice, though, nearly all readers recognize certain constraints on their interpretive freedom; there are limits on what we can make *Animal Farm* mean, for example, even if we disregard Orwell's commentary on it, his tendencies as a writer and thinker, and the circumstances in which he composed it. Indeed, in the preface that I have already cited, Orwell restrains himself from more extensive commentary on the narrative because, he asserts, "if [the novel] does not speak for itself, it is a failure" (406). One

---

18. Peter Berek has proposed an interesting way of reconciling the competing desires of the genetic critics and the reader-response critics—drawing a strict distinction between the act of interpreting an allegorical text and allegoresis, or the act of reading allegorically. "I argue," Berek writes, "that interpreting the meaning of allegorical texts, like interpreting the meaning of other writings, has a claim to validity resting ultimately upon evidence as to the writer's intended meaning. Allegoresis, on the other hand, though its practitioners make interpretive statements which at first sound much like those made by interpreters of allegorical works, ultimately makes claims to validity that have nothing to do with authorial intention, but rather with a truth the allegorizing reader knows which may well have been beyond the awareness, whether conscious or unconscious, of the work's author" (118).

senses here that Orwell looks at his own work as Gay Clifford understands allegory, and that is as a mode that "presupposes an audience who will respond to it in specific ways" (36). Eliciting that response depends on what is in the actual narrative, on what the narrative literally says.

A rhetorical approach to narrative—and by extension to allegory—seeks to allow for the intersection of the compositional and hermeneutic tracks via the concepts of purpose (which I discussed above in relation to the idea of aesthetic merit) and authorial audience. Returning to Phelan's conception of the rhetorical approach to narrative, we can see how the three apparently discrete variables I have been discussing operate together to allow for the emergence of meaning. Phelan explains that,

> for the purposes of interpreting narratives, the [rhetorical] approach assumes that texts are designed by authors in order to affect readers in particular ways [this would constitute "purpose" and would involve an understanding of genetic concerns]; that those designs are conveyed through words, techniques, structures, forms, and dialogic relations of texts as well as genres and conventions readers use to understand them [broadly considered, these are the "textual phenomena"]; and that reader responses are a function of and, thus, a guide to how designs are created through textual and intertextual phenomena. (*Experiencing* 4)

Phelan's model also works under the assumption that some readers of fictional narratives "[seek] to enter the authorial audience," an audience constituted by "the author's ideal reader" (4).[19] It is from this assumption that Phelan develops his account of "rhetorical reading." The reader, in such a schema, gains access to the authorial audience through a holistic approach to the text, one in which he or she takes into consideration the interplay of intention, context of composition, and textual phenomena.

The argument that I want to put forward regarding allegory—at least full-length allegories such as *Animal Farm*—is that they are by nature narrative rhetorical acts, and in order to understand them we must recognize the importance and the interrelatedness of all three of the aspects I have described above: genetic concerns, readerly concerns, and textual phenomena. When it comes to interpreting such narratives, Phelan's feedback-loop metaphor, which positions these three narratological issues at the points of a rhetorical triangle, can help us see how they tend to initiate and then to compound or reinforce a meaning for the text.

---

19. I will address the idea and the significance of the authorial audience in more detail in the following chapter.

The feedback-loop metaphor strikes me as particularly apt for allegorical narratives because an actual feedback loop involves a system in which a *transformation* occurs, and as I conceive of the term, transformation is a defining characteristic of the allegorical enterprise. But rather than trying to identify one agent—whether it be the author, the rhetorical situation, the text, or the reader—responsible for that transformation, I prefer to attribute the change to the interplay of some, most, or all of these elements. Regarding a work such as *Animal Farm,* one that I call a strong allegory, the "input" into the feedback loop tends to be overwhelmingly "positive." In other words, all of our acts in the reading process tend to produce results that positively reinforce the transformative impetus. In nontextual feedback loops, such a situation would lead to exponential growth (think of compounding interest, for example) or decline, whereas with a text, it leads to a particularly strong rhetorical effect.

As Phelan understands the hermeneutic process, the reader "may begin the interpretive inquiry from any one of [the] points on the rhetorical triangle, but the inquiry will at some point consider how each point both influences and can be influenced by the other two" (*Living* 18). Today, many—perhaps most—readers of *Animal Farm* will begin from the genetic point, knowing something about Orwell's intentions or the circumstances under which he composed the novel, or both. This information might come from teachers, from "Introductions" published with the actual novel, or simply from a cultural familiarity with the text. When this is the case, the reading process might become essentially an exercise in confirmation, one in which the textual phenomena are more or less simply and uncritically found to reinforce the stated desire of the author or to support the analysis of previous readers.

Similarly, a reader could begin the process of interpretation from a reaction to the text that precedes any actual engagement with it. For example, a reader with communist sympathies or socialist leanings might have formed an opinion of the work based on reactions to what he or she might have heard about the work and the politics of its author. Such an approach could certainly color one's response to and interpretation of the work. We would hope, however, that a careful and ethical reader would still be able to recognize the phenomenon that Orwell has transformed even if that reader does not share Orwell's particular worldview. From the other end of the spectrum, I could also imagine a reader raised on a farm who happens upon a novel called *Animal Farm* and who immediately finds him- or herself predisposed to like the work. It might take a while for this reader to recognize that Orwell's work is not really meant to be primarily about a farm, but, again, we would hope that the evidence provided by the text itself would bring this reader around to a valid interpretation of the text.

Finally, the possibility certainly exists that a reader—perhaps one completely unfamiliar with Orwell and his work or with life on a farm—might start by directly engaging the textual phenomena. Even in this case, though, most interpreters seem to have a basic desire to understand what a speaker or an author intends by an utterance, and most begin with what Hirsch calls a generic expectation that takes the form of a "type idea" and that functions as a heuristic device. When a narrative provides textual cues that point toward allegory, allegory becomes this kind of type idea, and it guides our interpretive activities at least until we have evidence that this idea is not or is no longer tenable (*Validity* 88). If the narrative bears out our initial guess and does not fit as well with alternative type ideas, then we can be reasonably sure that we have hit upon what Hirsch calls the "intrinsic genre," or "*that sense of the whole by means of which an interpreter can correctly understand any part in its determinacy*" (86, emphasis in original). Again, it is important to note that this "sense" resides in the interpreter and it manifests itself in that interpreter because of the rhetorical effect produced by a narrative (or a speaker). With strong allegories, this rhetorical effect is nearly overwhelming, and that makes the interpreter's guess about the intrinsic genre a fairly risk-free enterprise.

Applying these hermeneutic concepts to *Animal Farm,* we might say that the early appearance in the narrative of talking pigs raises some rather specific and powerful expectations concerning the type of meaning that Orwell intends to produce.[20] This is a preliminary rhetorical effect produced by a textual phenomenon, but it does not ensure that what the reader is reading is "an allegory." As the reader continues, new textual evidence arises that either strengthens or fails to strengthen this preliminary rhetorical effect. Despite the allegorical potential inherent in the personified animals, the narrative as a whole cannot result in a strong allegorical effect without the presence of other textual phenomena that reveal the author's thematic intentions. Obviously, corroborating narrative evidence in *Animal Farm* abounds. Indeed, as Old Major continues the speech that begins with "Comrades," his words serve only to strengthen Orwell's rhetorical effect. That speech is, as Orwell explains, essentially "Marx's theory from the animals' point of view," as it emphasizes the fact that man has been unjustly and cruelly exploiting the animals for their labor and keeping all that the animals have produced for their own consumption and profit.

---

20. One legitimate expectation, of course, might be that we have begun reading a work of children's literature. Such an expectation would not preclude the possibility of allegory; it might in fact heighten it. I address the role of children's literature in allegory more fully in chapter 3, "Weak Allegory."

As readers of *Animal Farm* progress through the narrative, the textual phenomena continually reinforce our early sense that Orwell has allegorical intentions and remain congruent with the theme of the communist revolution in Russia. At the same time, the import of this theme and the rhetorical situation that inspired it become increasingly clear as what started out as a noble and just cause becomes, in the hands (hooves?) of the unscrupulous, traitorous, and dictatorial pig Napoleon, a disillusioning power-grab. This is not a tract meant as a blanket condemnation of communism and socialism—indeed Old Major himself and his ideas are portrayed in strikingly positive terms—but rather a work meant to decry the misappropriation and misapplication of Marxist ideology by corrupt and illegitimate leaders. As Orwell claims in his preface to the Ukrainian edition, the work does "speak for itself," and what it reveals most clearly is the rhetorical situation that called it into being.

Recognizing Orwell's allegorical intent and identifying the fundamental theme of his narrative can make a reader confident in calling *Animal Farm* an allegory, but the case is strengthened even further when we are aware of the rhetorical situation that gave rise to it and makes clear the author's aims in addressing that situation. A narrative that produces the strongest allegorical effect also straddles the line between literature and pure rhetoric more precariously than do other narratives; this helps to explain the distaste for and distrust of allegory on the part of many literary critics. Whether one likes them or not, those works that strike us as the strongest examples of allegorical writing are also the ones that seem to address directly some kind of exigency, but they do so from within the framework of a fictional narrative. Given Bitzer's claim that the "exigence and the complex of persons, objects, events and relations which generate rhetorical discourse are located in reality, are objective and publicly observable historic facts in the world we experience, [and] are therefore available for scrutiny by an observer or critic who attends to them" (390), we would seem to have good reason for skepticism regarding my claim that the rhetorical situation plays such a central role in producing the allegorical effect. But fiction that produces a strong allegorical effect on the reader often needs a rhetorical situation as much as does the kind of discourse about which Bitzer theorizes. We must weaken Bitzer's claim that the constituent elements of the rhetorical situation must be "observable historical facts" if we are to apply the idea to allegorical fiction,[21] but we must also recognize that some real exigency—even if it is a general concern about the state of the human soul—gives rise to and manifests itself in allegorical narratives. This explains the pedantic quality of many works

---

21. Though in the case of *Animal Farm*, of course, they are.

that feel strongly allegorical; it also explains how Fredric Jameson can claim that, in some cases, the rhetorical situation *alone* is enough to produce a strong allegorical effect.

In the following chapter I will examine more carefully what I am calling "strong allegories," paying particular attention to the rhetorical effect produced when the hermeneutic feedback loop receives input that propels an interpretive transformation so powerfully in one direction. In addition to accounting for these strong allegorical transformations, the narrative-rhetorical approach to allegory that I am proposing will also help to explain how some works that seem allegorical—or that seem as if they *should* be allegorical—do not produce the same degree of certitude as does *Animal Farm*. I will address these weaker allegories in chapter 2.

Strong Allegory

Shirley Jackson

THE ANTIPATHY that many literary critics have felt for allegory applies most directly to what I am calling "strong allegory," a designation that encompasses those complete works of fiction that comprise the "genre" of allegory. Works such as *The Pilgrim's Progress, The Psychomachia,* and even *Animal Farm* clearly evince some characteristics that readers and critics generally associate with allegory. Yet these same characteristics—including the presence of personified abstractions or animals, the overriding sense that there is a "message" to be gleaned, and a pronounced antimimeticism—also serve as the metaphorical shovels that many critics have used to dig allegory's grave. Thus, before looking more closely at strong allegory, it will be worth our effort here to pursue what we might fittingly see as the figurative (more precisely, metaphorical) death of allegory.

Looking back over the course of the history of literary criticism, one will note that the numerous twentieth-century obituaries for allegory constitute what would seem to be the natural result of earlier decrees from literary scholars, many of which called for something like a death sentence for allegory. According to Hans-Georg Gadamer, for example,

> the demotion of allegory was the dominant concern of German classicism; that concern inevitably resulted from the emergence of the concept of genius and from art's being freed from the fetters of rationalism. Allegory is certainly not the product of genius alone. It rests on firm traditions and

always has a fixed, stable meaning which does not resist rational comprehension through the concept—on the contrary, the concept of allegory is closely bound up with dogmatics: with the rationalization of the mythical (as in the Greek Enlightenment), or with the Christian interpretation of Scripture in terms of doctrinal unity (as in patristics), and finally with the reconciliation of the Christian tradition and classical culture, which is the basis of the art and literature of modern Europe and whose last universal form was the baroque. With the breakup of this tradition allegory too was finished. For the moment art freed itself from all dogmatic bonds and could be defined as the unconscious production of genius, allegory inevitably became aesthetically suspect. (79)

The combination of the distaste for dogmatics and rationalism and the conception of the artist as genius ultimately manifests itself in the devaluation of allegory, as Gadamer shows, and the concomitant elevation of a highly idiosyncratic notion of the symbol. As opposed to allegory, the symbol was seen as a more natural trope, one that might spring organically from the mind of a true poet.

The allegory/symbol distinction was most famously articulated by Coleridge (who was strongly influenced by the German classicists), and it reflects Romantic ideas concerning the nature of the poet and his craft. "Of most importance to our present subject is this point," Coleridge writes, "that the latter (allegory) cannot be other than spoken consciously;—whereas in the former (the symbol) it is very possible that the general truth may be unconsciously in the writer's mind,—as the Don Quixote out of the perfectly sane mind of Cervantes, and not by outward observation or historically. The advantage of symbolic writing over allegory is, that it presumes no disjunction of faculties, but simple dominance" (qtd. in Fletcher 17). In this scheme, the symbol is preferable to allegory primarily because it is less calculated and more natural. According to Angus Fletcher, the trouble with allegory, as Coleridge uses the term, is that "there is always . . . an attempt to categorize logical orders first, and fit them to convenient phenomena second, to set forth ideal systems first, and illustrate them second" (18). Such planning and ordering works against the more naturalistic predilections of the Romantics, and might lead to the kind of "disjunction" to which Coleridge refers.

In *Dark Conceit: The Making of Allegory* Edwin Honig effectively demonstrates the extent to which Coleridge's ideas regarding allegory and symbol (and what differentiates the two) depend on Coleridge's personal aesthetic prejudices. "Coleridge's idea of the way symbolism works," Honig explains, "includes the notion of a general truth concealed in the writer's unconscious mind, having its origin there and growing spontaneously into the fictional work. But this view illustrates Coleridge's principle of organic form better than it does the symbolic principle" (46–47). It is not surprising, then, that allegory suffers, in Coleridge's system, from seeming less organic and more "denotative"; "its form must be imposed from the outside, 'consciously.' Hence allegory must be taken as a specimen of mechanical, and not of organic form" (Honig 47). Whatever the origin of Coleridge's particular biases, however, the end result was that allegory, in comparison to the symbol, emerged with the stigma of being less artistic because more artificial. This belief has been surprisingly persistent, despite the numerous rehabilitative efforts aimed at allegory since the middle part of the twentieth century.

The second complaint against allegory has grown out of these perceived shortcomings of allegorical works, but it also reflects a twentieth-century change in the emphasis of literary criticism. The problem with allegory, in this second scenario, has evolved from a concern with its suspect aesthetic credentials to a belief that it handcuffs the literary critic by too consciously limiting the text's signifying potential. In other words, the relationship between reader and allegorical text has too little mystery. This is precisely the point that Northrop Frye makes in *Anatomy of Criticism*: "The commenting critic is often prejudiced against allegory without knowing the real reason, which is that continuous allegory prescribes the direction of his commentary, and so restricts its freedom" (90). This is especially apparent in what Frye calls "actual allegory," which we have "when a poet explicitly indicates the relationship of his images to examples and precepts, and so tries to indicate how a commentary on him should proceed" (90). In a literary climate that prizes the autonomy, freedom, and creativity of the reader, a prescriptive mode such as allegory is unlikely to find favor with the very critics whom it "directs."

Like the argument against the aesthetic aspect of allegory itself, the argument against the interpretive limitations supposedly inherent in allegory has a second component. This second component involves what I will call the distaste for exhaustibility. The problem with allegory might not simply be that it controls and directs our commentary, as Frye argues, but also that once we have "correctly" commented on allegory we have done all there is to do. If allegory simply "says one thing and means another" (Fletcher 2), then once we have arrived at that other meaning we have exhausted the text. In the twentieth century, the ascendance of undecidability as both the aim and the result of much interpretation made such interpretive closure highly suspect.

The suspicion of closure has extended beyond recognizably allegorical texts, however, and encompassed the idea of interpretation more generally. As Fredric Jameson notes in *The Political Unconscious*, ". . . a criticism which asks the question 'What does it mean?' constitutes something like an allegorical operation in which a text is systematically *rewritten* in terms of some fundamental master code or 'ultimately determining instance.' On this view, then, all 'interpretation' in the narrower sense demands the forcible or imperceptible transformation of a given text into an allegory of its particular master code or 'transcendental signified': the discredit into which interpretation has fallen is thus at one with the disrepute visited on allegory itself" (58). At this point, the suspicion of closure is now cast in a different direction. It is not that allegory inherently closes off or too easily exhausts interpretive possibilities, but rather that readers, when they "interpret" a work, necessarily do this themselves. The result, however, is the same—a text and a reader that are both too easily exhausted.[1]

Regardless of where one stands on the issue of the aesthetic or hermeneutic value of allegorical narratives, we must recognize that when we are dealing with certain kinds of allegories the limits on interpretation are real and intentional. Despite the persistent claims by numerous theorists of allegory that it is, as Jon Whitman claims, "an oblique way of writing" (1), that it "conceals many of its secrets" (1), and that "it provides an initiation into a mystery" (2), there is often nothing particularly mysterious about the intended meaning of an allegory. That meaning, in fact, is often so obvious and so pedantic, so "sermonlike," that readers reject the narrative used to convey it precisely for this reason. As Fletcher points out, "By means of his 'message,' . . . the allegorical poet is . . . trying to control his audience. He seeks to sway them . . . to accept intellectual or moral or spiritual attitudes" (192).

As we saw in the previous chapter, Orwell's *Animal Farm* provides a good example of this particular bias. So, while I postulated that the interplay of genetic considerations, textual phenomena, and readerly concerns accounts for the allegorical nature of this novel, it seems clear to me that much of the "input" that makes that novel an allegory comes from Orwell himself and, through him, his text. We can safely call this work a strong allegory largely because we know that its author intended it as such and because he composed it in such a way that it would convey that intention fairly clearly to his readers. Those readers, then, find themselves in the position of discovering and verifying Orwell's meaning rather than creating it through the reading process, and this is the usual position of readers vis-à-vis strong allegories.

---

1. In "Allegory and Allegoresis, Rhetoric and Hermeneutics," Rita Copeland and Stephen Melville make the plausible claim that, since the work of Paul de Man to reenergize discussion of allegory, "The older polarity 'symbol-allegory,' which valued symbol over allegory, appears to have been replaced with the polarity 'allegory-allegoresis,' in which allegory stands as the preferred mode" (161–62).

To understand more clearly what I mean by the term "strong allegory" and the reader's role in realizing it, we need to return to my definition of allegory: that class of works that fulfills its rhetorical purpose by means of the transformation of some phenomenon into a figural narrative. In strong allegories, the reader has the overriding sense that the author both intends and does the work of the transformation, and this intuition activates, as I indicated in the previous chapter, what E. D. Hirsch calls the "intrinsic genre," or *"that sense of the whole by means of which an interpreter can correctly understand any part in its determinacy"* (*Validity* 86, emphasis in original). When the reader senses that the whole is allegorical, he or she will adopt a reading strategy that attempts to uncover the phenomenon that has been transformed into a narrative structure, or, if the author has made it clear what that phenomenon is, to verify its transformation by a process of reconciling the text and the phenomenon.

Such a reading strategy approximates what Peter J. Rabinowitz calls "authorial reading." In *Before Reading: Narrative Conventions and the Politics of Interpretation*, Rabinowitz proposes that we recognize three categories for the reader of fictional narratives: the actual audience, which is composed of the individual flesh-and-blood readers; the narrative audience, which Rabinowitz describes as a "role" in which the reader is willing to enter the world of the narrative on its own terms (95–96); and the authorial audience, or the hypothetical audience for whom authors have designed their works (21). In many cases, that authorial audience will be more sophisticated and more educated than the narrative audience, as this former group is expected to be capable of joining "a particular social/interpretive community," one whose membership includes the author him- or herself (22). This authorial audience is a construct that is presumed to be capable of "getting" the author's full intended meaning, even as members of the actual or narrative audience, or both, might not. As Rabinowitz makes clear, though, that meaning is determined by the author and his or her text, and, as far as the reader is concerned, is "found rather than made" (22).

Strong allegories, I submit, ensure a significant gap between the narrative and the authorial audiences;[2] they encourage readers to enter into the authorial audience, and, most significantly perhaps, actively facilitate that entry.[3] While it is conceivable that a reader (a child, perhaps) could miss the

---

2. Rabinowitz uses the distance that separates these two audiences as a way to characterize realistic versus antirealistic texts. In the former, he argues, the narrative audience and authorial audience are very close, whereas in the latter—which would include allegorical tales, I believe—there is a significant distance between the two (99).

3. Indeed, in some cases that entry is more or less guaranteed, and this is one of the aspects of allegory that has turned many critics against it.

figural aspect of *Animal Farm*, for example, both Orwell and his text guide us strongly toward an understanding that the real significance of the novel is not in the plot or characters, but rather in how that plot and those characters are really the transformation of a political conviction into a figural story. A sophisticated reader, then, would have to resist willfully moving from the relatively naïve position of the narrative audience (a position that would credit talking animals, etc.) toward the more informed position of the authorial audience, where he or she can "discover" the full meaning of the text and enter into a kind of community with the author. Wayne Booth points out an interesting distinction between allegory and irony in this regard. In *A Rhetoric of Irony* he claims that "A naïve reader who overlooks irony will totally misunderstand what is going on. A naïve reader who reads an allegory without taking conscious thought, refusing all invitations to reconstruct general meanings out of the literal surface, will in effect obtain an experience something like what the allegory intends: the emotional and intellectual pattern will be in the direction of what it would be for the most sophisticated reader" (25). When one becomes aware of the "second order of meanings" in allegory, Booth adds, "a mild pleasure is added, but the essential experience remains the same" (25). As Booth notes, with some allegories any reader who takes "conscious thought" and who recognizes the author's hermeneutic "invitations" will in all likelihood find his way to the authorial audience.

I disagree, however, that all that is at stake if the reader does not make that transition is the lost opportunity for the addition of "a mild pleasure" to the reading experience. Consider tennis as an analogy: does actually playing a tennis match add only a mild pleasure to the act of hitting balls back and forth as one does, for example, when warming up? A tennis court is a space the structure of which has been determined by a set of rules meant to encourage a specific activity; similarly, an allegorical narrative has a form that emerges from an author's intended purpose, and that purpose should guide the reader's engagement with the text. While this does not have to be the case (just as people do not have to use a tennis court to play tennis, properly speaking), two readers, one of whom understands or acknowledges the author's purpose and one of whom does not, will end up doing very different things with that author's text. A reader of Orwell's *Animal Farm* who remains confined to the narrative audience—a reader, that is, who is oblivious to the second order of meaning and who processes the novel only as a story about life on a peculiar farm for some animated animals—has, like the person simply returning volleys from a partner across the net, a very different experience with this narrative than does a reader (or tennis player) who truly engages with what he or she is meant to be doing. Orwell's stated aim, after all, was to "Expose the Soviet myth"; if the reader never makes the jump from pigs and sheep to Trotsky and Lenin, then the entire rhetorical premise of the act of narrative communication has broken down. We are not simply dealing with some measurement of how much fun one might be having—as Booth's comments would imply—but rather with basic issues of comprehension.

While we can acknowledge some validity to Booth's point that one can read an allegory from the perspective of the narrative audience and still derive some enjoyment from the activity, just as we can surely observe two people happily hitting a ball back and forth on a tennis court, successfully facilitating entry into the authorial audience strikes me as being an essential aspect of strong allegory, just as understanding the aims of tennis as a competition is an essential aspect of making full and good use of a tennis racquet and balls. As the anonymous author of the strongly allegorical medieval morality play *Everyman* avers, "The matter [of the play] is wonder precious, / But the intent of it is more gracious / And sweet to bear away" (7–9). To my mind, the author here implies that reading this play from the authorial position will result in not just a slightly more pleasurable experience, but rather in an experience that differs qualitatively from that experienced from the narrative perspective. Moreover, this claim, coming as it does at the outset of the play, serves as an invitation into the authorial community by facilitating recognition on the part of the reader-audience, a recognition that we are both welcome and expected to uncover the transformation that the "matter" of the play (the textual phenomena, in other words) represents.

The reader's recognition in cases such as *Animal Farm* has two components: that the literal text is the transformation of some extratextual phenomenon and that that phenomenon actually occupies a position of primacy even if it remains implied. When a reader recognizes allegory, she tends to realize at the same time that she is close to "meaning," in the sense that E. D. Hirsch uses that term in *Validity in Interpretation*.[4] Indeed, if we are to believe the author of *Everyman,* authorial intent is accessible and there to be borne away in allegory. The recognition that accompanies allegory sets in motion a distinctive hermeneutic reader response. The strongest allegories produce the strongest sense of recognition, and the stronger the recognition, the more certain the reader is of the ultimate nature of his or her interpretation—the more certain he or she is, in other words, of gaining access to the authorial audience. This dawning certainty activates a mode of interpretation that I will label concordant, a term that applies when the reader has clear

---

4. "*Meaning* is that which is represented by the text," Hirsch claims; "it is what the author meant by his use of a particular sign sequence; it is what the signs represent" (8, emphasis in original).

indications that the author and the author's text are paving a clear path from narrative to authorial reading. In the terms of the feedback-loop metaphor, such texts produce a positive feedback loop, one in which all of the inputs propel the interpretation in the same direction. As Rabinowitz notes, the authorial audience does not remain entirely passive in the reading process, but its job is not to invent or construct its own meaning; rather, it "makes what the author intended to be found" (28). In the case of allegory, what the audience makes are connections and concordance between the narrative and the implied phenomenon that has been transformed but not entirely effaced by that narrative.

Narratives that produce the strongest allegorical effect comprise a subset of narratives that also encourage and reward thematic interpretation. This is so because these narratives are generally constructed so that the disparate parts of an individual narrative work together to produce a strong sense of thematic coherence, something that is not usually characteristic of more mimetic narratives. Typically, when we think of "theme" we do so along the same lines as those proposed by Eugene Falk in his *Types of Thematic Structure*: "the term 'theme,'" Falk explains, "may . . . be assigned to the ideas that emerge from the particular structure of such textual elements as actions, statements revealing states of mind or feelings, gestures, or meaningful environmental settings" (2). Falk refers to these various "textual elements" as "motifs," and he concludes that "the idea that emerges from motifs by means of an abstraction" is a "theme" (2). Yet in the context of strong allegory, this conception of theme does not go far enough; I do want to propose that the authors of strong allegories construct narratives that not only facilitate the process of abstraction and that limit both the number and range of themes that might be abstracted from the various motifs, but I also suggest that the theme of a strong allegory includes what we might call a predicate, or a proposition, relating to the emergent idea. In other words, the rhetorical concept of purpose must guide our thinking about theme as it relates to allegorical—particularly strongly allegorical—narratives.

The dominant theme(s) of narratives that produce a strong allegorical effect can almost always also serve as the narrative's meaning or message, that which defines authorial purpose in my rhetorical approach to allegory. Falk, however, cautions against equating theme and message: "A message . . . is the result of reflections in which motifs are not under immediate consideration. The theme is a 'first intention,' whereas the message is a conception obtained through reflection upon a previous conception gained by abstraction from the motifs themselves. A message is thus a 'second intention'; and when we confuse a message with a theme we do so at the risk of assuming wrongly that a work is a preconceived embodiment of a 'philosophy'" (3).

Yet in the case of strong allegory, narratives often are the embodiment of a philosophy, an ideology, or some other authorial position, intention, or purpose. Strong allegory effectively collapses Falk's distinction between theme and message. Thus, as we will see below, when the reader of a work that produces a strong allegorical effect extrapolates themes from the textual phenomena (or "motifs"), he or she also uncovers the narrative's purpose.[5] With regard to such narratives, to say what they are about is also to say what the author intends by them. Such a hermeneutic move serves to take us deeper into the authorial audience and to cement our sense of community with the (implied) author and other readers.

At this point we would be well served by moving to a concrete example and some practical criticism as a means of anchoring this theoretical discussion. The text I have chosen for this task is Shirley Jackson's "The Lottery." Jackson's story, first published in June 1948 in the *New Yorker*, is the well-known and oft-anthologized tale of a small town's annual lottery, the "winner" of which is subjected to a brutal stoning that results in his or her death. The implied rationale for the lottery in Jackson's story harks back to the ancient practice of using scapegoating and ritual sacrifice as a way to appease a deity and, often, to ensure a good harvest. Yet Jackson has set the story in what seems to be contemporary times—at least as of her writing in the mid-twentieth century—and in the United States, so we cannot dismiss the ritualized scapegoating that she describes as the product of a time long past or of some benighted culture.

By nature more circumspect about the meaning of her work than was Orwell, Jackson was reluctant to offer much in the way of interpretive keys in her subsequent commentary on the text. Her reticence on this score proved troubling to many readers of the story, one that garnered, according to Jackson in a piece that she called "Biography of a Story," "more mail than any piece of fiction [the *New Yorker*] had ever published" (127), undoubtedly because the narrative's cold cruelty leaves many readers emotionally disturbed. As Judy Oppenheimer attests in her biography of Jackson, "No one, not then, not ever, would be able to read the story without having a powerful reaction. Its quiet tones and everyday setting only contributed to the force of its final, shattering climax" (128). Given the powerful emotional effect of "The Lottery," the incredulity and inquisitiveness of Jackson's readers make perfect sense, even if Jackson herself was left with the impression—based on the responses that she received—that "people who read stories are gullible, rude, frequently illiterate, and horribly afraid of being laughed at" ("Biography" 127). Jackson's rather harsh view of her reading public (the "actual

---

5. I treat the idea of theme in more detail in chapter 4.

audience" in Rabinowitz's terms), or at least the segment of it that bothered to write to her through the *New Yorker,* undoubtedly results from the fact that those readers proved largely incapable of making the interpretive transition from the narrative audience to the authorial audience. As a result, they are left with the nagging sense that other readers might be more in the know and therefore liable to mock their failure to understand the text,[6] and Jackson is left wondering if they are actually capable of reading with enough sophistication to be considered literate.

As I indicated above, the gap between the narrative audience and the authorial audience is large and significant in what Rabinowitz calls "antirealistic" texts. A narrative such as "The Lottery" does not announce its antirealism in quite the same way as does *Animal Farm,* for example, but rather leaves one with the disquieting sense—almost a hope, really—that what transpires in the story does not actually happen somewhere in modern America. Without the equivalent of Orwell's scheming and talking farm animals, though, the allegorical markers in Jackson's text prove less obvious, potentially putting even very astute readers on uncertain footing. Describing the period between Jackson's submission of her story to the *New Yorker* and its publication, Oppenheimer relates that

> Even *The New Yorker* must have sensed some of [the story's] potential for disturbance. The magazine bought it immediately, but fiction editor Gus Lobrano thought it prudent to call Shirley and ask if she had any explanation she would like to pass along. Editor Harold Ross, he said apologetically, was wondering—Ross had often said he would never publish a story he himself did not understand. Was there anything special she was trying to convey? Not really, said Shirley, who hated explaining her work, it was just a story. Well, said Lobrano, even more apologetically, did she think the story might be called an allegory which made its point by an ironic juxtaposition of ancient superstition and modern setting? Sure, said Shirley kindly (she had no use for that kind of fancy-pants academic drivel), that would be fine. Good, good, said Lobrano, that was what Ross thought it meant. (128)

This episode speaks to Hirsch's idea of the intrinsic genre (that "sense of the whole") that experienced readers of narrative fiction formulate as they make their way through "The Lottery." At the same time, it illustrates the fate of readers who fail to do so: the inability to access the authorial audience,

---

6. Many of those who wrote letters apparently demanded that they not be published, thereby convincing Jackson of their fear of being mocked ("Biography" 127).

the failure to have properly read the story, and a nagging sense of literary inadequacy.

Jackson's rather flippant and dismissive response to the question that Lobrano poses notwithstanding (if indeed Oppenheimer has presented it faithfully), the allegorical reading Ross proposes hits the mark and helps to explain why the readers who failed to see the story as an allegory seemed so hopelessly far off the mark; we are not dealing just with varying levels of enjoyment here, but rather with examples of misprision egregious enough to cause people to cancel their subscriptions to the *New Yorker* and, in some cases, to write abusive and threatening letters to the magazine and the story's author ("Biography" 127–28). The gulf separating those in the narrative audience—characterized by readers who wrote to Jackson curious about "where these lotteries were held, and whether they could go there and watch" ("Biography" 128)—and those who, like Ross, joined her in the authorial audience is wide indeed.

Although Jackson apparently preferred to let her work speak for itself rather than to interpret it for others, she did provide a revealing comment concerning her rhetorical aim to the San Francisco *Chronicle* on July 22, 1948, less than a month after her story had appeared in the *New Yorker* and during the height of the small maelstrom that it produced. "Explaining just what I hoped to say is very difficult," Jackson confesses. "I suppose I hoped, by setting a particularly brutal ancient rite in the present and in my own village, to shock the story's readers with a graphic dramatization of the pointless violence and general inhumanity in their own lives" (qtd. in Oppenheimer 131). Even if it does lack some of the traditional and obvious markers of allegory—personified animals or abstract qualities as characters foremost among them—"The Lottery" does contain numerous contextual and textual clues that, when we piece them together, reveal the narrative to be a strong allegory built to effect this rhetorical aim.

One of the reasons that the text has such a powerful effect on so many readers seems, at first glance, to be counterintuitive: Jackson's narrator adopts a style that exhibits little emotion and that abjures any kind of overt commentary on what is happening in the story. Such a style departs significantly from the kind of overt moralizing that we often associate with the strong, mainly religious allegories from the Middle Ages. Yet Jackson's intent also differs significantly from these earlier examples of strong allegory; rather than imparting a moralistic lesson, Jackson wants to provoke a particular reaction, and restricting her narrator to the matter-of-fact reporting of a series of increasingly disturbing events effectively serves that purpose.

As that description of the narration suggests, the allegorical nature of the story becomes apparent only through the relatively leisurely progression of the plot. This buildup to the work's climax (which coincides with the readers' recognition of the allegorical nature of the text) heightens the shock value that Jackson sought. Thus, Jackson has her story begin positively idyllically, in "the fresh warmth of a full-summer day," with flowers "blooming profusely," the grass "richly green," and children poised to break into "boisterous play" (291)—a description that could easily be occasioned by a Norman Rockwell *Saturday Evening Post* cover typical of the era.

The small-town agrarian setting further reinforces the Rockwell-like feel of the story's opening, a feel that relies heavily not only on the ludic qualities that attend summer vacation but also on the reassuring cadence of cyclical routine in the adult world, a cadence that is mirrored in both the content and the rhythm of Jackson's prose: "Soon the men began to gather, surveying their own children, speaking of planting and rain, tractors and taxes" (291). The lottery and the ritual behind it—including the continued use of a "shabby" receptacle for the slips of paper that function as the lots only because "no one liked to upset even as much tradition as was represented by the black box" (293)—contributes to the comfort that certain abiding rites or traditions can engender in a society.

Aside from its occasionally striking lyricism, the other distinguishing feature of Jackson's style is the distance that characterizes her narrator from the events that she tells. This distance—which takes the form of a remarkably disinterested reportorial style—characterizes the story even from the opening paragraph:

> The people of the village began to gather in the square, between the post office and the bank, around ten o'clock; in some towns there were so many people that the lottery took two days and had to be started on June 26th [the day before it occurs in the location Jackson describes], but in this village, where there were only about three hundred people, the whole lottery took less than two hours, so it could begin at ten o'clock in the morning and still be through in time to allow the villagers to get home for noon dinner. (291)

While the narrator is heterodiegetic, her detailed knowledge of the logistics of the lottery and, indeed, her initial reference to it simply as "the" lottery, with no additional information, also suggests that she is an insider relative to the community she describes, and this position affords her a certain authority in the mind of the reader. Thus, Jackson's narrator is able to invite us readers into what at first seems to be a very hospitable setting of which she (the narrator) has personal knowledge.

Even so, a careful reading of the language that Jackson employs reveals blemishes on this pastoral image of mid-century Americana, blemishes that should put readers at least slightly ill at ease about what we are reading, even if we do not yet know how the story concludes. As the men discourse on "planting and rain, tractors and taxes," for example, they stand together, but "away from the pile of stones in the corner, and their jokes were quiet and they smiled rather than laughed" (292). Even without full knowledge of the intended use of the stones, readers can sense the apprehension that dampens the men's jokes and prevents smiles from evolving into laughs. And later, as Mr. Summers prepares to get the lottery underway, we are told that he announces "soberly" that they had better "get started, get this over with" (295). We sense at this point that the winner of this lottery will not likely feel fortunate to draw the distinguishing mark. And finally, as the men of the families go about drawing their slips of paper from the black box, Jackson's narrator remarks that those who had already drawn were "holding the small folded papers in their large hands, turning them over and over nervously" (297).

By this point the slow progression of the narrative has heightened the suspense and anxiety that both characters and readers experience. Speaking for herself, her family, her entire community, and, I suspect, the majority of Jackson's readers, Mrs. Dunbar finally exclaims to her older son, "I wish they'd hurry . . . I wish they'd hurry" (298). The moment of release finally does come for all involved (characters and readers) when, after the "long pause, a breathless pause" that follows the last family's pulling of lots (298), Tessie Hutchinson realizes that her husband Bill has the tainted slip of paper. Tessie reacts so forcefully that no doubt about the endgame remains: "You didn't give him [Bill] enough time to take any paper he wanted," she protests to Mr. Summers. "I saw you. It wasn't fair!" (298). We know now how serious the consequences of the lottery truly are, but readers who participate in the authorial audience also realize that what is about to happen to someone in the Hutchinson family should not be taken literally; we strongly suspect we are dealing with allegory because we believe, at least intellectually, that nothing that could occasion Tessie's terrified response should be determined by random chance without some compelling and rational social need (which would not include superstitions about crop yield).

What doubt remains in the reader's mind at this point about Jackson's intentions dissipates quickly as the second stage of the lottery occurs. Now, each member of the Hutchinson family must choose lots among themselves to determine the sacrificial scapegoat. The image of "little Davy," too young to understand that he should pull just one slip of paper from the box, the thought of Bill and Tessie's two older children forced to confront the possibility of their own or a sibling's imminent death, and the anguish that the two parents must be experiencing, all drive the increasingly incredulous reader toward the necessary conclusion that this cannot be real. Yet this growing conviction of the text's "antireality" does not, I should stress, compromise the force of Jackson's narrative because by this point most readers have also been strongly drawn into the narrative audience, and in that place we feel the affective and ethical force of the Hutchinsons' situation.

Jay A. Yarmove helps us to understand the allegorical resonance that Jackson's story has for a mid-twentieth-century audience by providing an important contextual reading, one that addresses the rhetorical situation in which Jackson was working:

> The underpinnings of Shirley Jackson's famous post–World War II story "The Lottery" demonstrate that the work is far greater than the sum of its parts. The date of the lottery, its location, and the symbolic or ironic names of its characters all work to convey a meaning that is even more disturbing than the shock created by its well-known ending, namely, that despite assurances during the late 1940s that "it couldn't happen here," a microcosmal holocaust occurs in this story and, by extension, may happen anyplace in contemporary America.

Yarmove understands "The Lottery" as an allegory, and one that gains some of its force from its appearance just a few years after the Holocaust, when more and more information about the extent of the Nazi genocide was being discovered. Thus, even though Jackson's story is not a direct allegory of the Third Reich's final solution (the Christian villagers, after all, sacrifice one of their own members), it does, as Yarmove contends, "help to create the specter of a holocaust in the United States" because it forces readers to confront the fact that "custom and law, when sanctioned by a selfish, unthinking populace, can bring an otherwise democratic and seemingly just society to the brink of paganism."

As readers piece together the meaning of this text and thereby make sense of what it means to enter the authorial audience, we must also come to terms with the fact that Jackson invites us to discover her own distance from her narrator, a narrator who appears to have intimate knowledge of this microcosmic holocaust, but who chooses to accept it. Looking back with a full understanding of what the lottery accomplishes and what it means for the person who draws the unfortunate lot, we can draw two important conclusions: 1) the narrator understands the full meaning of the lottery from the outset without appearing to be disturbed by its implications and 2) refuses to question it. Indeed, so ingrained is this ritual that virtually the entire community—including the victim herself, who objects to the unfairness of the process but not the concept of the lottery—simply accepts it. The fact that Jackson's narrator appears to go along with the crowd in this regard makes the gap between her and the author enormous and leaves us with the distinct possibility that Jackson's work critiques such passive acceptance as much as it critiques a heartless and senseless act. Jackson folds both of these aspects of her rhetorical target nicely into a subtly horrific scene immediately following the revelation that Tessie is the Hutchinson to die. "Although the villagers had forgotten the ritual and lost the original black box," the narrator tells us, "they still remembered to use stones" (301). And more coldly to the point, without a hint of approbation or sympathy: "The children had stones already, and someone gave little Davy Hutchinson a few pebbles" (301).

These revelations and the certainty that we are dealing with a figural narrative force the reader into a radical reconfiguration of the earlier parts of Jackson's story. The reader's incredulity at the narrator's insensitivity only increases as events and descriptions previously encountered that should produce moral outrage, or at least prompt serious questions, mount. In the second paragraph, for example, the village children, recently released from school for the summer, begin to gather the stones that will be used as murder weapons to conclude the story, but the narrator describes this as if she were observing a group of kids about to enjoy a harmless snowball fight on an unexpected day off from classes: "Bobby and Harry Jones and Dickie Delacroix—the villagers pronounced this name 'Dellacroy'—eventually made a great pile of stones in one corner of the square and guarded it against the raids of the other boys" (291). And just a page later, the narrator connects this abhorrent lottery—albeit indirectly—with a trio of utterly inoffensive social rituals: "The lottery was conducted—as were the square dances, the teen-age club, the Halloween program—by Mr. Summers, who had time and energy to devote to civic activities" (292). Blithely associating the oversight of a ritualized stoning with "other" civic commitments surely offends the sensibilities of most contemporary readers.

And this is precisely the point: the narrator's general lack of emotional or ethical engagement is provocative, and its provocations contribute significantly to the feedback loop that produces the allegory for the reader. The narrator's flat affect focuses readers' first attention acutely on the events of the story; rather than getting caught up in an analysis or critique of the narrative's voice, readers are left to encounter the shocking and bare fact of the action that lies at its center. Jackson herself noted in "Biography of a Story" that early readers of "The Lottery" were somewhat transfixed by the story's signature event: "People at first were not so much concerned with what the story meant; what they wanted to know was where these lotteries were held, and whether they could go there and watch" (128). This rather morbid reaction does illustrate the power of the central action of Jackson's narrative and her ability to focus her readers' initial gaze on it.

Once the reader commits to this figural turn, the hermeneutic feedback loop provides nothing but positive reinforcement to the allegorical hypothesis, as we can see by looking at Jackson's use of character names. Mr. Summers oversees the lottery that occurs each summer, of course, and his name carries a seasonal appropriateness as well as a healthy dose of irony; his somber duty stands in stark contrast to the more positive connotations we associate with the summer season. Mr. Graves's name, on the other hand, captures perfectly the tenor of the story and its main event, and one can imagine a slight nod of Shirley Jackson's head as she penned the line "[Mrs. Graves] watched while Mr. Graves came around from the side of the box, greeted Mr. Summers *gravely*, and selected a slip of paper from the box" (297, emphasis added), confident that she was pointing readers in the right direction.

And of course we have Old Man Warner, who objects strenuously when Mr. Adams points that some communities have purportedly abandoned the ritual of the lottery, implying that perhaps their own could follow suit. "Nothing but trouble in that," Mr. Warner warns, convinced that it's the lottery and the scapegoat that it produces that are responsible for ensuring a good harvest every year (297). The scapegoat herself is called Mrs. Hutchinson, whose name necessarily recalls that of Anne Hutchinson, another New England woman who was victimized by what we now see as backward-thinking communal paranoia. Fittingly, Mrs. Hutchinson taps one Mrs. Delacroix on the arm "as a farewell" just before the former makes her way to the front of the crowd and toward the box that contains her fate. Meaning "of or from the cross" in French, "Delacroix" calls to mind for the careful reader the entire narrative of Christianity's most central wronged martyr/scapegoat/victim and functions as an effective bit of foreshadowing regarding what will ultimately befall Mrs. Hutchinson. The thematic potential in so many of the names in "The Lottery" makes it clear that Jackson's intentions were more figural than verisimilar and strongly reinforces the notion that we are dealing with allegory.

A short essay by Nathan Cervo illustrates the amplification of a figural hypothesis that occurs in the hermeneutic feedback loop of a strong allegory. Cervo agrees that the name "Delacroix" "plays a key thematic role" in the story, a role that has unmistakable religious overtones. This conclusion then helps Cervo to see equal significance in the date on which the story takes place, June 27. "That Jackson wishes to suggest the specifically

Christian parallel or intent of 'Delacroix'/'Dellacroy,'" Cervo contends, "is supported by the fact that the lottery takes place on June 27. Twenty-seven is three cubed. So what we have is the motif of the Trinity in a total, intensified interplay with itself, rather than the hypostatic interplay of the Three Persons comprising it."[7] I am less interested in the issue of whether Cervo is on target or overreading than I am in the way that his analysis illustrates the kind of interpretive activity prompted by the recognition that the story is a strong allegory. For Cervo, the name "Delacroix" invokes the theme of Christianity; the date on which the story takes place confirms and amplifies this invocation. From here it is a short step to the idea of the scapegoat and to Cervo's ultimate conclusion that Mrs. Hutchinson "is a parodic Christ-figure, slain to appease a demonic entity that is the personification of involuted . . . ignorance masquerading as primitivistic piety."

Finally, I want to return to Yarmove's interpretation of "The Lottery" and argue that we can extend the point he makes about the work being "far greater than the sum of its parts" to all strong allegories. In these works, the individual textual phenomena invariably produce an impact that exceeds the value of the sum of each individual textual unit. Authors consciously construct strong allegories so that the hermeneutic feedback loop amplifies the thematic value of such phenomena as names, dates, and so forth, ultimately producing a work whose intended meaning emerges clearly. Strong allegory results, in other words, when the careful reader picks up on the significant textual phenomena, understands how the details fit together, and thereby arrives at an interpretation that is concordant with the author's aims. This process is one of the hallmarks of an authorial reading.

As we saw at the outset of this chapter, many critics have viewed this process as overly contrived, mechanistic, or perhaps even stultifying for the ambitious reader, but as Yarmove implies and as readers' letters to Jackson testify in a different way, strong allegories can still have a profound, haunting, and chilling effect on the reader. Jackson set out to *shock* her readers through the transformation of a ritual of violence (in the form of the lottery) into a figural narrative that transcends the literal. The history of the work's reception and its continued relevance today speak to its ultimate success and, by extension, to the persistent vitality of allegory.

---

7. It is unclear whether Cervo is aware that the June 27 date was actually suggested by the editors of the *New Yorker* because it coincided with the release date of the issue that contained Jackson's story. Jackson, according to Oppenheimer, had originally set the story a few days earlier in June.

Weak Allegory

Kafka and a Carrot Named Coco

I OPEN this chapter with a brief discussion of a children's book, one that I am familiar with because I have two children, and one that can help to illustrate how we, as readers, arrive at the conclusion that an individual text we happen to be reading is an allegory. The book is *Coco the Carrot,* and other than knowing that this was a book meant for children,[1] I had no familiarity with the story before I read it the first time with my wife and my own children. As the title reveals, Coco is a carrot, and she is the protagonist of the story that bears her name. Had this book been located in the library's general fiction section rather than in the children's section, the mere fact that the narrative focuses on an anthropomorphized carrot would certainly alert the reader to allegorical potential. With a children's book, however, a talking carrot might be nothing more than a verbal vegetable, so at the outset I had no reason to suspect that Coco's creator had allegorical aims. But almost immediately my take on the narrative began to evolve.

Two related textual phenomena catalyzed this changed reader response: 1) Coco's status as a female character and 2) her dramatic situation as the narrative opens, which the author, Steven Salerno, describes as being unhappily confined to the refrigerator. Coco, it seems, has dreams of a life beyond the vegetable crisper. For this reader at least, the appearance of a female character who feels hemmed in by her domestic space and the expectation

---

1. Admittedly, this knowledge and how we come by it are not unproblematic, but this is an issue that, if pursued, would take me too far off track at this point.

that she stay there signals the strong possibility of allegory; we are only one page into the story, but we have good evidence that Salerno might be transforming at least a portion of the narrative of Western feminism into a redemptive allegory featuring a female carrot. And much of what follows this opening confirms this initial reaction. Coco escapes and boards a steam liner for Paris, where she mingles with the rich passengers and impresses them with the hat she has made for herself. Eventually, Coco becomes a successful and famous hat designer.

The plot, however, is complicated by a series of events that occurs between the ocean voyage and the onset of Coco's career as a hatmaker. On board the ocean liner, the ship's cook recognizes Coco as a carrot and attempts to force her back into the kitchen, where she will surely perish. Coco's attempts to elude the cook result in her falling overboard. After floating at sea for several days, she washes up on an island, where she befriends a monkey. Coco decides to make the best of her new situation and begins making hats for the passengers she met on the ship. Her monkey friend makes boxes for the hats and then they fling the boxes into the ocean with a tag marked "Hats by Coco." Amazingly, the hats reach their targets and the mysterious Coco becomes a renowned designer, even though nobody knows who or where she is. Ultimately, word of Coco's talents reaches a famous Parisian hatmaker, who spares no expense to locate Coco. Once found, Coco and her monkey friend go to work for the Parisian firm, where they become internationally known and respected, a true phenomenon in the world of *haute couture*.

The story ends with a twist, as both Coco and the monkey decide that their newfound celebrity does not adequately compensate for the stress and the demands of the hatmaking industry. They miss their island and decide to forgo the fame and fortune they have in order to return to the tranquility that their previous seclusion had provided them. The narrative ends with Coco and the monkey happy again, making hats and building boxes according to their own whims and on their own schedule.

Immersed as I was in my work on allegory, my first exposure to *Coco the Carrot* proved to be fortuitous, as it provided me with a kind of laboratory in which to test some of the ideas I put forward in this book. As I have indicated, the opening lines of Salerno's book alerted me to the possibility of allegory, and so I continued reading with that as my tentative "sense of the whole" (Hirsch, *Validity* 86). The progression of the narrative continually compelled me to reconsider this preliminary sense, and Coco's decision to abandon her career challenged my initial sense that Salerno intended to transform the ideal of a woman liberated from the domestic sphere and newly fulfilled by a professional life into his narrative. This ending makes it more likely that Salerno intends to put a more contemporary spin on this idea: woman is liberated from domestic sphere, finds success in the professional world, and ultimately liberates herself from the confines of *that* realm as well. Thus, the dominant theme of the work emerges as the *fully* emancipated woman completely in control of her own destiny and willing to define her success by her level of personal satisfaction rather than by her prowess in the kitchen or in the world of work.

Would, then, I label this work a strong allegory, as I did *Animal Farm* or "The Lottery"? As I pondered this question, two issues came to mind. The first involves the reader; more specifically, who is the implied reader of a children's book, and does the answer to that question have any bearing on the question of allegory?[2] Clearly, my five-year-old son and two-year-old daughter—the ostensible implied "readers" of this narrative—would be incapable of seeing the transformation that I just identified and, for that matter, would in all probability be completely uninterested in it were I to point it out. For these two readers, then, readers happy to remain exclusive members of the narrative audience (though I would guess that even they do not believe that a carrot could talk and make hats or that she would be likely to forge a friendship and a working relationship with a monkey), the work cannot be allegorical. Their input in the feedback loop of interpretation cannot stray from the literal, and this means that the narrative itself, in their eyes, will not be an allegory, no matter what the author's intentions were or what the textual phenomena seem to imply.[3]

But what about for me and my wife, readers who have the cognitive ability and the qualifying social and educational status to enter into the authorial audience? Do we constitute the real implied readership for this book, since we are, after all, the ones who have to do the actual reading? I suspect that on some level we are the ideal readers for this children's book, if only because another adult wrote it. A children's book might well *appeal* to children while also presupposing a readership composed of adults who can enter into the kind of authorial community that Rabinowitz identifies.[4] This

---

2. Readers interested in theories of the implied reader in children's literature can consult Aiden Chambers's "The Reader in the Book" and Neil Cocks's "The Implied Reader. Response and Responsibility: Theories of the Implied Reader in Children's Literature Criticism."

3. In the introduction I conceded that my definition of allegory, and in particular my claim that some phenomenon is intentionally transformed in an allegory, raised some difficult questions. Does allegory, for example, depend on an "elite" readership? Or can a work be an allegory—no matter what the author's intentions were—if it is not read as such, if, in other words, it is not read as an allegory? My encounter with Coco crystallized some of these issues for me. As for these particular questions, a rhetorical approach to allegorical narratives would hold that it does take an informed reader—one who makes his or her way into the authorial audience—to realize an author's allegorical intentions.

4. I have frequently had this experience while reading the works of William Steig with my

might be especially true of a children's book that belongs to the subgenre of juvenile fiction, as does *Coco*, because these narratives *require* an adult reader since the audience they ostensibly target cannot yet read, at least not sufficiently well to grasp the story. In short, it matters who the reader is, and who the implied reader is, as we think about allegory.

For the two juveniles to whom my wife and I were reading, *Coco the Carrot* cannot be an allegory because they have neither the experience nor the cognitive capacity to recognize that the narrative they are hearing could be the transformation of some other cultural phenomenon. This fact validates the kind of rhetorical approach to allegory that I am pursuing here because it illustrates that *recognizing* allegory depends both on the narrative text and on the reader. For the two adult readers, on the other hand, the nature of the narrative clearly presents the possibility of allegory, but we are left to puzzle through the question of what kind of allegory we are dealing with. Is this story a strong allegory?

The more I thought about *Coco the Carrot* the more convinced I became that this narrative does not have the allegorical strength of either *Animal Farm* or "The Lottery," for example. It took a while to put my finger on the reason for this, but eventually I began to focus my attention on the monkey; I just cannot quite make sense of him. The monkey "function" does not seem necessary for the plot; if Coco can make a hat, she can certainly make a box for it. And even if this function were necessary, why is the character that performs it a monkey? Wouldn't a coconut be a more fitting and appropriate helpmate for a carrot marooned on a desert island?[5] Are (adult) readers supposed to credit the possibility of a deep friendship—or even a working relationship—between two entities that do not even inhabit the same phylum? The possibility of something "romantic" is even more incongruous and troubling. Thus, in the interpretation of this story, the monkey functions as a source of negative feedback for an allegorical hypothesis. This one textual element does not eliminate the possibility of allegory, but it does give the interpreter pause. But, as we all know, and as the popularity of the *Curious George* books makes clear, *kids* like monkeys, and so the very element of the narrative that weakens the work's allegorical nature might strengthen its appeal for those who remain contentedly ignorant of the entire realm of allegory.

---

own children, both of whom adore *Sylvester and the Magic Pebble*, *The Magic Bone*, and *Rotten Island*, among others. While they enjoy the books, my wife and I *appreciate* them in ways that they are not yet able to do.

5. I actually talked about these issues with the members of a college class on literary theory and criticism that I was teaching at the time; one of the students suggested that the monkey makes sense because a monkey would not be a threat to eat Coco. I am not sure whether monkeys eat carrots or not, but even if they do not, I'm still not convinced.

If allegory is on our interpretive radar screens, I think we have to call *Coco the Carrot* a relatively weak allegory. To define this concept "weakness" in the narrative domain more clearly, I turn to Brian McHale, whose work on avant-garde narrative poetry (admittedly, about as far removed from *Coco the Carrot* as one can get) led him to coin the phrase "weak narrativity." Weak narrativity, according to McHale, "involves . . . telling stories 'poorly,' distractedly, with much irrelevance and indeterminacy, in such a way as to *evoke* narrative coherence while at the same time withholding commitment to it and undermining confidence in it; in short, having one's cake and eating it too" (165). The terms in this definition that at first blush sound negative ("weak" itself, "poorly," "distractedly," "irrelevance," "indeterminacy") are not intended to be pejorative, but rather serve to distinguish a certain kind and a degree of narrativity that McHale wants to contrast with the kinds of narratives that function as the exemplars of strong narrativity. I want to propose a similar contrast between strong allegory—examples of which I discussed in the two previous chapters—and narratives that manage to seem allegorical and not at the same time. Thus, I propose that weak allegory involves transforming some phenomenon "poorly" or distractedly, or with some or much irrelevance and indeterminacy, into a narrative structure. The result is a narrative that *evokes* allegory while at the same time withholding commitment to it and undermining confidence in it. To return one last time to *Coco the Carrot*, it is the irrelevance or the randomness of the monkey that weakens the allegory that the rest of the narrative clearly engenders.

And it just might be that a weak allegory serves the author Salerno's purposes better than a strong allegory would have. If we presume that the author intended his work to be enjoyed—if not actually read—by children, then we must recognize that he would have little concern with my (adult) inability to make his monkey track with some coherent secondary narrative. Anyone who has or has had children will recognize that their enjoyment of a book, movie, or television show does not depend on the "tightness" of the plot or on the exactness of allusions or figuration; in many cases, a certain randomness seems to produce immense pleasure in a young audience—think for instance of the bizarre plot twists of a typical Curious George book or the general incongruity of the television series *SpongeBob SquarePants*. Ultimately, Salerno almost certainly did not have the single, unified purpose in mind that my desire to read his work as a strong allegory demands. *Coco the Carrot* carries a message, certainly, and Coco the character has allegorical qualities, but, given his target audience, Salerno was undoubtedly not intent on producing a narrative that seamlessly transforms the ideal of a fully liberated woman who is comfortable in her own skin into a strong allegory. This is not a knock against the author or his book; on the contrary, if my kids' reaction is typical, the work is quite successful just as it is: a weak allegory.

⸻

In the realm of fiction for an adult audience, the figure of Franz Kafka stands out as the most prolific and effective purveyor of weak allegory. One can easily find critics on both sides of the fence, and a great many straddling the fence itself, regarding the question of Kafka and allegory.[6] Such diversity of opinion regarding the status of Kafka's fiction obviously says something about the enigmatic nature of the works themselves, but it also seems to say something about how we think about allegory. Perhaps rethinking allegory will better allow us to accommodate "problematic" texts and authors. Kafka will be our first test case.

Critics have long suspected that readers of Kafka's fiction might be the butt of some kind of perverse joke perpetrated by the author himself, that we are lured, in other words, into a vulnerable position expressly to have the rug pulled out from under us. As Clayton Koelb argues, for example, much of Kafka's fiction "cries out for interpretation," while it simultaneously "frustrates our expectations by offering no hint of a principle by which it could possibly be interpreted" (*Kafka's Rhetoric* 165).[7] That is not to say, Koelb continues, that no interpretation is possible, but rather to point out that none—even an allegorical one—will ever be wholly satisfactory: "There is no plausible allegorical reading that does not harbor a contradiction" (168). Such contradictions, however, are precisely what conventional allegories promise to eliminate. For Koelb, "the most likely allegorical meaning" of Kafka's work is, therefore, "one that actually denies the efficacy of allegory, so that the reader is sent back chasing his logical tale in a hopeless attempt to do what the story wants him to do" (168–69). Koelb proposes to skirt this Kafkaesque hermeneutic problem by arguing that this "antithetical gesture" is a fundamentally rhetorical one insofar as it "actualizes in a particularly

---

6. The authors of *A Franz Kafka Encyclopedia* provide a helpful historical look at the relationship between allegory and Kafka's body of work. They note four major stages in this relationship: Max Brod's influence on early Kafka scholarship resulted in a tendency toward theological-leaning allegorical interpretations. Erich Heller's work in the 1970s then shifted the emphasis away from allegory and toward the idea of symbolism. This view was picked up by Heinz Politzer, who argued that "Kafka's narratives were based not on any univocality of meaning, but were grounded instead in the multivocality and semantic tensions of paradox" (Gray et al. 7–8). Finally, Walter Benjamin's reinterpretation of allegory—a view that distances it from the sense of univocality that had characterized it—encourages new allegorical interpretations of Kafka.

7. Koelb limits himself to Kafka's parables in this chapter, but his claims can easily and effectively be extended to all of Kafka's fiction.

dramatic way the coexistence of two opposed systems of meaning in a single signifying structure" (169). Seen in this light, Kafka's corpus stands as a testament to the inherent intrigue of rhetoric as it is understood by a poststructuralist critic: it is perpetually "unreadable though longing to be read" (180).

While there is undoubtedly much truth to this claim, it does not help us to understand what I see as the artistry of Kafka's writing, his ability, in other words, to invite and deny, in one stroke, allegorical interpretation. Kafka's narratives, which exhibit all of the symptoms of allegory as "a totally achieved literary creation," tempt us toward allegorical interpretation but refuse us the "satisfaction" of feeling as though we have truly and definitively unlocked their meaning. The allegorical bait of a Kafka story takes the form of a narrative world filled with the kinds of exigencies that Bitzer describes, a world in which apparent injustice, confusion, and hopelessness are both endemic and epidemic. While not uncommon in allegorical works—think, for example, of Dante's *Inferno*—the representation of such a world in a conventional strong allegory always offers both a cure to our ills and a key to our understanding the narrative in which they are depicted. Kafka's texts, however, leave the reader in a predicament that in some ways resembles that of perhaps his best-known protagonist—Gregor Samsa. We feel immediately confused as the narrative opens, but eventually we stagger to our feet and begin to cope with the bizarre situation unfolding before us.

In *The Metamorphosis*, as Gregor, the pitiable young clerk who awakes to find himself transformed into an insect and locked in his room without the means to get out, makes some admittedly small steps toward a kind of reorientation he starts to feel himself "drawn once more into the human circle" by the sound of his family and by their decision to call a doctor and a locksmith. He has hopes "for great results from both," we are told, "without really distinguishing precisely between them" (80). For Gregor, the doctor and the locksmith represent highly pragmatic choices within the context of Kafka's narrative world, for these figures can diagnose and potentially cure his illness and provide access into and out of his room, respectively. But the doctor and the locksmith also seem perfectly suited for roles in an allegorical interpretation of this novella; they are figures that we can extend easily into the allusive realm because that which doctors and locksmiths do (healing and facilitating ingress or egress) has proved to be easily allegorizable. Thus, the claim that "there is something wrong with Gregor, and he is trapped" beckons us toward the allegorical while it functions adequately as a literal description of the situation as Kafka's novella opens. Like Gregor, we readers eagerly await the key and then the diagnosis and healing.

Conventional allegorical narratives rarely disappoint in supplying these hermeneutical perquisites. Indeed, in discussing what he calls "actual" allegory, Northrop Frye, as we have seen, argues that "A writer is being allegorical whenever it is clear that he is saying 'by this I *also* (*allos*) mean that.' If this is done continuously, we may say, cautiously, that what he is writing 'is' an allegory" (90). In this description of allegory the writer him or herself fulfills the role of the locksmith, providing the key to the door separating the literal and the figurative somewhere and somehow in the work itself. Usually, when the reader is reading strong allegories, his or her ability to pass from the literal to the figurative also provides him or her with access to the "doctor," that figure who can make us whole and healthy again if only we will allow ourselves to be healed.

This description of the interpretive path characteristic of conventional allegory would work as well if applied to the literal level of *The Metamorphosis*: through the intervention of the locksmith, Gregor will be able to see the doctor. This prospect is what gives Gregor hope and enables him to feel the potential to be drawn, by the grace of the doctor, "once more into the human circle." But when the voices on the other side of his door become silent, Gregor proves incapable of waiting, and so he decides to try to release himself. The act would have been much cleaner and far less painful, however, had the locksmith been on hand. Without hands of his own, Gregor must use his mouth to turn the key, but he has no teeth and must therefore rely on the brute strength of his jaws, with whose help "he did manage to set the key in motion, heedless of the fact that he was undoubtedly damaging them somewhere, since a brown fluid issued from his mouth, flowed over the key and dripped on the floor" (80). When he finally bullies the lock into yielding, Gregor feels greatly relieved and says to himself: "So I didn't need the locksmith" (81).

Reading one of Kafka's narratives leaves one with a similar feeling. We suspect that there must be someone, somewhere, who holds the interpretive key, but that figure never materializes. Nevertheless, readers always seem determined to force their way through the literal narrative and into the figurative realm; however, the process is invariably messy, imprecise, and even excruciating, just as it is for Gregor. Ultimately, once we have reached the other side of interpretation we are faced with the realization that our mere presence there will neither clearly diagnose nor cure our ills. In Kafka, it seems, we should hold out no hope for either the locksmith or the doctor. Is this deliberate, a kind of bait and switch? Gregor, for his part, thinks they must have come, for he wonders, some days after the reality of his metamorphosis has set in, "under what pretext the doctor and the locksmith had been got rid of that first morning" (93). In fact, we really have no evidence that they were ever actually called. And with Kafka more generally we must at least entertain the possibility that the predicament on the literal level is as real as Gregor's while the solace of the allegorical is perpetually chimerical.

But what makes it so difficult to settle the question of whether *The Metamorphosis* is an allegory or not? Why do we have critics who argue adamantly on both sides of the issue? The explanation for the persistence of the disagreement, and hence the answer to these questions, lies in the fact that we tend to use the term "allegory" rather too rigidly. At the heart of the problem with allegory has been our collective inability to see it other than in absolute and conventional terms—something either is or is not an allegory. When we read what I call strong allegory, such dogmatism poses few problems because we are finding what we expect to find from allegory: a trope that is some phenomenon transformed into a narrative.

What, then, happens in *The Metamorphosis*? At the story level, the narrative looks as if it is (or should be) an allegory. The entities and the events in Kafka's narrative are strikingly allusive. We have, first of all, the behind-the-scenes transformation of a human into an insect, an act of dehumanization *cum* personification that invites allegorical interpretation; Gregor, from the very beginning of the story, is an insect that (who?) possesses a human consciousness, though he slowly loses the human capacity for speech. In addition to Gregor, we find in the narrative a number of other figures who, ontologically speaking, offer allegorical possibilities; these include not only the doctor and the locksmith but also the father (and the family unit more generally), as well as the representative from the world of work. Though perhaps somewhat less obviously hospitable to allegory than those of some examples of strong allegory (especially Christian allegory), the events of Kafka's narrative also have considerable allegorical potential. The result of the transformation (Gregor's new state of being) itself proves to be the catalyst for nearly all allegorical readings of the story, but we also see Gregor striving to hold on to something slipping from his grasp, we witness the process of deterioration, and of course we encounter conflict between family members, particularly between father and son.[8]

So, if we have events and entities that seem to lead us toward allegorical interpretation, why have we not satisfactorily resolved the issue of whether the work is an allegory or not? And why, even among those who agree that *The Metamorphosis* is an allegory, is there so much difference of opinion concerning what the story actually allegorizes? Why, in other words, can we not more clearly identify the phenomenon that Kafka intended to transform

   8. This list of allegorical pointers should also, of course, include the concept of metamorphosis itself. For an enlightening discussion of the history of the relationship between this allegory and this concept, see Bruce Clarke's chapter "Metamorphic Allegory" in his *Allegories of Writing: The Subject of Metamorphosis*.

through and in his narrative? The answer is not to be found in a new allegorical interpretation that will supplant all the others but rather in a more general account of why Kafka would be drawn to weak rather than strong allegory. I believe, in fact, that on some level Kafka intended his works to be weak allegories, and with what follows I hope to show convincingly why this is so.

The Metamorphosis evokes allegory through its juxtaposition of the mimetic and the synthetic, the figurative and the literal. More specifically, as noted above, the tale evokes allegory through the precipitating event of Gregor's transformation, and through the presence of the numerous, highly allusive figures and relationships among these figures (father–son, individual–family, employee–employer, previous self–transformed self, etc.). But it withholds commitment to allegory by refusing to render a precise and coherent phenomenon from the interplay among the precipitating event and these various allusive figures and relationships. I suspect that the fact that Kafka has given us a weak allegory has two related explanations. The first explanation breaks no new ground and has been offered by others before. Kafka in all likelihood *intended* to be ambiguous, and a narrative that simultaneously invites and frustrates allegorical interpretations that are conditioned on the expectation of strong allegory suits his desires well.

When one looks both at this particular narrative and at the entirety of Kafka's corpus, one could make a good case that his overarching aim was to convey a pervasive and disquieting feeling or sense of indeterminacy about fundamental issues of, to invoke a Heideggerian phrase, being in the (modern, technobureaucratic) world. As Peter Rabinowitz has argued, "authors often attempt to communicate ambiguity itself," and, in the case of *The Trial,* "Kafka was consciously trying to confuse" (36). This strikes me as a perfectly reasonable assertion and as good a theory about what Kafka was trying to do through his fiction (including *The Metamorphosis* in addition to *The Trial*) as any other, provided we add that Kafka's ambiguity is directed toward larger ends: capturing something of the irrational, frustrating, angst-filled, and even unknowable features of modern existence. If this is the case, then we would hardly expect for him to have constructed strong allegories, which, by their very nature, tend to resolve ambiguity rather than to cultivate it. Seen in this light, the oscillation between figuration and mimeticism in Gregor's story that at first can be quite disorienting and even disquieting actually turns out to serve Kafka's rhetorical purposes quite effectively, because such seemingly irresolvable inconsistencies seemed to permeate Kafka's life and mind. Why wouldn't he seek to convey this general sense of angst and discomfort through his narratives? To expect Kafka's authorial guidance through the text and toward a strong allegorical interpretation would be to impose on him a demand that he never set out to satisfy, and, by all indications, one that he was constitutionally incapable of satisfying.[9] More than perhaps any other author, Kafka managed to turn ambiguity, ambivalence, and confusion—traits that emerge thanks to the weakness of his allegories—into a narrative strength.

The second explanation for Kafka's preference for weak over strong allegory relies on what I call the naturalist hypothesis. Given his abiding interest in the realistic approach to fiction championed by the naturalist movement, one would not expect Kafka to write a text whose primary or exclusive rhetorical purpose was figurative or allegorical. *The Metamorphosis* emerges from two competing drives, one allusive and one mimetic. This combination produces significant but not necessarily unwelcomed uncertainty for the reader regarding what phenomenon Kafka might have wanted to transform through his narrative, as this phenomenon holds the key to understanding how all of the disparate elements of the narrative might work together. We find enough allusive potential in this novel to encourage us to look seriously at the possibility of strong allegory, and to find it, we need to identify that phenomenon.

Most of Kafka's readers who pursue an allegorical reading focus on the concept of Gregor-as-vermin. What does the idea of vermin represent, and how does it reflect Kafka's figurative intentions? We do have ample biographical evidence that the image and idea of the subhuman were common for Kafka. As Reiner Stach illustrates, "The image of a person degraded into an animal had been familiar to him for some time, probably since his childhood. His father, who liked to pepper his speech with profanities, employed this device on a regular basis. Their clumsy cook was a 'beast,' the consumptive shop-boy a 'sick dog,' the son making a mess at the table a 'big pig.'" (192). So, Stach continues, "Kafka had likened animal imagery to the idea of horrendous degradation from an early age. As a keenly observant child, he must have concluded that it was a curse to be an animal" (193). With what we know about Kafka's difficult relationship with his father and about his general disposition toward self-degradation, one could easily join Stach and others in "the realization that the animal metaphor—specifically, the image of the lowliest animal . . . was central to his existence" (195). If this is so, then Kafka might have sought to transform his own sense of self through his narrative, thus providing the phenomenon that controls the narrative and making of Gregor a stand-in for Kafka himself. This hypothesis can then be

---

9. Every biographer of Kafka, and nearly every critic of his work, agrees on this basic point: Kafka was conflicted in his personal relations, frustrated professionally, and troubled emotionally. Kafka was confused and congenitally ambivalent. We might, therefore, reasonably expect to see these states of being reflected in his work.

extended in various ways as the interpreter tries to account for Gregor's relationship with his job and his family and for the progress of Gregor's devolution over the course of the narrative.

This hypothesis, however, is not the only plausible one, and Kafka seems to have intentionally given us other viable interpretive options, the presence of which keeps the interpretive feedback loop from overamplifying the allegorical. Readers' intense focus on the identity of Gregor makes it difficult to see the importance of the idea of transformation itself. In other words, readers of *The Metamorphosis* cannot be absolutely sure that the ontology of the vermin that Gregor becomes should control our interpretive efforts. The phenomenon that Kafka meant to transform through his narrative might not be a debased sense of self, but the transformation of a human into some (any) utterly alien state. The story's title certainly supports this hypothesis, though the text itself provides no definitive confirmation and Kafka himself seems at points to be so distracted by the prospect of describing the physical minutiae of what it might be like to become a vermin that he cannot devote all of his energies to developing the significance of that "thing." Moreover, a number of Kafka's narratives—including "A Report to an Academy" (in which an ape becomes essentially human), "A Dream" (in which a man inhabits his dead self), and *The Trial* (in which K.'s arrest changes his life in ways that are almost as profound as the changes Gregor experiences, though not quite so spectacular)—pursue a similar line. It might then be that the idea of radical metamorphosis itself is at least as central to our interpretive concerns as is the struggle to figure out what the idea of the vermin that Gregor becomes represents.

I detect in *The Metamorphosis* a desire on Kafka's part to experiment with the character that he has created, to see what happens when a being is forced to adapt to a situation that is almost inconceivably strange. The opening of the narrative in particular reveals an author who apparently relishes the imaginative challenge of describing a man who awakes to find himself so profoundly metamorphosed. How would he move? What would he want or be able to eat? How would he respond emotionally? In this intellectual respect, Kafka shares some narrative tendencies with the naturalists, and with Émile Zola in particular. In his preface to *Thérèse Raquin,* a novel that chronicles the ill-fated adulterous affair between the eponymous heroine and her lover, Laurent, Zola claims that his goal is to study "temperaments" not "characters"; in other words, he wants to emphasize what today we might call the biological imperative, treating people as, to a large extent, slaves to their animalistic natures, as beings "without free will, drawn into each action of their lives by the inexorable laws of their physical nature" (22). His two main characters, Zola continues, "are human animals, nothing more. I have endeavored to follow these animals through the devious working of their passions, the compulsions of their instincts, and the mental unbalance resulting from a nervous crisis" (22). Zola claims that he wanted to bring his two temperamental types together and more or less "observe" what happened: "I simply applied to two living bodies the analytical method that surgeons apply to corpses" (23). Such pronouncements situate Zola clearly in the scientific approach to literature advocated by the naturalists, and they also prove applicable to *The Metamorphosis*.

While Kafka's case certainly differs from Zola's in its specifics, the general approach that Zola describes in his preface likely captures at least a part of Kafka's intention as well. Kafka's text certainly validates the claim that he wanted to use art to effect a transformation that reality could not produce (human to insect) and to explore and document how the human would react and adapt to this radical change of state. If readers pursue this possibility, then the question of what the insect represents recedes in importance relative to the issue of the metamorphosis itself.

This naturalistic hypothesis is bolstered by evidence that the origins of Zola's theory of literature also had an impact on Kafka. According to Martin Greenberg, Klaus Wagenbach's biography of Kafka's early years detects "the influence of natural science in Kafka's exact, exhaustive notation of detail— thanks to an admired teacher of natural history who was a convinced Darwinist, the sixteen-year-old, otherwise without scientific inclination, read Darwin and Haeckel and came under the influence of scientific naturalism" (36). Wilhelm Emrich, in his literary critical biography of Kafka, traces this influence as well, ultimately positing that, "Improbable as it may sound, Franz Kafka's earliest writing can best be understood as stemming from naturalism rather than from expressionism. . . . For the early Franz Kafka, it is above all a matter of 'description' that records, and of exact reproduction of everything that exists, precisely as it is for that 'consistent naturalist' Arno Holz, for Émile Zola, and others" (26–27).

Kafka wrote *The Metamorphosis* at the end of 1912, when he was twenty-nine years old. While we cannot place this novel with his "earliest" writings, traces of his naturalistic tendencies certainly remain. The attention to detail and the vivid, precise descriptions are indeed hallmarks of this text. The premise of the novel is utterly fantastical and highly allusive, but the narrative execution hews closely to the mimetic. Such hybridity certainly contributes to the enigmatic nature of the text and to its hermeneutic allure; it also helps to explain why we can best classify it as a weak allegory: Kafka was never fully committed to a text that tilted too heavily toward the thematic or allegorical realm. If Kafka at times seems distracted from the symbolic aspects of his work by the mechanics of what it would be like to undergo the kind of transformation that Gregor endures, it is because he was interested in both of these aspects of the narrative.

These competing interests manifest themselves most clearly in the fundamental uncertainty about what phenomenon Kafka intended to transform through his narrative—a dehumanized sense of self or the reality of undergoing a radical transformation—and that uncertainty helps to produce a weak allegory. Yet evidence of Kafka's competing narrative desires runs even deeper, all the way down into the most intimate of narrative categories: voice. A careful investigation of this concept as it relates to *The Metamorphosis* will make the case for weak allegory even stronger.

In *Coco the Carrot* the textual phenomenon that weakens the allegory is a character; in *The Metamorphosis* it is Kafka's combination of the mimetic and the figural, a combination that keeps many readers guessing about his ultimate rhetorical aim. If the author's intention is not explicitly stated (as it often is in allegories), then for a narrative to be a strong allegory readers need to be able to agree on the intentions of an implied author, and Kafka's narrative technique consistently frustrates this possibility. In many instances, allegory obviates the need to imply an author because the author makes his or her intention clear, either through his or her own voice or through the voice of a narrator to whom readers grant textual authority. If we do not have a "received" author (the opposite of an implied or inferred author), then we need to imply one, and we need to do it collectively if we are going to be able to say that we are reading an allegory.

Although there is considerable debate concerning the concept of the implied author (definitional debate, debate about the utility of the term for narrative study, and even debate about the very existence of such a thing), I contend that we need this concept in order to talk productively about allegory.[10] Allegory provides a good example of a text that rewards what we call an intentional reading, a reading, in other words, that focuses on uncovering the intended meaning of the author. Absent some explicit statement from the actual author concerning his or her intentions, the best we can do with an intentional reading is to imply a viable author, a construct certainly related to the real author—and one who might in fact share the real author's worldview and mindset—though not necessarily identical to that real author.

Kafka's discourse frustrates our ability to imply a coherent author in

---

10. For a recent and helpful treatment of the debate about the idea of the implied author, see Phelan's *Living to Tell about It: A Rhetoric and Ethics of Character Narration*. In an attempt to "provide a coherent and widely applicable redefinition of the concept," Phelan proposes that "the implied author is a streamlined version of the real author, an actual or purported subset of the real author's capacities, traits, attitudes, beliefs, values, and other properties that play an active role in the construction of the particular text" (45).

several ways. First, and most obviously, Kafka does not tell us that he has written an allegory. Nor does he tell us how we should interpret the narrative, or even whether the narrative is something that we should interpret. Compare this lack of authorial direction with what we receive at the conclusion of the first part of *The Pilgrim's Progress:*

> Now Reader, I have told my Dream to thee;
> See if thou canst interpret it to me;
> Or to thy self, or Neighbour: but take heed
> Of mis-interpreting: for that, instead
> Of doing good, will but thy self abuse:
> By mis-interpreting, evil insues. (Bunyan 164)

Or even more tellingly, consider the end of the morality play *Everyman*, where we receive specific instruction regarding how to understand the work:

> This morall men may have in mynde.
> Ye herers, take it of worth, olde and yonge,
> And forsake Pryde, for he deceyveth you in the ende;
> And remember Beaute, Fyve Wyttes, Strength, & Dy[s]crecyon,
> They all at the last do Everyman forsake,
> Save his Good Dedes there dothe he take.
> But be-ware; and they be small,
> Before God he hath no helpe at all.
> None excuse may be there for Every-man.
> Alas, how shall he do than?
> For, after dethe, amendes may no man make,
> For than mercy and pyte doth hym forsake.
> If his rekenynge be not clere whan he doth come,
> God wyll saye: '*Ite, maledicti, in ignem aeternum!*'
> And he that hath his accounte hole and sounde,
> Hye in heven he shall be crounde.
> Unto whiche place God brynge vs all thyder,
> That we may lyue body and soule togyder. (297)

We receive no such guidance as we make our way through *The Metamorphosis,* nor through any of Kafka's narratives for that matter, and this relative lack of guidance makes it difficult for readers to feel confident that they have access to the authorial audience, even as certain elements in the narrative(s) imply strongly that such an audience does exist.

In addition to the lack of authorial direction, Kafka's narrative, despite the presence of the fantastical element—namely, Gregor—that tempts us toward an allegorical interpretation, adheres very closely to the conventions of realistic or mimetic fiction. As one critic has put it,

> [Kafka's] narrative point of view is . . . one that promises, perhaps falsely, that the reader is entering an ordered realm of discourse in which meaning is generated according to well-known models. One of Kafka's favorite strategies is to exploit this kind of narration that, after a century of realist writers, had come to be codified as a form of discourse that guarantees the truth and stability of the represented world at the same time that it seems to offer a transparency through which the absent narrator promises to make present an absent but anticipated otherness. (Thiher 37)

The apparent incongruity between Kafka's fantastic story and his realistic representation of it has long fascinated readers, and it is partly this incongruity that explains why *The Metamorphosis* is a weak allegory.

The kind of mimetic fiction to which Thiher refers here is characterized by a narrative structure that employs a complex discourse—usually voiced through a complex narrator—in order to present a fictional world that is itself complex enough to be self-sufficient, one, in other words, that neither requires nor solicits an allegorical interpretation. Yet Kafka pairs this kind of realistic discourse with Gregor, a figure who clearly has no place in a mimetic narrative. While a figure such as Gregor—one that unmistakably invokes the history of personification allegory, albeit in a somewhat perverted form (Gregor is dehumanized before he personifies)—tempts us toward an allegorical interpretation of the entire narrative, the narrative itself tends to undermine that hermeneutic effort.[11] In *Allegory and Violence* Gordon Teskey argues that such an adversarial relationship between personification and narrative has a long history, that in fact there was a "neoclassical assumption . . . that allegory should have as little to do with narrative as possible. In Johnson's allegories, for example," Teskey explains, "the thought represented by a series of personified abstractions is carefully worked out so that only the most rudimentary narrative is required to link

---

11. Kafka's version of personification baffles many readers largely because it does not fall into either of the two major kinds of personification that we tend to associate with allegory. Howard Schless identifies these two varieties as 1) starting with a human aspect and then making a person or an animal out of it and 2) taking actual historical figures and making them "representative of a vice or virtue, [making] them, in fact, a symbol, an embodiment, of a human pattern of behavior" (131). Dante pioneered this second variety.

the elements of the series together. It seems, then, that in allegory narrative and personification are inversely prominent" (23). Although Teskey does not explain precisely what he means by "narrative," I suspect that, in this context, it coincides fairly closely with "discourse," and, as he sees it, a strong allegory will compel its discourse to toe the line of its author's intentions: "The more powerful the allegory, the more openly violent the moments in which the materials of narrative are shown being actively subdued for the purpose of raising a structure of meaning" (23).[12] In *The Metamorphosis*, however, Kafka's narrative discourse attains the position of power, subduing any definitive "structure of meaning" by refusing to grant authority to any particular interpretation, partly because it cloaks itself in a mimetic illusion.

This odd tension between the figural and the mimetic in *The Metamorphosis* is in evidence from the very start of the story. Readers, for the most part, are a relatively accommodating bunch. We accept Gregor's highly unrealistic transformation, but in order to do so we want to see it as symbolic or allegorical, as an element, in other words, of a recognizable "structure of meaning." Yet Kafka refuses to make evident for us what that meaning might be and, through his discourse, he presents obstacles to our reading Gregor himself as an allegorical element by allowing Gregor's "personal issues" to remain a central focus. This is a problem because Gregor will not accept his own transformation and, because so much of the narrative discourse is focused through Gregor, readers are constantly held back from exploring the larger significance of the metamorphosis. Instead of thinking about what Gregor *represents,* we must contemplate—with him—what he will *do,* given his perplexing situation:

> His immediate intention was to get up quietly without being disturbed, to put on his clothes and above all eat his breakfast, and only then to consider what else was to be done, since in bed, he was well aware, his meditations would come to no sensible conclusion. He remembered that often enough in bed he felt small aches and pains, probably caused by awkward postures, which had proved purely imaginary once he got up, and he looked forward eagerly to seeing this morning's delusions gradually fall away. That the change in his voice was nothing but the precursor of a severe chill, a standing ailment of commercial travelers, he had not the least possible doubt. (71)

---

12. Yet this raises an important question: is realism—as it manifests itself at the level of discourse—simply incompatible with allegory? Not necessarily, I think. In fact, much of George Orwell's fiction draws on the same realist tradition, yet we have no trouble calling *Animal Farm,* for example, an allegory. We can do this because the story told in this novel so closely matches a historical narrative. This is not the case with Kafka's story, obviously.

This focus on the effects of the transformation rather than on its significance complicates the reader's desire to participate in that other kind of transformation—the allegorical one.

Further contributing to the allegorical weakness of *The Metamorphosis* is the narrative's tone, or more precisely the difficulty we readers have in deciding what the tone actually is. As Frederick Crews shows in an essay in the *New York Review of Books*, a combination of editorial decisions by Max Brod (Kafka's literary executor) and world events during the first half of the twentieth century, when critics first began to take note of Kafka, encouraged readings that "[emphasized] solemn themes and prophetic insight" (4). While later critics have demonstrated a lighter side to Kafka, noting a more ludic quality in the writer who "seems to have relished the role of trickster" (4), we are still, to a large extent, influenced by the more somber version of Kafka. As a result, we are left with a schizoid vision of the author, something that is reflected in and reinforced by the tone of his works.[13] Writing about the experience of reading Kafka generally, the French critic Michel Dentan has argued that "On voudrait reconnaître une intention de l'auteur, mais le texte reste parfaitement ambigu; et le lecteur engage sa propre responsabilité dans la manière dont il perçoit le ton des récits" [One would like to uncover an authorial intention, but the text remains completely ambiguous; and the reader takes on the responsibility himself for the way in which he perceives the tone of the narratives] (9, my translation). Dentan explores specifically how Kafka's ambiguous narratives raise the question of when Kafka is being serious and when he is being humorous, but it also helps to explain why we have trouble determining whether he intends to be allegorical or not. Not surprisingly, most of the allegorical readings of *The Metamorphosis* either downplay or overlook the humor that Dentan finds in it.

Kafka's manipulation of narrative perspective largely explains the difficulty we have in identifying a tone and also goes a long way toward explaining the weakness of his allegory. Kafka employs a third-person narrator in *The Metamorphosis*, but Gregor's perspective tends to dominate the narrative. Indeed, some critics—most notably Friedrich Beissner—have gone so far as to claim that Kafka's narrator *always* relates only Gregor's point of view. Dentan and others have clearly shown that this is not so, but we can agree, I think, that until his death, Gregor serves as the guiding consciousness for the reader. Nevertheless, the story is not completely his, and even this slight indeterminacy concerning perspective complicates the issue of allegory. The inconclusiveness that we do experience in reading this narrative results pri-

---

13. This undoubtedly contributes to our difficulty in fashioning a satisfactory implied author as well—more on this below.

marily from Kafka's use of the *erlebte Rede* technique, which we also know as *style indirect libre* or free indirect discourse. Clayton Koelb points out in his work on Kafka that this is a form of third-person narrative that "is not necessarily a very far step from the first-person narrative" because "its perspective is normally limited to the point of view of a single character" ("Kafka Imagines" 347). Even if the distance between first- and third-person narration in free indirect discourse is small, however, that gap can be a significant one to overcome as one attempts to understand what an allegorical story ultimately means.

Thus, perspective in *The Metamorphosis* presents us with two serious problems. First, since we are so close to Gregor's perspective for most of the narrative, we have little advantage over him in understanding the significance of his predicament. We understand that Gregor's willingness and capacity to make sense of his situation are limited, but like tourists who intuit that their guide might not be the sharpest or most knowledgeable person for that position, we do not have any alternative sources of information or insight readily available. I am not proposing that one needs a third-person omniscient narrator who clearly and authoritatively speaks for the author in order to have an implied author, nor am I saying that one needs such a narrator in order to have an allegory; indeed, many allegories are first-person narratives (viz. *Piers Plowman* and *The Pilgrim's Progress*). In these first-person accounts the narrator has achieved some kind of critical distance (usually because the events narrated are ostensibly a dream) and thus is able to reflect on the significance of the happenings in such a way as to present them as a kind of heterodiegetic first-person narrator. This distance allows the first-person narrator to make sense of things in a way that Gregor—for whom we are told on the first page that "It was no dream" (67)—is not.

Like Gregor, then, we are frustrated and, in a way, trapped. And this raises the second problem with perspective: our narrator does not provide much help. Even at the points in the text when we sense that the narrator might provide us with a perspective or a voice that differs from Gregor's, we still receive little interpretive guidance. One passage from *The Metamorphosis* that has historically been one of the most carefully dissected and analyzed brings these issues to the fore precisely because it forces us to consider the issues of voice and perspective in Kafka's discourse. This passage occurs near the end of the novella and it describes an important event in the story. After Gregor's transformation his family has taken in three boarders in order to help defray some of their expenses and to compensate for the loss of Gregor's salary. One evening Gregor's sister—Grete—begins playing the violin in the kitchen and the boarders express a desire to listen to the music. To accommodate this, Gregor's father moves her music stand into the living area so that Grete can resume her playing in closer proximity to the three men. Gregor is also intrigued, however, and despite being "covered with dust" and trailing "fluff and hair and remnants of food," he crawls out of his room and inches his way into the living room (120). "To be sure," Kafka writes,

> no one was aware of him. The family was entirely absorbed in the violin-playing; the lodgers, however, who first of all had stationed themselves, hands in pockets, much too close behind the music stand so that they could all have read the music, which must have bothered his sister, had soon retreated to the window, half-whispering with downbent heads, and stayed there while his father turned an anxious eye on them. Indeed, they were making it more than obvious that they had been disappointed in their expectation of hearing good or enjoyable violin-playing, that they had had more than enough of the performance and only out of courtesy suffered a continued disturbance of their peace. From the way they all kept blowing the smoke of their cigars high in the air through nose and mouth one could divine their irritation. And yet Gregor's sister was playing so beautifully. Her face leaned sideways, intently and sadly her eyes followed the notes of music. Gregor crawled a little farther forward and lowered his head to the ground so that it might be possible for his eyes to meet hers. Was he an animal that music had such an effect upon him? He felt as if the way were opening before him to the unknown nourishment he craved. (120–21)

Even if we agree that the narrative is focalized through Gregor, or that it is Gregor's perspective that dominates, we are still left with questions concerning voice. Think about the claim that Gregor's sister was playing so beautifully. Whose voice is this? Does it matter? I cannot answer the first question definitively, but, as for the second, I would argue that it does matter, because inconclusive passages such as this one make it difficult to identify either the tone or the values of the narrator. And without a firm grounding in these areas we cannot really be sure of how the narrator feels about Gregor, his plight, and his family. Booth claims that "Our sense of the implied author includes not only the extractable meanings but also the moral and emotional content of each bit of action and suffering of all of the characters. It includes, in short, the intuited apprehension of a complete artistic whole; the chief value to which *this* implied author is committed, regardless of what party his creator belongs to in real life, is that which is expressed by the total form" (*Rhetoric of Fiction* 74). In this story, we do not know the chief value to which even the narrator is committed, and this makes it a matter of pure guesswork to decide to what values the textual authority is committed; this thwarts our attempts to imply an author. James Phelan has argued that voice is a "synthesis of style, tone, and values" ("Editor's" 2). In identifying allegory, tone and values are particularly critical, and they go a long way toward allowing us to form some image of an implied author. But in *The Metamorphosis* a determinative voice is difficult to identify.

Kafka's decisions bearing on the narrative's discourse produce critical uncertainty on the reader's part. We know that Gregor's point of view dominates, but we are equally aware of the countervailing presence of the narrator. At times it is impossible to say unequivocally whose voice we hear and what values are inflected by that voice.[14] In the passage cited above, if Gregor is (solely) responsible for the positive evaluation of his sister's musical performance, then we can—and probably should—interpret this as just another example of the vermin deluding himself, as further evidence of his inability to deal with his bizarre reality. If, on the other hand, the voice is that of the narrator, then Gregor comes out looking far better; ironically, he—the beast—would be the only one truly possessing a refined aesthetic taste, and the others, in comparison, would seem shallow and coarse. Given the indeterminacy of Kafka's discourse, both readings are plausible. Such indeterminacy does not preclude the possibility of allegory, of course, but it does alter the degree of allegoricalness; it contributes to this narrative being a weak rather than a strong allegory.

Thus, what readers often expect from Kafka, and what we get in works that are strong allegories, is a narrative discourse that helps us to configure the story elements in such a way as to make clear what it is the author has transformed into his narrative. This happens in historical allegories (*Animal Farm*) and in what Frye calls "actual" allegories, but it does not in *The Metamorphosis*. There is no implied author whose views are clearly discernible or whose views are consistent with all that transpires in the narrative itself. Such a figure is required in this case because, although we do have a story that has allegorical potential, the pieces of that story (the events and entities) do not add up to anything that resembles a pre-existing historical narrative, nor do we have an "authoritarian" voice guiding us toward the significance

---

14. This hermeneutical challenge pervades Kafka's fiction. In his discussion of *The Trial* Philip Weinstein makes a claim that buttresses my argument vis-à-vis *The Metamorphosis*. According to Weinstein, "there are two ways of misreading the opening sentence of *The Trial*. The first is to believe one is reading third-person realism and thus to trust the narrative voice (someone did in fact traduce Joseph K., and we will in time find out who and why). The second is to believe one is reading first-personal modernism and thus to distrust the narrative voice (he *says* he was traduced but we suspect he lies, and will in time discover why). Both ways produce cogent interpretations. Both likewise miss the intrinsic instability of that voice's reference, its bid for readerly trust joined with its betrayal of such trust—a bid and a betrayal inseparable from the text's peculiar deployment of the subject in space/time. One finishes the book exactly as one began, in confusion" (136).

of the narrative. In short, readers struggle to determine the specific phenomenon that has been transformed. As a result, we are left more or less on our own, per Kafka's design and due to his penchant for narratives that are both and simultaneously allusive and naturalistic, to make sense of something that needs interpretation. Strong allegories, I would argue, do not leave us on our own like this, waiting for a locksmith and a doctor who might or might not have been summoned.

Many readers, of course, actually prefer to go it alone and enjoy the process of breaking through a text in the same way that Gregor forces his way through his locked door. Many of these readers are the same ones who harbor such animosity for strong allegory, and many of them constitute a group of critics who actually prize allegory, but do so on their own terms, terms that we might call poststructuralist. Although they do not use the terminology that I have adopted, many poststructuralist critics who work with allegory seem to start from the premise that weak allegories—those defined by indeterminacy, incompleteness, and distraction—are paradigmatic of this trope, the rule rather than a variation on the historical norm of the strong allegorical narrative. Walter Benjamin and Paul de Man in particular renewed interest in allegory by recasting it in terms that would be more appealing to a twentieth-century audience and that do echo what I have said about weak allegory.[15]

As I mentioned in the introduction, poststructuralist critics—led by de Man—recognize the centrality of narrative to allegory. De Man sees in all language a "tendency toward narrative," and he conceives of allegory as a trope within the realm of language. Thus, allegory participates in this "tendency." The connection between allegory and narrative is more accidental or coincidental for de Man than I think it really is, but the connection itself remains significant, and it plays two important roles in de Man's conception of allegory. First, it allows de Man to focus on allegory as a particular use of language, a rhetorical trope. Second, it allows him to emphasize what he sees as allegory's crucial temporal dimension. Together, these moves define the poststructuralist approach to allegory.

De Man treats allegory as a trope within a text, focusing on what he calls the "allegorical sign." Like any sign, the allegorical sign, according to de Man, comprises both a signifier and a signified, and, as we would expect from one of his critical persuasion, de Man argues that the connection between these two components is neither necessary nor completely harmonious. Thus, de Man argues in *Blindness and Insight* that "The relationship between the

---

15. Benjamin's signal contribution to the theorizing of allegory comes in the chapter "Allegory and Trauerspiel" in *The Origin of German Tragic Drama*.

allegorical sign and its meaning (*signifié*) is not decreed by dogma; in the instances we have seen in Rousseau and in Wordsworth, this is not at all the case. We have, instead, a relationship between signs in which the reference to their respective meanings has become of secondary importance" (207).

Essentially, for de Man, allegory becomes a trope designating hermeneutic failure as is made evident in his well-known claim in *Allegories of Reading* that "allegorical narratives tell the story of the failure to read" (205). As Jim Hansen points out in "Formalism and its Malcontents": "In [de Man's] writing, allegory marks out the space of the failure of referential meaning, the space in which, as he explains, representation 'does not stand in the service of something that can be represented'" (665). Equally illustrative is de Man's claim in *Blindness and Insight* that in allegory, as well as in irony, "the relationship between sign and meaning is discontinuous, involving an extraneous principle that determines the point and the manner at and in which the relationship is articulated. In both cases, the sign points to something that differs from its literal meaning and has for its function the thematization of this difference" (209). Allegory, for de Man, stands as testament to the unbridgeability of this difference separating signifier and signified, or meaning.

According to Hansen, "For de Man, allegory gradually became the key rhetorical figure in a particularly relentless strain of deconstruction" (665). I would argue in addition that allegory becomes a symbol (not, we should note, an allegory) for signification in the vernacular of deconstructive criticism: a sign points only to some other sign, not to some extralinguistic signified with which it has some fixed relationship. Freed of these representational restraints, allegory becomes the ideal structuralist and poststructuralist signifying structure,[16] and it is no surprise that de Man would prefer it to the idea of symbol, which, he claims, "postulates the possibility of an identity or identification" between signifier and signified (207). As Hansen argues, for de Man, "in opposition to the symbol, allegory consciously points to its own temporality and, in so doing, embarrasses its own claims to truth" (672).

One can easily see how the indeterminacy and the lack of closure that I ascribe to weak allegory resonates with the approach to allegory adopted by de Man and like-minded twentieth-century critics influenced by post-

---

16. According to Joel Fineman, "we can see why, for contemporary structuralism, allegory would be the figure of speech *par excellence*. No other figure so readily lays itself out on the grid constructed out of the hypothesized intersection of paradigmatic synchrony and syntagmatic diachrony, which is to say that no other figure so immediately instances the definition of linguistic structure which was developed by Jakobson out of Saussure and the Russian Formalists, and that has since been applied to all the so-called 'sciences of man,' from anthropology (Lévi-Strauss) to semiotics (Barthes) to psychoanalysis (Lacan)" (32).

structuralism and deconstruction. These critics locate markers of allegory (allegorical signs, to use de Man's language) and then explore the significance—and the failure of significance—of these signs within the larger work of literature. This leads to what Roland Barthes would call a "readerly" approach to allegory and, as a result, to some fascinating examples of strong readings of weak allegories.[17] I call this kind of reading a strong reading because even a deconstructive approach—with notions of indeterminacy and multivalence fully baked in—to a text that seems allegorical tends to close the interpretive loop in such a way as to amplify the allegoricalness of the text beyond the author's probable intention. What follows is a description of one such reading of *The Metamorphosis* and an analysis of that attempt that will show how and why the weak allegorical designation for Kafka's novel is preferable to a strong reading that views allegory through a poststructuralist lens.

In *The Commentators' Despair: The Interpretation of Kafka's "Metamorphosis,"* Stanley Corngold argues that there are two primary modes of interpreting this enigmatic text. The first such reading Corngold calls "symbolic," and it is characterized by a belief that "Gregor Samsa remains an intact moral personality," but that he is also "homeless," an "outcast social man," and one whose "life is empty of meaningful work, friendship, sexual love, family loyalty" (33). "In sum the symbolic reading asserts," according to Corngold: "1. the continuity of the empirical personality of Gregor Samsa with the monstrous vermin; 2. the meaningfulness of the metamorphosis in terms of intentions and effects taken from ordinary experience; 3. the deficiency and remediableness [through death] of the experience with which *The Metamorphosis* is correlated; 4. the prescriptive and prophetic bearing of the work, hinted at in Gregor's and the family's end" (34). In short, we might surmise that Gregor, according to this interpretation, functions as a symbol for alienated, modern humankind, and that his metamorphosis underscores and exacerbates that sense of isolation.

The allegorical reading, on the other hand, Corngold offers, "opposes the symbolic reading in every detail. It takes literally the metamorphosis, the radical disjunction separating Gregor Samsa from the vermin. It considers the work as literally constituting an uncanny, unsettled existence" (35). Essentially, this variety of allegorical reading takes the same kind of ontological tack favored by de Man (and Benjamin before him): "Mainly because this reading stresses the absolute interval between Gregor Samsa and his new situation—his unbeing—it can be called *allegorical* according to Walter Benjamin's definition of allegory as the nonpresence—that is to say

---

17. Barthes lays out his distinction between readerly and writerly texts in *S/Z*.

the nonexperienceable character—of what is signified" (35).[18] Corngold has apparently accepted the deconstructive approach to allegory as the definitive one and is thereby able to call *The Metamorphosis* an allegory because it represents the disjunction between human existence and the absence of human existence.[19] What finally distinguishes what Corngold calls the symbolic interpretation from the allegorical one is the willingness of the latter to take seriously (and literally) the existential rift that Gregor experiences.

Corngold believes that *The Metamorphosis* is really about language and Kafka's ambivalent and ambiguous relationship with it. At the outset of this short novel, Corngold points out, Kafka literalizes a metaphor (Gregor is—literally—vermin), and in so doing he betrays his problematic relationship with symbolic language; Kafka, Corngold asserts, was neither good nor comfortable with metaphors, so instead of using them in his writing he transforms them into literality. Gregor, then, suffers from problems that produce some of the same symptoms that plague the author who conceived him. "The negativity of the vermin has to be seen as rooted," Corngold explains,

> in an absolute sense, in the literary enterprise itself, as coming to light in the perspective which the act of writing offers of itself. Here the activity of writing appears only autonomous enough to demand the loss of happiness and the renunciation of life. But of its own accord it has no power to restitute these sacrifices in a finer key. Over Kafka's writing stands a constant sign of negativity and incompleteness. (26)

In this sense, we can say that Gregor embodies the angst and alienation that Kafka supposedly experienced, but we cannot say—or at least Corngold would strongly resist saying—that Gregor "stands for" Kafka. It is an

---

18. This comes very close to what de Man says about allegory's ontological component: for de Man, as for many critics committed to deconstruction, the step between hermeneutics and ontology is a small one, and this is made clear by de Man's ideas regarding allegory. Indeed, we see in *Blindness and Insight* how easily de Man moves from the hermeneutic to the ontological: "Whereas the symbol postulates the possibility of an identity or identification, allegory designates primarily a distance in relation to its own origin, and, renouncing the nostalgia and the desire to coincide, it establishes its language in the void of this temporal difference. In so doing, it prevents the self from an illusory identification with the non-self, which is now fully, though painfully, recognized as a non-self" (207). Here, de Man seems to make analogous the relationships signifier–signified and being–nonbeing, thereby closing the circle of hermeneutics and ontology.

19. It is perhaps worth quibbling here. Is it really correct to say that Gregor-as-vermin is an "unbeing" or a "nonpresence"? This does not seem quite right to me, especially since death seems to provide a clear opposition to existence. De Man appears to be on firmer ground when, in *Blindness and Insight,* he reads one of Wordsworth's Lucy poems as an allegory because it plays with the difference between life and death (223–25).

analogy of condition, of alienation from life that springs from a "distortion of ordinary language" (27), that most interests Corngold:

> It is this dwelling outside the house of life, "*Schriftstellersein,*" the negative condition of writing as such, which is named in *The Metamorphosis;* but it cannot name itself directly, in a language that designates things that exist, or in the figures that suggest the relations between things constituting the common imagination of life. Instead, in *The Metamorphosis* Kafka utters a word for a being unacceptable to man (*ungeheuer*) and unacceptable to God (*ungeziefer*), a word unsuited either to intimate speech or to prayer. This word evokes a distortion without visual identity of self-awareness— engenders, for a hero, a pure sign. The creature of *The Metamorphosis* is not a self speaking or keeping silent but language itself (*parole*)—a word broken loose from the context of language (*langage*), fallen into a void the meaning of which it cannot signify, near others who cannot understand it. (27)

Thus, Gregor-as-vermin, at least in Corngold's reading, functions as a sign that points to language, and indeed to a conception of language that sounds strikingly similar to that held by deconstructionists.

Yet Corngold seems to sense that an allegorical analysis cannot end with the identification of what the critic calls an allegorical sign. Thus, he asks the question that must be asked: "What, then, is allegorized in *The Metamorphosis?* What intention finds its correlative in the metamorphosis of a man into an *Ungeziefer,* an unbeing?" (35).[20] Even if we can overlook the fact that vermin, while not human, are a kind of being, albeit an odious one, we are hard-pressed to buy completely into Corngold's answer. "It [the correlative-seeking intention] is," he contends, "first of all, Kafka's intention to exist as literature, to write fiction; for this intention to write—to paraphrase Collingwood—is realized only insofar as it both lives in the historical process and knows itself as so living. In this story writing reflects itself, in the mode of allegory, as metamorphosis, literality, death, play, and reduction—the whole in a negative and embattled form" (35).

Corngold's argument here essentially runs as follows: Kafka was intensely committed to his writing, but as he wrote he "came to realize more and more sharply the impoverishment, reduction, and shortcoming which writing entails" (35). Writing, therefore, is antithetical to life, and so the writer

---

20. Corngold deserves credit for asking this question. De Man, on the other hand, never broaches the topic of what the works he interprets are allegories of. Instead, he is content to operate more locally, on the level of the signifier within a text. Traditionally, though, when we talk about allegory, we want to know, like Corngold, what the entire work allegorizes.

experiences a kind of death. For the committed Kafka, there is no alternative; he must, as a writer, constantly endure this "radical estrangement from life" (36). What Corngold calls Kafka's recognition of "the root separateness of literature and life—indeed the antithetical character of literature and life conceived as *Bildung*, as an extensive totality of experience," is reflected in "the vermin's [Gregor's] gradual reduction and impoverishment, his loss of eyesight and loss of locomotion" (36–37).

If Corngold's claim was that Gregor functions as a substitute for Kafka himself and thus enacts an allegory of Kafka's tortured existence, then we might be persuaded to follow his line of reasoning, even if there is no compelling textual evidence to support such an autobiographical approach (Gregor, after all, is no writer), and even if we are not completely convinced that writing did have the kind of deathly implications for Kafka that Corngold supposes it did. Perhaps because of these issues, Corngold does not make this claim. Instead, he puts forward an argument that sounds, today, like a parody of deconstructive criticism: "The sorrow belongs to the being who is literature, who is engaged in an exemplary way in the passage from particularity to generality and as a consequence must suffer death after death without hope of a goal. The emblem of literature in its desire for generality and its condemnation to particularity is its literality, the literal being the allegory of the literary" (36). Although it is difficult to say with certainty what Corngold intends by this, he seems to be making the claim that both the vermin and Kafka lead literary lives and are therefore condemned to lead lives that are only literal, lives, in other words, that provide no means of escape from the text and no hope of transcendence or meaningfulness. Kafka leads such a life by choice; he ties himself to the literary and the literal by being a writer. Gregor suffers such a life because, according to Corngold, he is a character in a work of literature who is constantly denied access to the symbolic:

> The constitution of tragic, allegorical consciousness in *The Metamorphosis* includes the representation of symbolic consciousness. This occurs whenever the vermin erroneously asserts his identity with Gregor Samsa and tries to restore his old situation within the family and again whenever his reflections appear to justify the metamorphosis as punishment. That the symbolic mode is a seduction and an error emerges through the vermin's attempts to speak in metaphorical language. Kafka's aversion to the metaphor is constant, but in the few places in *The Metamorphosis* where this language occurs, the reader patently finds himself inside an inauthentic consciousness.... It cannot be this creature's fate to know a symbolic unity with his world. (37)

Thus, Gregor and Kafka resemble each other because each feels alienated from his respective world, mired in a literary existence that impoverishes and reduces his being. While all of this might have some truth behind it, the grounds for Corngold's comparison are quite weak and depend entirely on the peculiarly deconstructive notion of allegory, one that inextricably ties it to *linguistic* failure, alienation, and meaninglessness. This is signaled, according to Corngold, by Kafka's "aversion to metaphor" and by what Corngold claims is the fact that "the vermin's attempt to come to terms with his experience through metaphor inspires derision" (37).[21]

For readers less under the thrall of deconstruction and its single-minded focus on linguistic indeterminacy and failure, however, Corngold has not provided enough evidence to prove that it was Kafka's *intention* to allegorize his own desire to "exist as literature," even if we can understand what this desire would be and can grant that it is plausible that Kafka experienced it (neither of which is a given). Rather than demonstrating that *The Metamorphosis* is an allegory of this sort, Corngold has rather imposed an interpretation on it that transforms it into a symbol for deconstruction. It is not my intention here to discredit entirely Corngold's reading of Kafka, but rather to claim that his reading does not justify calling the narrative a strong allegory. Like de Man, Corngold believes that the presence of an "allegorical signifier" (or the perceived predominance of allegorical signifiers over symbolic signifiers) within a text justifies applying the term allegory to the work as a whole. The mere presence of such signifiers, however, even if we do agree that they are "allegorical," seems to me to be insufficient evidence of strong allegory more generally. And when Corngold attempts to make the leap from sign to text, he must rely too heavily on inference, on questionable conclusions about Kafka's psyche, and on arguments that he does not adequately support with textual evidence. In short, Corngold has produced a very strong allegorical reading of a weak allegory.

If Kafka's text were a strong allegory, then an interpretation of it would not allow for as much readerly latitude as Corngold takes. Nor would it allow for competing and even contradictory allegorical interpretations. But in the case of *The Metamorphosis,* such alternative readings do exist. In addition to Corngold's claim that Kafka's text is the transformation of the author's intention to "exist as literature," we have Honig's claim that the narrative represents the transformation of the problem of the individual's identity relative to others (Gregor "has no vital mission; he has cut himself off from society" [68]), the commonly expressed opposite view that this tale is an allegory

---

21. Although Corngold does not cite de Man in this section of his explication of *The Metamorphosis,* he does credit de Man's "The Rhetoric of Temporality" when he discusses allegory earlier in the essay, and his conception of allegory clearly owes much to de Man.

of modern society's dehumanizing effect on the individual, and the claim that the story is yet another allegory of the Freudian Oedipal conflict. The number of varying allegorical interpretations of *The Metamorphosis* attests to the presence of allegory in this narrative and also stands as compelling evidence that the narrative itself cannot be called a strong allegory.

The weakness of Kafka's allegory, and the number of strong readings that this weakness has engendered, have together resulted in an interesting backlash against an interpretive approach to Kafka more generally. Benjamin first outlined this anti-interpretive approach in his essays on Kafka (collected in the volume titled *Illuminations*), but others came later to champion the cause. In a review of one such approach (*K.*, by Roberto Calasso), Robert Alter makes the case against interpreting Kafka succinctly: "To interpret Kafka's fiction is to coerce it into a framework of stable meaning—sliding down the slippery slope toward allegory—that the work itself seems devised to unsettle" (31). Although Alter's language betrays an abiding dislike for allegory (one is at pains to interpret "the slippery slope toward allegory" positively), his claim bolsters the case for calling Kafka's work weak allegory. Many of Kafka's narratives—certainly *The Metamorphosis* among them—lead the reader down a path toward allegory, marking the way with textual phenomena that appear tantalizingly allusive and figural, but then never allow for the kind of closure or determinacy that strong allegories invariably deliver. Thus, interpretations of his work tend to seem forced and a little messy. We should not be surprised that some would prefer not to follow that interpretive path at all.

All of this points, finally, to the conclusion that many readers remain uncomfortable with the kind of confusion and ambiguity that Kafka and his works beget. Some would argue that effecting such confusion in the reader is Kafka's aim and, perhaps, a part of his genius, but I see this confusion as stemming from a misunderstanding of Kafka's rhetorical purpose. This purpose, as I argued above, was simultaneously mimetic and figural, and the category of weak allegory gives us the perspective and the tools we need to understand and appreciate Kafka's rare achievement.

3

Embedded Allegory

I HAVE heretofore focused my attention on entire works of fiction—whether novels or short stories or parables—that we can label one kind of allegory or another (strong or weak), but allegory does not always and only manifest itself as a complete, self-contained narrative. Indeed, I contend that some of our problems in dealing with allegory, and some of our resistance to it, stems from our general insistence on applying the conventional designation "allegory" or "allegorical" only to entire works. As Honig claims, "The form of an allegory must also be the form of the medium (prose or poetry, drama or novel) conveying it. But in whatever medium, it is a form that characterizes the allegory as a totally achieved literary creation" (14). I resist the idea that allegory must be "a totally achieved literary creation" (though this is *possible*, as in the case of the strong and weak allegories I discussed in the preceding chapters) and submit instead that especially in modern and contemporary narrative fiction, allegory is more often than not an important *aspect* of other such creations. Recognizing this fact will allow us to see allegory as a complex feature of literature and will allow us to make better sense of certain modern texts that have proved especially challenging to interpretation.

Moving toward a rhetorically inflected approach to allegory can help us make sense of a variety of narratives that make use of allegory in some way but that do not produce the same kind of allegorical effect that more traditional allegorical narratives do. We commonly find allegory present in a work of fiction, for example, as a narrative embedded in but marked off from the primary narrative.[1] Such embedded narratives—which might take the form of dreams, stories related by characters or narrators, or speeches—raise important issues about our treatment of allegory, the most germane of which is whether the presence of such an embedded allegory necessarily makes the primary, host narrative allegorical. Honig broaches this question early in *Dark Conceit* when he wonders "whether in [Shakespeare's] *Coriolanus* Menenius' famous body-versus-belly speech is an allegory or in any sense allegorical" (10). Honig decides that the speech is allegorical primarily for two reasons: because it appeals to an "ideal" concerning the operation of government,[2] and because it "functions as a trope on at least two levels of meaning. The anatomical analogy makes of a civil insurrection and a physiological disorder one and the same thing" (10–11). Thus, Honig declares the speech to be allegorical; however, he resists calling it an allegory because he reserves that term for "the full-length, inclusively figurative work [i.e., Shakespeare's play] and [for] the literary type which comprises such works" (11).

Honig treats the allegorical speech in *Coriolanus* as if he were adopting the kind of rhetorical approach I am advocating. Immediately after stipulating that his work will focus only on the genre of full-length allegorical narratives, he notes that "Menenius' speech shows how an allegorical trope extends itself and, further, how it serves as a guiding motif in a longer work" (11). This speech, he continues, "[exerts] a . . . pressure of figurative predetermination" in the context of the entire play (12). But this is all that Honig has to say on the subject of this embedded allegory, and I believe the concept deserves fuller treatment. In examining other examples of embedded allegories we will see that a rhetorical approach can help to explain that "pressure of figurative predetermination" in the cases where such pressure does exert itself, but it will also allow us to recognize that not all embedded allegories do function within the primary narrative in the way that Honig's claims imply that they do.

When we shift our discussion from allegory *as* narrative to allegory *in* narrative, we must look at allegory in a very different way; embedded allegories are themselves textual phenomena, part of the feedback loop of interpretation. My aim in this chapter is to document the various kinds of embedded allegories and to explore the range of rhetorical impact that each produces, both on the reader and within the context of the primary narratives in which

---

1. In Gérard Genette's terms, such an embedded narrative would be a metanarrative ("a narrative within the narrative") that constitutes a metadiegesis ("the universe of this second narrative") (228). As I find Genette's use of "meta" to be somewhat misleading, however, I will simply use the term "embedded" in the discussion to follow.

2. This concept of an "ideal" is central to Honig's understanding of allegory. Indeed, he characterizes the allegorical genre as one that "refers to many different works that engage an ideal encompassing the problematic nature of human existence" (14).

they are framed. I identify three varieties of embedded allegories. For the first two, I fall back on the grammatical terms "independent" and "dependent" as classificatory aids. As with clauses in a sentence, independent and dependent here distinguish elements that can and cannot exist alone. Thus, an independent embedded allegory is conceivable as a separate narrative, one that could exist autonomously, while a dependent embedded allegory cannot function without the structure in which it is embedded. I call the third type of embedded allegory "interdependent," a designation that refers to an intertextual figural narrative, one that an author borrows from another author and embeds in his or her own story. These embedded allegories are changed and often reinvigorated in their new narrative surroundings, but they also remain tied to—and to some extent defined by—their original context.[3]

There is some overlap between what I am calling embedded allegories and the phenomenon that has come to be called *mise-en-abyme*, a term generally credited to André Gide that derives from ancient heraldry and that refers, in literature, to the instances in which some smaller part of a larger work reflects that larger work. Lucien Dällenbach, whose *The Mirror in the Text* stands as the most comprehensive work on this topic, defines *mise-en-abyme* as "*any aspect enclosed within a work that shows a similarity with the work that contains it*" (8, emphasis in original).[4] In the examples of embedded allegories below, we will find instances that meet the criteria necessary to be labeled *en abyme*; this will be most apparent in my sections on independent and dependent embedded allegories.

Despite the affinities between several of my categories and examples of embedded allegory and *mise-en-abyme*, I do not want to adopt this term—which, as McHale notes, "is not a very felicitous [one]" (189)—for my work on allegory because it describes what seems to me to be considered a largely monolithic narrative phenomenon. The term *mise-en-abyme*, in other words, does not currently allow for different kinds of embedded narratives, or at least for the different kinds of embedded narratives that I have identified. Dällenbach does devote a short chapter to different types of *mise-en-abyme* (chapter 8, "The Emergence of Types"), but I do not find his categories

---

3. For the most complete general discussion of the concept of embedded narratives, see William Nelles's *Frameworks: Narrative Levels and Embedded Narrative*. Nelles's work is very helpful from a descriptive standpoint.

4. Other critics have modified this definition. Moshe Ron, for example, claims that "Any diegetic segment which resembles the work where it occurs, is said to be placed en abyme" (436). Brian McHale identifies two criteria that characterize the phenomenon: "First, there must be a demonstratable relation of analogy . . . between the part *en abyme* and the whole, or some substantial aspect of the whole. . . . [And] the part *en abyme* must be inset one or more levels 'down' or 'in' the primary world" (190). Whatever the specific definition, critics are in general agreement that the embedded piece must somehow reflect or mirror the larger narrative in which it is placed.

conducive to the sort of rhetorical analysis to which I am committed because his categories depend on "*the degree of analogy between the 'mise-en-abyme' and the object it reflects* [typically the larger narrative]" (110, emphasis in original). I have found, on the other hand, that I need to subdivide the concept of embedded allegory according to the *nature of its relationship* to the embedding narrative. This method of distinguishing types of embedded narratives better enables me to describe the rhetorical impact of the different types of embedded allegorical narratives that I have identified.

A rhetorical approach to the phenomenon of narrative embedding—a broad category that would include both *mise-en-abyme* and embedded allegory—might add an important dimension to our understanding of this narratological category. The adjectives "dependent," "independent," and "interdependent" that I employ below might ultimately prove not just to be helpful in analyzing embedded allegories but also to be relevant and useful in the future theorizing about *mise-en-abyme*. At the same time, I do recognize that the work that has been done on this phenomenon can augment my own theoretical enterprise, and I will indicate below the various points at which I see my ideas intersecting with those that have been put forth in the service of developing a theory of *mise-en-abyme*.[5]

Independent Embedded Allegory: Achebe and Kafka

As Edwin Honig rightly claims, an allegorical tale that has been embedded in a larger narrative tends to exert an appreciable hermeneutic force on both the reader and the text; this is what he calls the "pressure of prefigurative determination." There might be a natural tendency on the part of readers to be influenced by this pressure because it facilitates a complementary relationship between the embedded narrative and the primary narrative. Such a relationship undoubtedly has a certain hermeneutic appeal, the appeal of finding the meaning of the entire narrative packaged neatly in a metonymic allegorical interlude. This is an expectation, I suspect, that has been reinforced—if not fostered—by the way in which critics have tended to talk about *mise-en-abyme*. Dällenbach proclaims, for example, that "its essential property is that it brings out the meaning and form of the work" (8),[6] and two of the three "dimensions of modeling" that McHale identifies take us in a similar direction—toward using the embedded narrative as a way of making

---

5. I am grateful to Brian McHale, who initially pointed out the convergence of my theory of embedded allegories with the idea of *mise-en-abyme*.

6. Ron lists this claim as one of his "Nine Problems in the Theory of Mise-en-Abyme" and asks some penetrating questions regarding it, including, "what if it fails [to do so]?" (419).

sense of the larger text. We can see the lure of this approach by examining the effect produced by such an embedded narrative in two well-known novels, Chinua Achebe's *Things Fall Apart* and Franz Kafka's *The Trial*.

Achebe's novel focuses on an Igbo man named Okonkwo whose personal story intersects with the beginning of European colonial expansion into Africa and, more specifically in this case, Nigeria. In Achebe's narrative, Okonkwo's personal trajectory is downward. He begins as a respected member of his village and the surrounding region, a man whose "fame rested on solid personal achievements" (3). As the novel progresses, however, Okonkwo struggles with some personal demons (issues with his dead father and with a son of whom he does not entirely approve) as well as with the changes occurring within his tribe and his culture as the twentieth century draws near. At the midpoint of the story Okonkwo inadvertently shoots and kills a fellow clan member and, as punishment, accepts exile for a period of seven years from his village. He relocates, with his family, to his mother's village to serve out his sentence.

When Okonkwo finally returns to his own village, he recognizes that both it and his position in it have changed during his seven-year absence. Personally, he has lost his place as one of the traditional "nine masked spirits who administered justice in the clan" and the respect that would have allowed him "to lead his warlike clan against the new religion, which, he was told, had gained ground" (171). That new religion, of course, explains the changes in the village itself; the Christian missionaries have made inroads, attracted followers (including Okonkwo's son), and brought with them a government and their own system of justice. Okonkwo is eventually arrested and imprisoned for his part in destroying a Christian church. His detainment and his treatment at the hands of the interlopers serve to increase his anger and, after his release, he exacts his revenge by killing a messenger who has come on behalf of the white men to break up a meeting of the clan. When the district commissioner arrives with a small group of his men to arrest Okonkwo, we learn that he (Okonkwo) has committed suicide by hanging himself.

Okonkwo is generally seen as a tragic figure, a good—though certainly not perfect—man who proves incapable of dealing effectively with his changing situation. In this regard, he also seems to represent the Igbo society more generally. As Arlene Elder argues, even more than being an interesting individual character, Okonkwo has a "larger symbolic function in the novel as representative of the suicidal fragmentation of Igbo society" (64). This fragmentation and its potentially devastating results are thematically central to Achebe's novel. Summing up the problem as the narrative draws to a close, Okonkwo's friend Obierika laments the insidiousness of the white man's presence among the Igbo as he rebuts Okonkwo's argument in favor of fighting: "How do you think we can fight when our own brothers have turned against us? The white man is very clever. He came quietly and peaceably with his religion. We were amused at his foolishness and allowed him to stay. Now he has won our brothers, and our clan can no longer act like one. He has put a knife on the things that held us together and we have fallen apart" (176). Since no clear consensus on how—or even whether—to combat the colonizers emerges from the clan members, Okonkwo decides to act individually if necessary, a decision that leads to his tragic ending.

As is the case with most good tragedies, a certain amount of ambiguity survives the narrative's end, even if the protagonist does not. Could the outcome have been different for Okonkwo and his people? How could the Igbo have prevented the fragmentation of their society that seems to have opened the door to the missionaries? Given the presence of these white men, how could the native peoples most effectively resist them? Achebe offers no clear answers to any of these questions, and from that silence springs the ambiguity. Yet perhaps because we are dealing with a text that involves political issues of colonialism by an African writer, readers tend to assume that Achebe must be trying to make some political point (it is difficult to imagine that he intended for *Things Fall Apart* to be "simply" the mimetic representation of the existence of one fictional character at a given historical moment); therefore, we look either to transcend the ambiguity through allegorical interpretation (what is ambiguous on the literal level might clearly signify on the allegorical) or to weave the ambiguity into an allegorical interpretation, as some critics do with the weakly allegorical Kafka. If Achebe is trying to make some larger point, but has not overtly told us what that point is, then many readers will find themselves tempted to view the work as an allegory.

One way to arrive at an (allegorical) interpretation of the entire narrative is to extrapolate from one's interpretation of an embedded narrative. In *Things Fall Apart* we find an independent embedded tale that has the potential to be revealing. Ekwefi, one of Okonkwo's wives, relates the fable of "The Tortoise and the Birds" during an evening in which each of Okonkwo's wives and their children tell folktales. In this tale, the birds are preparing to attend a feast in the sky during a time otherwise marked by famine. Tortoise, who has "not eaten a good meal for two moons" (96), notices the preparations and devises a way to get himself included. He convinces the skeptical but good-hearted birds that he has reformed from his days of cunning and mischief, and they each give him a feather out of which he fashions two wings. Prior to the feast, Tortoise, who is obviously a skilled orator, is selected to be the spokesman for the group, and he convinces the birds that custom dictates that each of them take a new name for such a special occasion. Tortoise takes for himself the name *All of you*.

When the group arrives at the feast, Tortoise asks the hosts for whom they have prepared the repast, and the reply is "For all of you" (98). Reminding the birds that this is his name, Tortoise eats first, leaving only the scraps that he has thrown on the floor for the others. The angry birds retaliate by repossessing the feathers they had "lent" him, leaving Tortoise "in his hard shell full of blood and wine but without any wings to fly home" (99). Trying to figure a way out of his predicament, Tortoise asks the birds to take a message to his wife. Each predictably refuses until Parrot, "who had felt more angry than the others, suddenly changed his mind and agreed to take the message" (99). Tortoise wants Parrot to tell his wife to construct a landing pad of soft material from their house, but Parrot instead tells her to bring out all of their hard items, which she does. The list includes "hoes, machetes, spears, guns, and even [Tortoise's] cannon" (99). Unable to discern from above the nature of his landing site, and trusting that Parrot has delivered the message he intended, Tortoise jumps. He survives, but shatters his shell, which is pieced back together by the neighborhood medicine man.

The story is a traditional tale that purports to explain "why Tortoise's shell is not smooth" (99). As such, this fable falls into the category of strong allegory; it transforms a phenomenon of the natural world (the appearance of the tortoise's shell) into a highly figurative narrative for an explanatory purpose. This embedded allegorical story is also an independent one because it can stand on its own as a narrative, and indeed has its own history as a fable in African culture.

But, as Barbara Harlow asserts, "In the context of *Things Fall Apart*, the traditional fable of the tortoise and the birds represents more than indigenous folk wisdom and its interpretation of the natural phenomena of the village world" (74).

According to Harlow, Achebe's novel is

> an analysis of the colonial moment in African, Nigerian, and Igbo history in which the traditional folktale of the tortoise and the birds is recoded as an allegory of resistance. In such an allegory, Tortoise represents colonial power. The birds, who are his victims, signify the colonized population that remains subject to manipulation until it learns to command the weapons the colonizers have used against it: words, machetes, spears, and a cannon. The folk wisdom of the animal fable reveals a political message: both rhetoric and armed struggle are crucial to an oppressed people's organized resistance to domination. (75)

Although Harlow's allegorical interpretation does not work in every detail,[7] her general claim that the meaning of the embedded narrative changes when it is viewed in relation to a primary narrative seems to me to be a valid one.[8] This change itself, however, is less interesting—after all, arguing that context can affect interpretation is not exactly a radical claim—than the fact that the allegorical status of the embedded narrative produces such a strong rhetorical impact; the embedded allegory in Achebe's novel can determine the interpretation of the entire narrative.

This effect in *Things Fall Apart* is so pronounced because Achebe has clearly set off the allegorical tale from the main story. The action of Achebe's primary narrative is interrupted, the fable is presented entirely and without comment regarding its potential connection to that primary narrative, and the primary narrative resumes following a clearly marked end to the embedded story. The lack of any exegetical commentary from author, narrator, or character that would tie the "why story" to the novel's primary narrative ensures that neither the ontology nor the meaning of the embedded narrative has changed simply as a result of its inclusion in the larger work.

That is not to say, however, that Harlow is unjustified in claiming that the tale of the tortoise and the birds does take on new meaning in the context of Achebe's novel. Nor is it to deny that Achebe seems to invite a particular (re)interpretation simply by including this particular fable, as opposed to some other. The agonistic relationship between the characters and the theme of retribution or revenge for a group that has been wronged both have

---

7. I say that the interpretation is not entirely convincing because it works only in the most general sense. One can accept, perhaps, that the tortoise and the birds might represent, respectively, colonizer and colonized. And Harlow's belief that "the birds' refusal to provide [the tortoise with the help he needs to get back down], once they understand the conditions it entails, is . . . a radical critique of the continued cultural and economic dependency fostered by Europe's 'underdevelopment' of Africa" (78) seems plausible enough if we accept that the tortoise and the birds do in fact stand for Europe and Africa. Harlow's claim that the birds use rhetoric against Tortoise, on the other hand, strikes me as dubious. Parrot does deceive Tortoise's wife, but that requires no clever use of words, and certainly nothing approximating the rhetorical acumen that Tortoise demonstrates. Similarly, the claim that this fable somehow demonstrates that the birds have engaged in and embraced "armed struggle" as a means of resistance is not borne out by the embedded narrative itself. The birds never actually possess or employ the weapons mentioned; in fact, it is the Tortoise's own wife who chooses to bring out the machetes, spears, guns, and so forth. Moreover, Ekwefi's commentary at the end of the story points only to its explanatory powers—its ability to explain why the tortoise has a shell that is not smooth—and not to any lesson concerning the power dynamic that obtains between Tortoise and the birds, although we should note that this embedded allegory precedes the arrival of the missionaries in Achebe's narrative.

8. Jacques Derrida makes a similar claim regarding Kafka's "Before the Law" parable, which I will discuss below. Outside the primary narrative of The Trial, Derrida states, the embedded narrative becomes "another institution" (140).

obvious connections to a novel about colonial Africa. Nevertheless, the act of recoding the fable is left to the reader, and Harlow has recoded this particular one in order to make the embedded narrative complement what she believes Achebe is "really" trying to express through the primary narrative.

In order to sustain a reading that makes the embedded allegory complement the primary narrative, Harlow must assume that both of these narratives bear the mark of the author and are meant to work together to convey his rhetorical purpose. Despite the fact that the embedded narrative is characterized by what Genette calls external focalization (the narrator simply re-presents the story that Ekwefi tells), Harlow refocuses it through what she imagines to be the point of view of the author.[9] The assumption that the point of view must ultimately be the author's is what we might call the assumption of an implied, fixed focalization, and it of course rests on certain assumptions about the implied author. If this assumption is plausible, then the embedded narrative can be made to stand in a synecdochical relationship to the narrative in which it is embedded, thereby allowing the reader to obviate at least some of the latter's ambiguity.

In this regard, the embedded narrative that has been transformed from a fable that explains *why* the tortoise's shell has the texture it has into an allegory about *how* best to resist colonial rule allows Harlow to transform the primary narrative from one that deals primarily with *why* Okonkwo falls into one that, like the embedded narrative, is about *how* to resist. For Harlow, in short, the embedded narrative has assumed the role of the master narrative. In a claim that indicates the extent to which her allegorical reading of the embedded narrative has colored her interpretation of the primary narrative, Harlow states that "The final incidents of Okonkwo's life and the resistant history of the other villagers reenact the fable of the tortoise and the birds" (78). In order to make this analogy work, however, Harlow has to claim that Okonkwo's suicide at the end of *Things Fall Apart* "causes the people of Umuofia to debate their strategies of resistance to the colonizers' increasing influence" (78). But we cannot validate this claim with any direct textual support. Indeed, Okonkwo's suicide could be seen as a response to what he assumes is the clan's decision not to resist. After he murders the

---

9. This might help to explain Harlow's inaccurate claim that Okonkwo "dismisses the parrot's story, which demands the overthrow both of inherited paradigms and of the colonial system, as a tale told by women" (76). In fact, there is no mention of Okonkwo's reaction to this story, though it is true that he is dismissive of "women's stories" generally. Harlow believes, however, that for Achebe, "Okonkwo's personal failure represents the inadequacy of recalcitrant traditionalism in responding to the exigencies of the present or elaborating a vision of the future" (76). If this is so, then Okonkwo's rejection of the story as Harlow has allegorized it would make sense. There is, however, no textual basis for this assertion.

messenger, Okonkwo, the narrator tells us, "knew that Umuofia would not go to war. He knew because they had let the other messengers escape. They had broken into tumult instead of action. He discerned fright in that tumult" (203). Although war is obviously not the only means of resistance, there is, Harlow's claim notwithstanding, no mention of a discussion of possible alternatives in what remains of the narrative.

When we draw on a case such as this one to reconsider allegory, we can see the utility of using the narrative and rhetorical frameworks that I have been advocating. As a textual phenomenon, an embedded allegorical narrative strongly inclines readers toward allegorical interpretation more generally. In the case of *Things Fall Apart*, the allegorized interpretation of the embedded narrative can be extended to the primary narrative and can literally determine one's interpretation of the entire text. To read the embedded fable as Barbara Harlow does also seems to be in keeping with the "Jamesonian" approach to narratives written from the perspective of the colonized. It can be difficult for readers to imagine that Achebe does *not* have some broader political aims in writing this novel, so when we combine our knowledge of the historical context of the novel and its author with an allegorical fable such as the story of the tortoise and the birds, we wind up with significant positive feedback for an allegorical interpretation. Ultimately, Achebe's presentation of the fable allows for, perhaps even encourages—even if it does not completely validate—the recoding of the story in the manner that Harlow has chosen.[10]

My own sense is that Harlow has granted the embedded allegory too much "prefigurative determination," to go back to the phrase that Honig used in his discussion of Shakespeare. While the fable of the tortoise and the birds certainly alerts readers to allegorical potential, the other sources of "feedback" do not, in my opinion, fully justify Harlow's strong figurative reading. Achebe himself and his narrative style are the two elements that most mitigate the allegorical potential introduced by the fable. Achebe does not actually advocate for anything in this novel, and his detached style of

---

10. Julian N. Wasserman's essay "The Sphinx and the Rough Beast: Linguistic Struggle in Chinua Achebe's Things Fall Apart" indirectly opens up a second path to arrive at a similar allegorical reading. Wasserman does not spend much time on the tale of the tortoise and the birds, but he does offer it as an example of the kind of "folk oratory" that characterizes Achebe's novel (81). According to Wasserman, "linguistic etiquette among the Ibo, as with most oral cultures, is characterized by a verbal strategy of indirection rather than directness in speech. . . . Within Ibo speech, objects are not only called by names other than their own but subject matter is often introduced by seemingly irrelevant material" (80). If we accept this anthropological claim about the context from which the author of the novel emerged, then we might deduce that Achebe's use of the tale is an indirect way of making the very point that Harlow claims for him; however, I am not inclined in this direction.

narration conveys to me a mimeticism that contrasts sharply with an allegorical novel. The embedded fable seems to me more likely to be a representation of the kinds of stories that the Igbo people tell, and the contexts in which they tell them, than a figurative pronouncement from the author about how to resist colonial rule.

At the same time, the fact that Harlow can see the relevance of this fable to the general political situation that obtained at the turn of the twentieth century in Nigeria can hardly be a coincidence. I suspect that Achebe does want his readers to see armed conflict and subterfuge as options, and thus to have the fable resonate with those readers—as it surely would have with Okonkwo, if he were inclined to listen to the stories that women told—but I am not convinced that Achebe's purpose was to advocate a particular mode of resistance, and I do not find *Things Fall Apart* to be allegorical, despite the presence of an embedded allegorical narrative.

My primary point here is that the kind of extension or extrapolation exhibited in the Harlow interpretation of the fable and its relationship to the narrative in which we encounter it might be a "natural" reaction of readers long accustomed to making this hermeneutic move. In fact, I contend that we have been conditioned to make such moves by our repeated exposure to texts that invite them and by the kind of interpretive work that has emerged from the study of *mise-en-abyme*. From Homer and the Homeric simile to the most thoroughly postmodern narratives, we repeatedly encounter texts in which extended metaphors, parables, fables, dreams, and the like, are unmistakably meant or are made to be representative of the larger, primary narrative, or both. As the example of *Things Fall Apart* illustrates, we are not always meant to make this interpretive move. Another of Kafka's texts, on the other hand, will present us with an example of an embedded narrative that does speak for the larger narrative.

We encounter another well-known example of an embedded allegorical narrative in Kafka's *The Trial*, but before getting to the import of that embedded allegory we need to analyze the novel as a whole. This is a work, of course, with a famously disquieting first line: "Someone must have been telling lies about Joseph K., for without having done anything wrong he was arrested one fine morning" (1). And the remainder of the narrative revolves around K.'s attempts to uncover why he has been arrested—even though his "arrest" does not stop him from going about his daily activities—and to navigate the bizarre and obscure legal system of the unnamed jurisdiction in which he lives. Of course, things do not end happily for K.; and as for the readers, we are left in an interpretive predicament similar to the one we experience while reading *The Metamorphosis*.

Like much of Kafka's work, *The Trial* is an enigmatic novel, highly allusive and inviting of thematic readings. As a result, Ingeborg Henel has claimed, "The question has repeatedly been raised whether we are dealing, in Kafka's works, with allegories, with symbols, or with a special kind of myth" (40). While critics have yet to agree on a definitive answer to Henel's question, the fact that she lists the three possibilities that she does tells us much about Kafka's reception. The three terms "allegory," "symbol," and "myth" all point to narratives that are highly figurative and intensely thematic. My own reading locates *The Trial* in the realm of weak allegory, one of those works that transform some phenomenon "poorly" or distractedly, or with some or much irrelevance and indeterminacy, into a narrative structure. As we saw in my chapter on weak allegory, such narratives *evoke* allegory while at the same time withholding commitment to it and undermining confidence in it.

A quick glance at a cross section of Kafka criticism leaves little room for doubt that his novels and stories do indeed evoke some kind of allegory. Critics such as Henel have long noted a quality in Kafka's works that draws us toward an allegorical reading, or something approximating it. Henel herself concludes that "Kafka is far less a realist, a surrealist, or a purveyor of mere absurdities than he is an allegorist or symbolist" (40). Edwin Muir—an influential figure in introducing Kafka to English-speaking readers through his translations—claims that Kafka's evocation of allegory springs naturally from the kind of thinker he was. In Muir's mind, Kafka was a "profound religious thinker" whose thoughts manifested themselves "in concrete images" (33). These allusive images, then, form the basis of his fiction. Thus, Muir contends that the author's "semiallegorical stories are really the most simple and unaffected expression that could be found for his genius; not in the least a form of mystification, though to many people they must read somewhat like that. Given Kafka's special kind of imagination and complete honesty in following it, something like this was inevitable, and there is no help for it" (34). Muir's term "semiallegorical" might well convey the same phenomenon that I am trying to get at with "weak allegory." Kafka's concrete images tempt readers into a game of trying to figure out what, in the context of an entire narrative, they represent. What, in other words, is the big idea that Kafka wants to transform through his narrative? The fact that many (perhaps even most) readers find something allegorical in Kafka's works combined with the lack of a definitive answer to the question of what his works are allegories of provides strong empirical evidence in support of the designation weak allegorist.

When we turn to *The Trial* as a specific example, we see broad agreement that this novel is on some level and to some degree allegorical. Heinz Politzer contends that "The novel is a parable" and that Kafka intended it to be "a simile of human existence" (173). It is fitting, therefore, that Politzer understands Joseph K. as "an Everyman" (165). Kafka, according to Politzer, "has given him [K.] only as many of his own individual characteristics as were necessary to prevent the figure from dissolving into the mist of abstraction" (165). Likewise, Charles Osborne finds this novel to be "a huge, exhausting and tragic parable of the human condition . . . which can have only one outcome" (76).[11] Though they are both obviously correct in asserting that we all die, even if our deaths do not play out in the same ignominious way that K.'s does, Politzer and Osborne must share a rather gloomy outlook regarding the human condition if they want to maintain that K.'s experience is a representative one.

Other critics, however, offer some resistance to the idea that Kafka is fundamentally an allegorist, and this resistance bolsters my claim that Kafka's narratives, including *The Trial*, present us not with strong allegories, but weak ones. Disagreement on the matter of whether what we are reading is an allegory or not reinforces the notion that a work has allegorical aspects but lacks the strength necessary to consolidate critical opinion. Ronald Gray gives voice to the allegorical skeptics in his critical biography, *Franz Kafka*:

> The universal applicability some readers find [in *The Trial*] was not put there by Kafka. That most men undergo a trial is not a sufficiently close parallel to justify seeing in his novel a parable of the human condition. On the other hand, the false trial to which many submit at one time or another, substituting imagined guilt for real guilt, supplies enough affinities to give this novel a telling power. The rest of us do know what this trial of K.'s is; what is required is that we should not confuse it with a more generally significant one. (125)

---

11. Osborne and Politzer take a very general approach in their interpretations, a fact that that I believe bolsters my claim that *The Trial* is a weak allegory. Arguing that this novel is a "parable of the human condition" makes the phenomenon transformed (the human condition) a very large one indeed. The fact that we cannot be more precise in identifying what it is that Kafka allegorizes indicates to me a certain weakness in the allegory itself. Osborne notes, interestingly, that "Whether one understands [the phenomenon at the center of Kafka's novel] as the gnawing away of a fatal disease, or as neurosis worsening into self-destructive psychosis, or as man struggling with his original sin, its poetic and emotional meaning is unaffected. What it says may well be conveyed in different ways by different words, but meaning lies beyond words, and the meaning of Kafka's profound and gloomy creation is irrefutable" (76). I am not as sure as Osborne is that Kafka's narrative produces such an obvious meaning, although it might do so if we could be certain that the author meant to transform the effects of a fatal disease, the deterioration of a neurotic man, or the modern effects of original sin into a fictional narrative. If we could do this irrefutably, then we would have a strong allegory.

Kurt Fickert in *Kafka's Doubles* likewise stands firm against the allegorical tide, but he also understands the temptation to allow it to sweep one away: "Equating guilt with a fall from grace or establishing it as the measure of man's distance from God," Fickert remarks, on the possibility of reading *The Trial* in the same way that we read *Everyman* or *The Pilgrim's Progress*, "the interpreter of *The Trial* is free to conclude that Kafka is close to presenting an allegory about the sinful state of man, according to which Josef K. is an everyman and a pilgrim in search of grace" (56). But he also acknowledges other possibilities, recognizing that "Because of the novel's open symbolism there are occasions for insisting, as does Osborne, on the viewpoint that Kafka has transcribed a nightmare or has written a case history about a victim of dementia praecox or tuberculosis" (59). Like Gray, Fickert pushes back against these allegorical approaches and argues for a tack that would work well with my conception of weak allegory: "In fact," he concludes, "*The Trial* deserves to be read for what it suggests rather than for what it means . . ." (59). What it suggests, I would add, is allegory, but what exactly Kafka transforms through his narrative—what it "means"—remains somewhat obscure.

But why does *The Trial* suggest allegory, and why do so many critics want to call it a parable? Unlike *The Metamorphosis* this narrative does not involve an insect with human consciousness, the kind of personification that usually functions as a clear marker of allegory. And why do so many critics see Joseph K. as a modern incarnation of Everyman? After all, despite Politzer's claim that K. comes perilously close to "dissolving into the mist of abstraction" (165), he often looks surprisingly like a character whose mimetic qualities predominate.[12]

To answer some of the questions the novel raises about allegory, we can start with the plot, for *The Trial*'s plot contains elements that make the narrative as a whole seem conducive to an allegorical interpretation. These elements include an arrest, an impending trial, a struggle with bureaucracy, and a death. In addition to being central components of the plot of Kafka's novel, these elements also tend to appear with some frequency in what H. Porter Abbott calls masterplots, which he defines as "recurrent skeletal stories, belonging to cultures and individuals[,] that play a powerful role in questions of identity, values, and the understanding of life" (192). From the perspective of plot, then, *The Trial* appears to be a strong candidate to

---

12. For example, K. has a real job; he has particular relationships with women; we know exactly how old he is (thirty at the time of his arrest, thirty-one at the time of his death). We do not, it is true, have much in the way of detail regarding K.'s physical appearance, but this could be as much due to the fact that K. is the focalizer of the narrative as to any allegorical lack of specificity on Kafka's part.

be called "an allegory" because the events of the narrative correspond to a familiar, cultural, extradiegetic narrative.

When we move beyond the rudimentary elements of the plot, however, and examine the progression of that plot, the case for calling *The Trial* a strong allegory becomes less convincing. Unlike *Everyman*, Kafka's narrative does not develop in such a way as to reveal the phenomenon that the author seeks to transform through his narrative. In *The Transformations of Allegory*, Gay Clifford argues that the concept of the Law in *The Trial* is a symbol and that "K.'s involvement in the process of law" is an allegory (12). I contend, on the other hand, that the concept of the Law makes it seem as if K.'s involvement with it should produce a strong allegory, but that it finally fails to do so. K.'s "arrest," his subsequent appearances before the "court," and his meetings with legal counsel do follow the general trajectory of an individual's experience with the law, but, as we have seen in the varying interpretations of the text, we have no consensus that this experience is what Kafka intended to transform into an allegory.

The allegorical difficulty with *The Trial* is exacerbated by issues of character. It is never entirely clear who K. is supposed to be or to represent, and this makes it difficult to derive a satisfactory secondary narrative from the literal one that Kafka has provided. Abbott argues that "A masterplot comes equipped with [character] types" (45). This is indeed often the case with what I call strong allegories, but not so for weak ones. K., for example, does not seem to fit any particular type. Nor, as I argued above, does he seem to be something like an "Everyman"; he is too idiosyncratic—with his distinguishing sexual "issues" and slightly abrasive personality—to be a character that readers are likely to accept as a symbol for all of Western society. On the other hand, if we take K. to be a representation of the author himself (which would at least partly explain and justify the idiosyncrasies), then we are left with a kind of psychological (persecution) narrative that falls short of "allegory" in the way that we usually think of that term.

In *The Trial* we confront a novel that suggests allegory but frustrates allegoresis. We have allegorical images, to use Frye's terminology, but they never coalesce into a coherent narrative that makes clear what has been transformed. One can, I think, legitimately claim that Kafka's protagonist finds his experience with the law confusing and frustrating and that he finds life in a bureau-technocratic society perplexing, senseless, and dehumanizing. Similarly, we might legitimately make the same claims about our lived reality. The simple fact of that correspondence, however, does not make Kafka's narrative a strong allegory. At the end of *The Trial* we are left, just as we are at the end of *The Metamorphosis*, with a weak allegory, and this weakness can be troubling to readers precisely because we want to know with some certainty what phenomenon Kafka intends to transform through his figural narrative. Just as we often use narratives to make sense of our worlds and our lives, so too do we use narratives—often the secondary phenomena transformed through allegory—to make sense of other narratives.

This issue of the use of narratives to comment on other narratives brings me to what I consider to be the piece of textual evidence in Kafka's novel that does the most to convince other readers that this work is a strong allegory— a famous short parable known as "Before the Law" embedded in the novel. The "Before the Law" section of *The Trial* has all the trappings of traditional allegory: it is narrative, and its use of concepts such as the Law and traditionally symbolic images such as doorways and doorkeepers make it obviously suggestive of meanings beyond the literal.[13] Furthermore, the allegorical passage is followed by interpretive commentary that seeks to resolve the strangeness and ambiguity of the embedded narrative.[14] The narrative itself is simple and in keeping, thematically, with the primary narrative of Kafka's novel: a man seeks admittance to the Law, but a doorkeeper informs him that he cannot enter "at this moment" (213). The man, hoping eventually to gain access to the Law, waits for years, occasionally trying to bribe the doorkeeper, but in vain. Finally, as death closes in, the man asks the doorkeeper why no one else, during all the time he has been waiting, has tried to gain entry to the Law. The doorkeeper responds, chillingly: "No one but you could gain admittance through this door, since this door was intended for you. I am now going to shut it" (214–15). Following the story, K. and the priest who relates the parable-like tale engage in a discussion concerning its ultimate meaning.

Not surprisingly, given his own difficulties negotiating the labyrinthine legal system that has forced him to defend himself against unspecified charges, K.'s initial response is to believe that the man has been deceived by the doorkeeper. The priest, on the other hand, offers an academically informed history of the various interpretations of "commentators," a history of often contradictory readings that stand in stark contrast to K.'s "hasty" judgment. The end result of the priest's lengthy exegetical survey is K.'s confusion and exasperation: "He was too tired to survey all the conclusions arising

---

13. Prior to the novel's appearance—which occurred only after Kafka's death—the author extracted "Before the Law" and published it separately as a piece of short fiction in the collection titled *A Country Doctor.*

14. In *The Transformations of Allegory,* Gay Clifford suggests that a certain sense of strangeness is central to allegory. The strangeness of allegories often "derives not from exoticism, but from the fact that they are so neutral, so indefinite, and yet immediately suggest that they mean something important" (2). I find this an apt description of the feeling one gets from reading the "Before the Law" section of *The Trial.*

from the story, and the trains of thought into which it was leading him were unfamiliar. . . . The simple story had lost its clear outline, he wanted to put it out of his mind . . ." (220–21).

In this case, the embedded narrative has a clear connection to the larger narrative of the novel; indeed, the two story-worlds present some striking similarities, including, most obviously, a protagonist struggling to gain access to—or at least some understanding of—a vague and confusing entity called the Law. The strong connection between the two narratives has made this a very common example in works on *mise-en-abyme*. A second, no less important similarity is an ultimate sense of indeterminacy, a failure to find conclusive meaning in a narrative that invites us to search for it at every turn. In the case of *The Trial* and its embedded allegory, therefore, the embedded allegory has a complementary relationship with the primary narrative; the diegesis of the embedded narrative synecdochically represents the main diegesis.[15] This is the type of relationship that Edwin Honig examines in *Dark Conceit*, and he finds such embedded allegories significant primarily because they demonstrate how "an allegorical trope extends itself and, further, how it serves as a guiding motif in a longer work" (11). In terms of their effect on the primary narrative, Honig finds, as we have seen, that the embedded allegories "exert a . . . pressure of figurative predetermination" (12). In other words, the message carried in a part of the narrative corresponds with the meaning of the entire narrative.

How do we explain, on narratological grounds, this correspondence? There are several contributing factors. First, as I have already indicated, the two diegeses share the same thematic content—the inaccessibility of the Law. Second, the essential plot structure of the two narratives is similar: a relatively benighted man seeking something (access, knowledge, redemption) is frustrated by an impenetrable and inscrutable "system" and dies with his desire unfulfilled.[16] Third, and I think this might be the most crucial point, the primary narrative and the embedded allegorical narrative are both filtered through the same third-person heterodiegetic narrator. And although the story of the man from the country and his struggle to cross the threshold of the Law is related by the priest, Kafka's narrator provides only the direct speech of this figure, denying the reader any access to his thoughts.

---

15. Heinz Politzer has argued that "the parable serves as a symbolic master plan for the novel as such. The initial situation of the novel is repeated here; this time it is couched in the form of an intellectual exercise, rather than as a part of the plot. K. loses out both here and there" (180).

16. The two plots are not, however, identical. One significant difference is that K. is forced to confront the Law because of his arrest, while the allegorical protagonist's motivation is unexplained.

As a result, the focalization remains fixed and internal. The reader, in other words, is still closely aligned with K. and has access only to his thoughts and feelings. We know, for example, that K. is tired by the end of his exegetical discussion with the priest and that "he *wanted* to put [the story] out of his mind" (emphasis added). As far as the priest is concerned, we never know with any certainty what he is thinking, only what he says.

The closest we come to the priest's internal consciousness is the narrator's claim that the priest, in allowing K. to stop talking and thinking about the allegorical story, has shown "great delicacy of feeling ... although undoubtedly he did not agree with" K.'s decision to do so (221). (The original German tells us that the priest "mit seiner eigenen Meinung gewiß nicht übereinstimmte" [188].) The "undoubtedly" (*gewiß*) here indicates the suppositional quality of the claim; given the circumstances and what the Priest has already said, the narrator seems to be saying, one can only assume that he would disagree with K. in this instance. Ironically, a word that is meant to convey certainty functions, in this case, as a means for marking a guess or supposition. More importantly, however, it maintains the integrity of the internal focalization that characterizes Kafka's text and that contributes to the complementary relationship that obtains between the primary and the embedded narratives.

The importance of maintaining the internal focalization of the narrative becomes even more evident when we learn, at the end of the chapter in which we find the allegorical embedded narrative, that the priest is actually the prison chaplain (*Gefängniskaplan*), a fact whose significance is implicitly underscored by his own interpretation: "'That means I belong to the Court,' said the priest" (222). Both K. and the reader might logically assume that the priest, as a part of the legal system to which K. is trying to gain access, possesses potentially helpful information, information that, if he does indeed have it, he withholds. This puts the priest in the role of the doorkeeper, which gives added significance to the final—as in last, not definitive—interpretation of the allegory that he puts before K. The priest claims, ultimately, that the doorkeeper may be "incomparably greater than anyone at large in the world. The man is only seeking the Law, the doorkeeper is already attached to it. It is the Law that has placed him at his post; to doubt his dignity is to doubt the Law itself" (220).

Honig's approach of treating the embedded narrative as a synecdoche for the primary narrative works relatively well with Kafka, and with *The Trial* in particular, because the embedded allegorical narrative potentially bears out Honig's claim that Kafka is putting on trial, figuratively speaking, the reality experienced by his heroes. "[It] is this world that is on trial," Honig writes, "with its superstitious worship of bureaucracy and its inert irrationality which the hero attempts to understand; but its nature is inexorably to defeat him just when he is about to receive some revelation that would have done him no good even if he had succeeded in receiving it" (162). Such an interpretation is certainly plausible both for the "Before the Law" section of *The Trial* and for the novel as a whole.

But as we have seen, there are other, contrariwise, interpretations of both the novel and the parable. Ingeborg Henel, for example, shares the view that the parable rightly determines how one should read the novel, but she arrives at a dramatically different interpretation of both. She rejects outright Honig's claim that Kafka's novel has something to say about his "world," arguing instead that

> Kafka is ... far removed from a critique of his age or his society. After Josef K., at his first interrogation, has concluded his speech of accusation against the court, the Examining Magistrate points out to him that he has, with his speeches, deprived himself of the advantage of a first examination: Instead of exploring his inner self, he has criticized the external world. K.'s accusing words constitute, then, not a valid criticism of the authorities, but a cover-up of his own guilt.... (49)

In Henel's reading, this novel—and, indeed, all of Kafka's work—emerges from the author's attempts to deal with his personal feelings of guilt, and readers who fail to recognize this, Henel argues, will miss the point of his fiction entirely:

> In contrast to most confessional novels, Kafka's works are neither the apologia of the hero nor that of the author, but rather a judgment on himself. This demands a new attitude from the reader. He must not naively identify with the hero, as Josef K. identifies with the man from the country; for then he falls into the further error of Josef K. (into which in fact many readers and critics repeatedly do fall) of indicating the negativity, absurdity, and devilishness of the world, instead of "endorsing the world" and carrying out the judgment on oneself, as Kafka insists. (54)

To say, however, that Kafka "insists" on such a reading surely overstates the case. Granted, Henel supports her claim with reference to some relevant passages from Kafka's diaries and from his other works of fiction, but the "Before the Law" parable stands as her primary piece of evidence; this "legend," she contends, "becomes the key to the novel" (54), and so her reading of the parable will determine her reading of the narrative writ large. Her explication of the novel and the parable's significance in it is in many ways a brilliant one, but its brilliance does not make it determinant. We would be well advised to keep in mind Henel's comments regarding the presentation of the parable through the priest as we consider her own exegeses of it: "As in the Bible, Kafka has the exposition follow the parable. But his explanations do not have the same status as Jesus' interpretations of his parables: They are mere learned exegeses, and thus lacking in authority, ambiguous, and even contradictory. Hence they must be understood, not as absolutely valid statements, but rather as experimental attempts to lead the listener, through assertion and counter-assertion, to an independent judgment" (41–42).

The parable itself, because it is a weak allegory and thus inherently indeterminate, naturally produces readings that might themselves be ambiguous and even contradictory. This is the case not only in the text, as the priest relates different interpretations of the legend, but also outside of the text, as different critics of Kafka's novel arrive at different conclusions about the meaning of the parable. As I proposed in my earlier discussion of *The Metamorphosis,* I doubt that Kafka wanted to provide us with an interpretive "key"; the entire trajectory of the novel tends toward confusion and ambiguity. The net effect of Kafka's embedding in *The Trial* a weak allegory that shares so many structural and thematic similarities with the larger narrative is to encourage readers to see it as a kind of synecdoche for the novel as a whole, and thus to read the novel as an allegory. Like the embedded allegory, the embedding allegory turns out to be a weak one, and this is, I suspect, as Kafka intended it.

In cases such as this one the presence of an (obvious) independent allegorical narrative—even if it is a weak one—as a textual phenomenon within the primary narrative seems to function as an interpretive clue pointing the reader toward the conclusion that the entire work must be allegorical, and that its deeper meaning must be related to the allegorical meaning conveyed through the embedded narrative; this is precisely the dynamic that, according to critics who focus on the *mise-en-abyme,* often obtains when the larger narrative is "reflected" in the embedded narrative. Henel takes this one step further, proposing that we can use Kafka's parables as a kind of key to deciphering his corpus as a whole. "On the basis of his short parables," she argues, and these parables of course include "Before the Law," "which at least stylistically present no puzzles, it should thus be easier to gain an understanding of the images of Kafka's world" (40). The temptation to see the relationship between an embedded allegory and its host narrative in this light is indeed strong, but even if we follow this interpretive path, we end up at a point of profound uncertainty regarding the meaning of Kafka's parable and the text in which he has embedded it.

Recalling Peter Rabinowitz's claim in *Before Reading* that Kafka might well have been "consciously trying to confuse" in *The Trial* can help us to recognize the use-value of an embedded weak allegory for his purposes. Weak allegory holds out the general promise of significant meaning but withholds commitment to any particular interpretation, and this state of affairs suits Kafka perfectly. As Kafka's perceptive biographer Reiner Stach attests, "Kafka points, but if we follow his finger with our gaze, a veil descends on the spot. His court [in *The Trial*] has a visible surface; what we see only refers to things that are both essential and unimaginable: 'the supreme judges,' 'the law.' The less we know, the more we speculate" (474). This combination of things both essential and unimaginable is characteristic of weak allegory, and the speculation that the combination engenders speaks to its power.

It is precisely this speculation without the promise of resolution that Kafka sought to wring from his readers, and that seems to have characterized his own state of mind throughout much of his life. "The more striking the semiotic phenomenon," Stach continues, "the greater the obscurity that lurks behind it. Every detail says, 'I mean something, but I am not saying what'" (475). This statement applies not only to details such as "the law" and "the judges," but also to the textual phenomenon of the embedded allegory. The presence of this weak allegory incites heightened speculation from both the protagonist and the reader, but neither can solve the riddle that it presents. Kafka uses the embedded allegory as a means of allowing the reader to identify with the character's hermeneutic plight, if not his legal one. Indeed, Kafka pushes us toward such identification by using the embedded narrative to put his protagonist in the position of the reader trying to make sense of an enigmatic text. Ultimately, this rhetorical situation helps to underline Kafka's primary rhetorical purpose—the creation of a text laden with "significant" semiotic and textual phenomena that refuses to yield any final, determinative meaning.

Dependent Embedded Allegory: Barth

At the other end of the rhetorical continuum I would place dependent embedded allegories. These I will classify as essentially mundane allegories situated within a larger narrative. I use the term "mundane" to connote a nontranscendent quality to these embedded allegories. In other words, unlike the other embedded allegories we have analyzed thus far, a dependent embedded allegory confines itself to the story-world of its host narrative; that is the sense in which it is mundane.

This distinction offers another opportunity to point out the overlap between my conception of embedded allegories and some of the theoretical work that has been done on *mise-en-abyme*. In his essay "*En Abyme*" Brian McHale makes a signal contribution to this area of study by pointing out the "cognitive potential of *mise-en-abyme*" (191), and he identifies "three dimensions of modeling by *mise-en-abyme*," each of which can contribute to the reader's understanding of some entity (191). McHale analyzes "cases where *mise-en-abyme* yields knowledge of the text itself by modeling its form"; "cases where *mise-en-abyme* yields knowledge of how the reader engages with the text—in other words, where it models the reading process"; and cases where *mise-en-abyme* can yield knowledge of the extratextual world, serving to model or map that world cognitively" (191). While I would not want to delimit what my different conceptions of embedded allegory have the potential to do for readers, I do see some potential correspondence between McHale's cognitive functions and my types of embedded allegories; dependent embedded allegories are likely to contribute to textual understanding, while independent and interdependent embedded allegories might tend more toward the transcendent. To delve further into these and related issues, I turn to John Barth and his first novel, *The End of the Road*.

The End of the Road chronicles approximately six months in the life of Jacob Horner, a thirty-year-old former graduate student in English literature who takes a job teaching grammar and composition at a Maryland teachers college at the suggestion of his therapist, who believes that the structure of a regular job will benefit his patient. Jacob serves as both the protagonist and the narrator of his story, a story that focuses on his relationship with Joe Morgan—a teaching colleague—and Joe's wife, Rennie. The plot's climax involves Jacob's adulterous affair with Rennie; a pregnancy and unresolved questions concerning paternity; and, finally, Rennie's death following a botched abortion.

The catalyst of the plot is Jacob's mental condition, one that leaves him occasionally "immobilized" as the result of a paralyzing realization that "there is no reason to do anything" (323). When this knowledge weighs too heavily on Jacob, he literally shuts down, as happens for the first time at Baltimore's Pennsylvania Station. On his twenty-eighth birthday, Jacob, who has just completed his oral exams but has yet to begin his master's thesis, checks out of his university-owned room with his bags packed and his mind made up to "take a trip somewhere" (322). He credits "simple birthday despondency" for the desire to leave, recounting that, at that instant, "I had no self-convincing reason for continuing for a moment longer to do any of the things that I happened to be doing with myself as of seven o'clock in the evening of March 16,

1951" (322). As a result, Jacob inquires of the ticket agent the furthest destinations—by bus—to which his twenty dollars will grant him access. Informed that his choices are Cincinnati, Crestline, Dayton, or Lima, Ohio, Jacob retires to a bench to "make up [his] mind" (323). "And it was there," he relates, "that I simply ran out of motives, as a car runs out of gas" (323).

After spending the night immobilized on the bench, Jacob is finally roused by a doctor who serendipitously happens by and who will become his therapist. The doctor, an unnamed African American, operates a "Remobilization Farm" where he employs what we might generously call unconventional methods of treatment on paralytic patients. These unsanctioned methods, combined with the doctor's race, force him to maintain a low profile and to relocate his clinic with some regularity. Nevertheless, Jacob becomes a regular patient, and he clearly has some confidence in the doctor's motives and abilities, even if he is not always comfortable with or confident in the means he employs. The novel opens with Jacob the narrator writing from one of the Remobilization Farm's dormitories, looking back on the Jacob Horner who took the doctor's advice about two years earlier to find a career, "a lifework" (257). As the Farm and the teachers college were in the same town at the time of Jacob's initial treatment, the doctor suggests applying there, but he directs Jacob not to teach literature—the focus of his graduate studies—because, as a discipline, it lacks discipline. "There must be a rigid discipline," the doctor advises, "or else it will be merely an occupation, not an occupational therapy" (259). The doctor finally settles on grammar, but insists on prescriptive rather than descriptive grammar: "No description at all. No optional situations. Teach the rules. Teach the truth about grammar" (259).

The doctor's insistence on prescription over description is intended to minimize Jacob's exposure to situations in which no clear choices exist; this pertains to what he calls "Informational Therapy," which relies on the premise that knowledge of the world can, in some cases, mitigate the need to make choices. The doctor illustrates his point by asking Jacob to think about how many people Cleveland's Municipal Stadium seats: "If you don't simply *know* how many people can sit in the Cleveland Municipal Stadium," he explains, "you have no real reason for choosing one number over another, assuming you can make a choice at all. . . . But if you have some Knowledge of the World you may be able to say, 'Seventy-seven thousand, seven hundred,' just like that. No choice is involved" (330). Armed with enough information, Jacob just might be able to avoid his spells of choice-induced immobility.

Avoiding situations that require choices, however, will not, the doctor indicates, solve Jacob's problem, for, he explains, the inability to choose "is only theoretically inherent in situations, when there's no chooser. Given a particular chooser, it's unthinkable" (331). In other words, steering clear of certain situations might allow Jacob to reduce the frequency of his symptoms, but it will not cure him. As the doctor explains, regarding Jacob's first bout of paralysis, "the fault lies not in the situation but in the fact that there was no chooser. Choosing is existence: to the extent that you don't choose, you don't exist" (331). In Jacob's case, the doctor wants to simplify the patient's life, to reduce the number and the complexity of choices so that one, such as Jacob, who struggles to make them can still function as an agent. The overarching term for the treatment that Jacob's doctor prescribes is "Mythotherapy."

"Mythotherapy," according to the doctor's description of it, is a combination of existentialist philosophy and pragmatist utility. It is, he explains, "based on two assumptions: that human existence precedes human essence, if either of the two terms really signifies anything; and that a man is free not only to choose his own essence but to change it at will. Those are both good existentialist premises," the doctor tells Jacob, "and whether they're true or false is of no concern to us—they're *useful* in your case" (336). These premises are potentially useful to Jacob because the doctor has used them as the foundations of his Mythotherapy, which is a way of living a "fictionalized" version of one's own life. One who practices Mythotherapy adopts a role for him or herself and allocates supporting roles to those with whom he or she comes into contact. When Jacob became immobilized at the bus terminal, the doctor hypothesizes, he was simply "no character at all" (338). The solution, then, is to convince and enable the patient to adopt any number of different life-scripts and to don the mask appropriate to that script. Knowing who he is supposed to be in any given situation and knowing where the plot of any particular script leads will allow Jacob to act in any given circumstance and allow him to function in society as if he had a viable self. The doctor believes that with Mythotherapy as a way of managing his personal life and teaching grammar as a way of grounding his professional life Jacob should manage to function—more or less effectively—in the world.

As we have already seen, Jacob's doctor posits making choices as an ontological necessity ("Choosing is existence: to the extent that you don't choose, you don't exist" [331]); Jacob's difficulty in making choices, therefore, threatens him, at least according to the doctor, not only with immobility but with annihilation as well. But the issue of choices is only part of a larger existential conundrum for Jacob, one that is signaled by the opening line of the narrative: "In a sense, I am Jacob Horner" (255).

Jacob's decision to hedge his bets as to his identity works, then, on two readily apparent levels: it is in keeping with a "character" that is inconsistent and wholly unable to commit to much of anything, and it is in keeping with certain prevailing twentieth-century notions of identity and selfhood, which manifest themselves in character and in (literary) characters. For the most part, however, very few make the leap from the idea that we do not have a stable, immutable, and persistent self to the claim that we do not exist. Rather, we have learned to accept that words such as "self" and "identity" work better metaphorically than literally; we cannot say that they denominate some "thing" precisely and unerringly, but we can be relatively certain that we know what tenor we intend to conjure when we utter our own names as vehicles. *The End of the Road,* however, presents Jacob with problems that transcend those related to identification, going so far as to call into question his actual existence.

Fittingly, Barth provides Jacob with a dream that functions as an embedded allegorical narrative to illustrate his existential dilemma. As Jacob describes it, he once "had a dream in which it became a matter of some importance to me to learn the weather prediction for the following day" (286). In order to find the forecast he tries newspapers, the radio, the telephone company's weather number, and even the weather bureau itself, but without success. Finally, he calls the chief meteorologist at home, only to learn that "There isn't going to be any weather tomorrow" (287). The concept of weather in this short anecdote corresponds to what Jacob calls his "moods," and he uses the strange dream narrative to demonstrate a shortcoming in the commonly employed weather–moods analogy as well as to illustrate what he recognizes to be a personal oddity: "a day without weather is unthinkable, but for me at least there were frequently days without any mood at all" (287). On these days without moods, he tells us, "Jacob Horner, except in a meaningless metabolistic sense, ceased to exist, for I was without a personality. Like those microscopic specimens that biologists must dye in order to make them visible at all, I had to be colored with some mood or other if there was to be a recognizable self to me" (287). As an intellectual, Jacob admits to being aware of the fact that his "successive and discontinuous selves were linked to one another by the two unstable threads of body and memory," of the fact that "in the nature of Western languages the word *change* presupposes something upon which the changes operate," and of the fact that just as the "dye is not the specimen," neither is the mood the self (287). These facts, however, hold no interest for him; on his "weatherless days" he feels bereft of self.

In the context of the novel, Jacob's subconscious has transformed the phenomenon of his intermittent sense of existence into a meteorological narrative. What, then, should we make of Jacob's dream, which functions as a dependent embedded allegory? We should begin by noting that the dream itself has all of the markings of strong allegory. Jacob's own exegesis makes it clear that he reads the dream as the transformation of the idiosyncratic role of moods in his life into a narrative in which "weather" represents those moods. The dream seems strange to Jacob and to us because it presents us with a bizarre possibility: a day without weather. And while Jacob claims that he uses this dream to illustrate a shortcoming in the weather–moods analogy, his explanation and interpretation indicate that the dream of a weatherless day corresponds exactly to an occasional state of his existence: a day without moods. Furthermore, we have no evidence to suggest that we readers should not accept this interpretation, thus effectively eliminating the possibility that Barth's narrator speaks in a voice that would oppose his own authorial one.

Despite its strength, however, this embedded allegory remains entirely dependent on the narrative that houses it. In other words, the dream helps us to understand Jacob, but it is not applicable to anything beyond him; this embedded allegory is primarily a tool of characterization. Unlike the "Before the Law" section of *The Trial* or the story of the tortoise and the birds in *Things Fall Apart,* Jacob's dream does not offer the possibility of transcendence, the prospect of being transported beyond the confines of the narrative into another realm. Moreover, unlike these other two embedded narratives, the allegorical nature of Jacob's dream depends on its context. Certainly, the *metaphor* of being "weatherless" makes sense outside of *The End of the Road,* but the dream narrative relies on the particular character established in the embedding story for its full allegorical effect. Kafka's "the man from the country," by way of contrast, can be interpreted as standing in for K., but the designation is sufficiently vague to apply to anyone. Indeed, the priest who relates the parable to K. makes it clear that the story predates K.'s own existence, appearing in "the writings that preface the Law" (213). And, moreover, Kafka actually published the parable as an autonomous short story. Thus, any attempt to equate K. and the frustrated figure in the parable becomes an exercise in finding correspondences *ex post facto,* as it were. In Barth's story, on the other hand, the person in Jacob's dream is—and can only really be—Jacob.

Even if we interpret Jacob as a figural rather than as a mimetic character, as a number of critics have, then the embedded allegorical dream still lacks the hermeneutic import of the independent embedded allegories cited above. One could argue, for example, that Jacob and Joe are so simplified as to be little more than one-dimensional stand-ins for certain ideas or philosophical positions. Jacquelyn Kegley, in fact, finds that "Barth makes no attempt to delineate characters.... The central characters, in fact, have stock and symbolic names: Jacob Horner, who sat in the corner and mindlessly pulled out plums, and Joe Morgan, whose name probably alludes to J. P. Morgan, the tough, energetic American financier" (116). If Kegley is correct in her assertion,[17] then we might see the weather dream as way of ensuring that Jacob Horner represents the idea that Barth intends. In works such as *The Pilgrim's Progress, Everyman,* and the *Psychomachia,* traditional strong allegorical narratives, the characters bear the names of particular qualities, and the fates of these characters are invariably determined by the relative merits of the qualities that give them their names. Thus, in Prudentius's *Psychomachia,* virtuous qualities including Faith, Modesty, and Patience engage their respective nemeses Idolatry, Voluptuousness, and Anger on a field of battle and ultimately defeat them.

The very names they bear serve to overdetermine these characters; they are what they are, and never anything more or less. Moreover, these characters are, by definition and by nature, static. In a strong allegory, Faith cannot *naturally* or mimetically become something other, and Idolatry cannot recognize the error of her ways and gain a measure of redemption.[18] This overdetermination, therefore, results in a feeling that the characters are underdeveloped, at least in comparison to those who inhabit the more mimetic fiction to which readers have grown accustomed. When Prudentius describes Faith, for example, each of her various aspects serves as a way to elaborate her most salient trait; the progressive revelation of character does add to our knowledge of that character, but it does so primarily by adding depth to our understanding of that central trait rather than adding breadth and complexity by revealing the character's multiple traits. Thus, we learn that Faith moves toward her battle with Idolatry in "careless rustic dress, with shoulders bare, / With flowing locks and naked arms exposed; / For in her sudden zeal for new conflicts, / She takes no thought of weapons or of shield, / But trusting her stout heart and unclad limbs, / She risks the hazards of a savage fray" (22–27). That Faith does not feel compelled to gird herself in the customary way for battle attests to her faith, to the confidence that lies in her "stout heart." We do not learn what Faith as a "person" is like here, but we do learn something about that quality that she represents and that ultimately (over)determines her.

As S. Georgia Nugent argues in *Allegory and Poetics: The Structure and*

---

17. Kegley does not speak for all readers when she claims that Barth's characters in this novel are essentially allegorical. Indeed, Bernard J. Paris contends that "often characters seem unrealistic simply because we do not comprehend their motivations and personalities" (81), and that, when read carefully we can see that, in this novel at least, Barth's "characters are brilliant mimetic portraits" (64).

18. That is not to say that change is impossible in allegory; however, this kind of change, when it does occur, usually happens through divine or magical intervention.

Imagery of Prudentius' "Psychomachia," the representations of these characters "becomes largely a matter of securing univocality" (17). In order to guarantee the unambiguous nature of his characters and what they represent, "Prudentius loads attributes on his allegorical warriors with a heavy hand. He understands that, in the rhetorical economy of allegory, it is only by such an excess of apparently anomalous—and therefore telling—detail that one can certify meaning" (17). Ultimately, the overdetermination of character allows Prudentius to ensure that his figures clearly and faithfully convey what he intends them to convey: "The careful orchestration of each adjective and verb to harmonize in one monochromatic whole enables Prudentius to transform a state of mind into a condition of the body" (17).

Seen from this perspective, the reader might construe Jacob's dream as providing one of those "anomalous" and "telling" details of the character's true identity. Even so, Barth's embedded allegory reinforces our understanding of a character but does not fundamentally shape how we interpret the entire narrative. Dependent embedded allegories such as this one operate as aspects of some textual phenomenon (character, in this case) rather than as independent textual phenomena.

Interdependent Embedded Allegory: Barth and Coetzee

To this point I have been working with discrete examples of embedded allegories in respective texts. Fictional narratives, however, might well contain multiple instances or several kinds of embedded allegorical narratives. Barth's *The End of the Road,* in fact, employs both dependent embedded allegories and what I am calling interdependent embedded allegories. Interdependent embedded allegories are intertextual figural narratives, ones that an author borrows from another author or another narrative and embeds in his or her own story.[19] Given Barth's interest in embedded narratives and

---

19. In her excellent work *The Language of Allegory,* Maureen Quilligan identifies a similar phenomenon that she calls a "pretext," which she defines as "the source that always stands outside the narrative . . . ; the pretext is the text that the narrative comments on by reenacting, as well as the claim the narrative makes to be a fiction not built upon another text. The pretext thus names that slippery relationship between the source of the work and the work itself" (97–98). Quilligan's insights are valuable and clearly relevant to my own ideas. I have not adopted her terminology, however, for two reasons. First, the term "interdependent" works better in conjunction with the two related terms—independent and dependent—that I am also putting forward. Second, Quilligan understands the pretext as being a pretext for another allegory. I submit that interdependent embedded allegories can be found in texts that are not themselves allegorical.

with literary history,[20] we should not be surprised to find such a textual phenomenon in his own narratives. So, we return to *The End of the Road*.

Armed with the doctor's advice, the occasionally moodless Jacob submits a letter of application to be an instructor at the Wicomico State Teachers College, and, following an interview, he is hired. At the interview, Jacob meets the college's history teacher, Joe Morgan,

> a tall, bespectacled, athletic young man, terribly energetic, with whom one was so clearly expected to be charmed, he was so bright, busy, and obviously on his way up, that one had one's hands full simply trying to be civil to him, and realized at once that the invidious comparisons to oneself that he could not for the life of him help inviting would prevent one's ever being really tranquil about the fact of his existence, to say nothing of becoming his friend. (268)

Despite the pessimistic nature of his first impression of him, Jacob does become friendly with Joe and with Joe's wife, Rennie, as well; the relationship among these three is the primary concern of Barth's novel and Jacob's narrative.

The friendship begins auspiciously, with Jacob deciding after their first social engagement that he would have to revise his first impression of Joe, attesting that "it was clear in a very short time that if I remained in Wicomico we would be friends" (284). The characteristics that immediately appeal to Jacob are Joe's intelligence, his deliberative nature, his analytical acumen, and his ability to live by his philosophy. That philosophy rests on classic twentieth-century antifoundationalism and the concomitant recognition of relativism, and contingency. "In my ethics," Joe explains, "the most a man can ever do is be right from his own point of view" (296). The closest that Joe comes to holding an absolute, as Jacob points out to him, is his belief that one must always take others and their ideas seriously (296). And, indeed, Joe does adhere to this prescription; he works tirelessly to articulate his own position on any matter and to understand that of his interlocutor; in this regard, he displays intellectual strength and energy reminiscent of Socrates, strength and energy that one must have if one is to lead the kind of "examined life" that both men advocate. As Joe explains,

---

20. See, for example, his "Tales Within Tales Within Tales."

the more sophisticated your ethics get, the stronger you have to be to stay afloat. And when you say good-by to objective values, you really have to flex your muscles and keep your eyes open, because you're on your own. It takes *energy:* not just personal energy, but cultural energy, or you're lost. Energy's what makes the difference between American pragmatism and French existentialism—where else but in America could you have a cheerful nihilism, for God's sake? (298)

Joe applies his philosophy not only to his own life, but to his marriage as well, and this results in an interpersonal dynamic that looks strange from the outside. "I'm not a man who needs to be married under any circumstances," Joe explains to Jacob, "—in fact, under a lot of circumstances I couldn't tolerate being married—and one of my conditions for preserving any relationship at all, but particularly a marriage relationship, would be that the parties involved be able to take each other seriously" (296). For Joe, taking people seriously entails both being able to "respect" them and "not making allowances" for them (296); he must be able to consider them his equals in all respects. Toward this end, Joe can justify having "popped [Rennie] one on the jaw" when she acted in such a way as to threaten his ability to take her seriously (297). His hitting her is, in his mind, a demonstration of his respect for her (treating her as an equal rather than as "merely" a woman) and his way of showing her that she has acted in way that he would interpret as being beneath her. The result of Joe's application of his philosophy to his marriage is a wife who, as Jacob remarks, seems to be his own creation, a modern version of Pygmalion's Galatea (283). Despite his professed belief that he can only ultimately be right from his own point of view, and that other points of view are potentially no less valid than his own, Joe proves unwilling to take seriously anyone who does not share his general perspective, anyone, in other words, who does not reason through things as he does. One would not necessarily have to arrive at the same conclusions, but the process itself is nonnegotiable. Recognizing this, Rennie felt compelled, early in her relationship with Joe, to effect radical changes in herself in order to meet his standards: "I think I completely erased myself," she explains to Jake, "... right down to nothing, so I could start over.... I'd rather be a lousy Joe Morgan than a first-rate Rennie MacMahon" (311–12).

Jacob, like most readers, I imagine, has some difficulty embracing Joe's approach to his marriage, even if he can appreciate, in theory, the fact that Joe strives to live a life consistent with his principles and refuses to accept the intellectual laziness of others. As the novel progresses, Jacob becomes increasingly skeptical of Joe's applied philosophy and Joe's unrelenting seriousness about it. As a result, Jacob begins to take Joe less and less seriously, finally finding something "silly" about such a dogmatic adherence to a philosophy—even if it is based on tenable principles—that leaves no room for irony or whimsy and that countenances no truck with social convention. Both Joe and Rennie recognize Jacob's growing skepticism, and Rennie in particular finds it threatening: "What scares me," she admits, "is that anybody could grant all of Joe's premises—our premises—understand them and grant them and *then* laugh at us" (314). Although she assumes that Joe is strong enough to withstand the threat that Jacob represents, she is scared by the prospect that someone could be astute enough to understand what she and Joe are doing and ultimately not take it—and them—seriously.

Rennie's fears ultimately manifest themselves in an embedded allegory, one that becomes central to our understanding of the novel from this point forward. Because Joe spends much of his free time working on his dissertation (he teaches at the teachers college as an ABD [All But Dissertation]), he suggests that Rennie offer Jacob horseback riding lessons on her parents' nearby land. During one of their rides, Rennie relates that she has either dreamed or imagined while daydreaming, "that for the last few weeks Joe had become friendly with the Devil, and was having fun arguing with him and playing tennis with him, to test his own strength" (317). Jacob obviously corresponds to the Devil in what Jacob rather patronizingly calls Rennie's "pretty conceit" (317), and Rennie has already made it clear that, even though she recognizes that Jacob will find it "ridiculous," "[she] think[s] of Joe as [she'd] think of God. Even when he makes a mistake, his reasons for doing what he did are clearer and sharper than anybody else's" (312).

Rennie's dream clearly alludes to a previous cultural narrative—the struggle between ultimate good and ultimate evil—and so its resonance and its rhetorical impact depend on the reader's familiarity with that previous story. Yet while Kafka and Achebe put forth the "Before the Law" parable and the story of the tortoise and the birds, respectively, as autonomous narratives simply nested in the primary narrative, Barth has woven the story of the battle between God and Satan—a story that is well known to a Christian audience—into the host narrative in such a way that it does not function as a "story within a story." Instead, the prior Manichaean narrative—which might not be allegorical at all, depending on one's theological inclinations—has been rewritten in terms of the embedding narrative; the character-pairs Joe–God and Jacob–Satan have been overtly conflated, and both the setting and the plot of the story have been altered to suit the purposes of the embedding narrative. This act of narrative integration does not efface the preexisting narrative, but rather brings it into a state of interdependence with its host.

We should note that—as was the case with *The Trial*—the basic structure and the primary figures of this embedded allegory are similar to what we find in the primary narrative. In both cases, a figure who is an invited interloper—the Devil or Jacob[21]—has a destabilizing effect on Rennie and Joe's relationship even as the actual existence of that figure is called into doubt.[22] Would we be justified then in accepting Rennie's characterization of the roles played by the various figures? And if so, would this embedded allegory have the same force as those that we have examined in the Achebe and Kafka texts? Or is its effect more localized, as we saw with the dependent embedded allegories?

The amount of hermeneutic force that interdependent allegories carry depends on how readers see them squaring with the implied author's perspective. These embedded narratives can produce a strong allegorical effect even as they lack the mystical or transcendent appeal of the independent embedded allegories if they can be made to resonate with the values or aims of the implied author. Thus, Barth's interdependent embedded narrative has the potential to produce readings such as Kegley's, readings in which the characters appear one-dimensional and flat. Such interpretations indicate that Kegley and the numerous other critics who read Barth's novel in this way have succumbed to the same temptation that we saw in the case of Barbara Harlow's interpretation of *Things Fall Apart*. Kegley, for example, argues that *The End of the Road* is essentially a novel about order versus chaos, and that Barth has constructed one-dimensional thematic characters to play out this battle. I, on the other hand, find Kegley to be too willing to allow Rennie's "pretty conceit" to stand for the larger narrative.

In Kegley's defense, there is considerable pressure to adopt just such a reading; indeed, the doctor's "prescription" for Jacob is precisely to view the world in similarly clear-cut binary terms and to simplify his own sense of self, to become something akin to what E. M. Forster has called a "flat" character (68), a character, in other words, who is unburdened by complexity or ambiguity and who never surprises because he or she always follows a predictable script. The true import of the novel for me lies in the fact that it shows finally and clearly that this "black and white" approach to life, or

---

21. In the embedded allegory, Joe invites or conjures the Devil in order to test his strength, and one has a sense that Joe might have done the same with Jacob, whom he does perceive as a worthy intellectual challenge. And it is the case that Joe and Rennie are more eager to develop a relationship with Jacob than he is; he admits, in fact, to having no other friends and to being generally disinclined to maintain close relationships with other people. Thus, he does play the role of an interloper, but he has also been prodded, enticed, and encouraged to do so.

22. Although I do not have the space to examine it in detail here, the question of Jacob's particular existence—and what it means to exist more generally—is a central theme in this work. This is reflected not only in Jacob's bout of immobilization and the doctor's counsel about "choosing," but also, as I mentioned earlier, in the enigmatic opening line of the narrative: "In a sense, I am Jacob Horner." (255).

to interpretation, or to other people, or to ourselves, cannot be maintained without doing violence to those entities. The progression of the novel, with all its revelations and its complications, both produces and reveals cracks in such a mind-set. No matter how much someone might want them to be, no matter how hard someone tries to make them so, "things" just are not that simple. The allure of a straightforward and strong key to the relationships among the characters in the novel (such as the one that Rennie provides and that Jacob will later adopt) and to the narrative more generally seems clear, but, at the end of the road, we will realize, just as characters in Barth's novel must realize, that the pursuit of this key has led us to a dead end.

Still, Barth's interdependent embedded allegory and its direct allusion to the biblical figures certainly raises our awareness of allegorical potential. As Stephen Barney declares, if an allusion such as this one "is extensive, especially if it resides in the whole plot of the text, it tends towards allegory. The correspondence of the presented text to the old, authoritative text encourages the reader to look for a *tertium quid,* a principle of interpretation to which the correspondence points. Since the literary monuments—the Bible, Virgil, Ovid—have submitted to allegorical interpretations of their own, the *tertium quid* may not be far to seek. The fact that the antique text *has been criticized* makes it a fit support for allegory" (16–17, emphasis in original). An allusive embedded narrative such as the one we find in *The End of the Road,* then, can be read as a signal of allegorical intent and can result in the reader moving toward allegoresis.

Barth has in a sense encouraged this move by having his narrator pick up and extend Rennie's interdependent embedded allegory, effectively allowing the allusion to "[reside] in the whole plot of the text" (Barney 16). Late in the narrative, after Rennie has had an affair with him, Jacob actively adopts the satanic role that Rennie has envisioned for him. Having learned of the affair, Joe perversely sends the repentant Rennie back to Jacob's apartment so that she can have sex with him again, ostensibly to decide exactly what she thinks about adultery, about Jacob, and about her marriage. Surely at least partly to spite Joe, Jacob does take Rennie to bed, but he contends that

> I was able to do so only because, for better or worse, enough of my alertness was gone to permit me to dramatize the situation as part of a romantic contest between symbols. Joe was The Reason, or Being (I was using Rennie's cosmos); I was The Unreason, or Not-Being; and the two of us were fighting without quarter for possession of Rennie, like God and Satan for the soul of Man. This pretty ontological Manichaeism would certainly stand no close examination, but it had the triple virtue of excusing me from having to assign to Rennie any essence more specific than The Human

> Personality, further allowing me to fornicate with a Mephisthophelean relish, and finally making it possible for me not to question my motives, since what I was doing was of the essence of my essence. Does one look for introspection from Satan? (377)

This "pretty ontological Manichaeism" clearly recalls Rennie's "pretty conceit" that casts Jacob as Devil and Joe as God (317). Moreover, the fact that Jacob—Barth's autodiegetic narrator (a first-person narrator who is also the protagonist of the story)—picks up the conceit gives it more force than it has coming from one of the more minor characters. This force derives from the tendency of most readers to seek out an authoritative voice in and for the narrative. Susan Lanser has argued—and I think convincingly—that "Voices with the greatest mimetic authority . . . are more likely to be equated with, or to coconstruct, implied authorship; voices carrying both diegetic and mimetic authority will have the edge" (156). As a character who both dominates the story-world (mimetic authority) and has control of the narrative (diegetic authority), Jacob fits the description of an authoritative voice, one that *might* echo the sentiments of the implied author.

We would be well advised, however, to take seriously Jacob's warning that this extended conceit "would certainly stand no close examination," because such scrutiny will reveal the rhetorical limitations of this kind of embedded allegorical narrative. In this case, the good–evil opposition that the embedded narrative fleshes out seems overly simplistic, a fact that even Jacob recognizes. Jacob's most egregious act of bad faith is to convince himself—or to allow himself to be convinced by his therapist—that life demands such incessant reductionism. Relying on a structuralist linguistic metaphor to explain Rennie's confusion about whether she loves him or abhors him, Jacob reasons that getting on in the world requires us to distort reality in ways that enable us to avoid becoming bogged down by what appear to be irresolvable conundrums:

> I'm sure, as a matter of fact, that what Rennie felt was actually neither ambivalent nor even complex; it was both single and simple, like all feelings, but like all feelings it was also completely particular and individual, and so the trouble started only when she attempted to label it with a common noun such as *love* or *abhorrence*. Things can be signified by common nouns only if one ignores the differences between them; but it is precisely these differences, when deeply felt, that make the nouns inadequate and lead the layman (but not the connoisseur) to believe that he has a paradox on his hands, an ambivalence, when actually it is merely a matter of *x*'s being part horse and part grammar book, and completely neither. Assigning names to things is like assigning roles to people: it is necessarily a

distortion, but it is a necessary distortion if one would get on with the plot, and to the connoisseur it's good clean fun. (389)[23]

For the second time, but in a different context, we hear Jacob making an implicit Aristotelian argument that plot should be our chief concern and, further, that the progression of a plot depends on one's ability to distort reality through simplification, and ultimately claiming that such an activity can be both harmless and fun.

Jacob is at least consistent on this score, if not others. Indeed, slightly earlier in his narrative he has an epiphany concerning his one real conviction, and it is one that explains even if it does not ethically justify his rather cavalier attitude toward Rennie's emotions. "Articulation!" he exclaims,

> There, by Joe, was *my* absolute, if I could be said to have one. At any rate, it is the only thing I can think of about which I ever had, with any frequency at all, the feelings one usually has for one's absolutes. To turn experience into speech—that is, to classify, to categorize, to conceptualize, to grammarize, to syntactify it—is always a betrayal of experience, a falsification of it; but only so betrayed can it be dealt with at all, and only in so dealing with it did I ever feel a man, alive, and kicking. It is therefore that, when I had cause to think about it at all, I responded to this precise falsification, this adroit, careful myth-making, with all the upsetting exhilaration of any artist at his work. When my mythoplastic razors were sharply honed, it was unparalleled sport to lay about with them, to have at reality. (367)

Despite the frustrating qualifier that immediately follows ("In other senses, of course, I don't believe this at all" [367]), the reader of Barth's novel must take Jacob's confession about articulation seriously, because it helps us to understand his character and how he seeks to manipulate the world so as to make his way through it as painlessly as possible.

When we take the long view of Barth's novel and Jacob's role in it, the interdependent embedded allegory that pits Jacob against Joe emerges as an example of the tendency of the characters in this work to falsify and to oversimplify. Thus, despite the reliance on the compelling narrative of good versus evil that the God–Satan narrative provides us, the interdependent embedded narrative that emerges from it has little power to transcend the confines of the narrative that houses it. Indeed, it seems almost laughable to equate such fallible and petty characters as Jacob and Joe with the monu-

---

23. This idea of "getting on with the plot"—and what getting on with the plot requires one to do or not to do—will be echoed and expanded in Barth's short story "Click." See chapter 6, "The Presence of Allegory," for a discussion of this story.

mental figures of Satan and God. Jacob can only be a one-dimensional character—as Kegley argues he is—if we allow him to oversimplify himself and if we fail to recognize that things are far more complicated than he allows them to seem. Thus, Bernard J. Paris contends that "often characters seem unrealistic simply because we do not comprehend their motivations and personalities" (81), and that, when read carefully we can see that, in this novel at least, Barth's "characters are brilliant mimetic portraits" (64). The apparent contradiction between Kegley's and Paris's interpretations of the characters can be explained by the amount of faith they put in the embedded allegory and by how seriously each takes Jacob as a reliable narrator, one who essentially speaks for the implied Barth.

If there is a general lesson to be drawn from this example of an interdependent embedded allegory, it is that this kind of textual phenomenon can have a significant impact on how we interpret a work of narrative fiction. Like other textual phenomena, however, interdependent embedded allegories are only a part of the feedback loop of interpretation, so readers should not blithely assume that they are a direct revelation of authorial intention or that they can be made to stand for the primary narrative. As is the case with Barth's characters, they are often more complicated than they first appear. This fact will be made even more evident as we examine another case of interdependent embedded allegory from a different novelist.

J. M. Coetzee's *Elizabeth Costello* is another text that employs interdependent embedded allegory, but rather than following Barth's lead and drawing on a foundational cultural–religious narrative, Coetzee weaves the weak allegories of Franz Kafka into the fabric of his narrative. This tactic produces a different rhetorical effect from that which we see in Barth's work because Coetzee's use of narratives that are themselves allegorical amplifies the allegorical quality of the embedding text. Given that the connection between the embedded narrative and the embedding narrative is so strong in interdependent embedded allegory, this amplification might even be greater than what we encounter with independent embedded narratives that are allegorical.

My reading of Coetzee will reveal that the embedding of an allegorical narrative can function not only as a tool that an author might use to structure a reader's response to or interpretation of the primary narrative, but also as a means of summoning or channeling the spirit of the embedded narrative or author. We see this effect to some extent in Kafka's use of "Before the Law," the feeling of which seems to dominate the close of *The Trial*. Both of these narratives, however, are Kafka's creations, so the net effect is still entirely

Kafkaesque. In *Elizabeth Costello*, by way of contrast, Coetzee makes use of *Kafka's* narratives and in so doing manages to engage with the spirit of those weak allegories—to capture, in other words, the essence of the Kafkaesque without merely emulating Kafka through Coetzee's own weak allegory. Here, Coetzee seems to be exploring the possibility of using fictional narratives[24] to perform what at least one version of literary criticism has historically tried to do: to sympathetically convey the essence of another author.[25]

Coetzee divides his novel into eight "Lessons," each of which issues from the mind or words of the eponymous protagonist, a sexagenarian author from Australia. A decorated and prolific novelist, Elizabeth Costello remains most famous for her 1969 novel *The House on Eccles Street*, a work in which she takes Marion Bloom—the wife of Leopold Bloom, hero of Joyce's *Ulysses*—as her subject. When her own story—the one written by Coetzee—begins, the passing years have nudged Elizabeth past the tipping point that we all face somewhere in the middle of life and into physical decline.

The novel opens with Elizabeth leaving her home in Australia for a trip to Pennsylvania, where she will receive a prize, deliver an acceptance speech/lecture at a college, and submit to the requisite media interviews. She is accompanied by her son John, a lecturer in physics and astronomy at a school in Massachusetts. "Elizabeth has become a little frail," Coetzee's narrator reveals, and "without the help of her son she would not be undertaking this taxing trip across half the world" (2). John does worry about the toll that the trip will exact from his mother, recognizing that she does not have the physical strength or stamina that she did when she penned the work that made her famous. As he reflects on her condition and her prospects for surviving the ordeal, we readers get the first of a number of allusions to Kafka: "He [her son] is here, with her, out of love. He cannot imagine her getting through this trial without him at her side. He stands by her because he is her son, her loving son. But he is also on the point of becoming—distasteful word—her trainer" (3). The use of the word "trial" to describe Elizabeth's visit speaks both to the suffering that her public performance will no doubt

---

24. Coetzee has also approached Kafka in his literary criticism. See for example his collection of essays titled *Stranger Shores*.

25. Coetzee practices in this novel something close to what Mark Edmundson has claimed should be the goal of all teachers of literature. "The standard for the kind of interpretation I have in mind is actually rather straightforward," Edmundson explains. "When a teacher of literature admires an author enough to teach his work, then it stands to reason that the teacher's initial objective ought to be framing a reading that the author would approve. The teacher, to begin with, represents the author: he analyzes the text sympathetically, he treats the words with care and caution and with due respect. He works hard with the students to develop a vision of what the world is and how to live that rises from the author's work and that, ultimately, the author, were he present in the room, would endorse" (62).

cause her, but it also, of course, brings to mind the Kafka novel of the same name. The reader might never make this latter connection, however, if Coetzee had not written an acceptance speech for his protagonist that makes the link more pronounced, a link that depends on the "distasteful word" that describes what John seems to feel is his role relative to his mother.

John, Coetzee writes, "thinks of [his mother] as a seal, an old, tired seal. One more time she must heave herself up on to the tub, one more time show that she can balance the ball on her nose" (3),[26] and he is her trainer. But in her acceptance speech Elizabeth alludes to another animal, the ape in Kafka's short tale "A Report to an Academy." Elizabeth uses this story to get at the theme of her talk (itself a kind of a report to an academy)—realism—and to make the point that sometime in the twentieth century something changed in the way we read literature; she sees Kafka as an exemplar of that change. "If you know the [Kafka] story," she tells her audience, "you will remember that it is cast in the form of a monologue, a monologue by the ape. Within this form there is no means for either speaker or audience to be inspected by an outsider's eye. For all we know, the speaker may not 'really' be an ape, may be simply a human being like ourselves deluded into thinking himself an ape, or a human being presenting himself, with heavy irony, for rhetorical purposes, as an ape..." (18). From this example, Elizabeth draws the broader conclusion that such undecidability or indecipherability now characterizes all of literature and our reading of it. The time of knowing for certain what something was or meant has passed, she asserts:

> The word-mirror is broken, irreparably, it seems. About what is really going on in the lecture hall your guess is as good as mine: men and men, men and apes, apes and men, apes and apes. The lecture hall itself may be nothing but a zoo. The words on the page will no longer stand up and be counted, each proclaiming "I mean what I mean!" The dictionary that used to stand beside the Bible and the works of Shakespeare above the fireplace, where in pious Roman homes the household gods were kept, has become just one code book among many. (19)

And from hermeneutic contingency comes ontological contingency: "There used to be a time, we believe, when we could say who we were. Now we are just performers speaking our parts. The bottom has dropped out. . . . There is every reason, then, for me to feel less than certain about myself as I stand before you" (19).

---

26. A few pages later, when John reflects on the insight with which his mother writes, he changes his assessment and thinks she resembles a cat more than the typically amiable seal (5).

This issue of belief and Elizabeth's inconsistent relationship with it returns forcefully in the penultimate section—and final "Lesson"—of the novel. This chapter of the text is called "At the Gate," and it is a striking example of an interdependent embedded allegory. With no contextualization from the narrator, the reader of this section finds him- or herself looking on as Elizabeth—sunburned and perspiring—alights from a bus in the middle of a busy town square. "Past the pavement tables, past the young folk, the wheels of the suitcase rattling over the cobbles, she makes her way to the gate where a uniformed man stands drowsily on guard, propped on the rifle he holds butt down before him" (193). When she asks the guard to open the gate for her (neither she nor the reader seems to understand why she senses that she should go through it), he informs her that she must first make a statement of what she believes. At this, we are told, "There is no more doubt in her mind about where she is, who she is. She is a petitioner before the gate. The journey that brought her here, to this country, to this town, that seemed to reach its end when the bus halted and the door opened on to the crowded square, was not the end of it all. Now commences a trial of a different kind" (194). The invocation of a trial at this point in the narrative calls our attention back to the opening chapter, in which Elizabeth's son worries about her as she faces the professional ordeals that arise from her celebrity. If Kafka's novel was a vague allusion at that juncture, it has now been fully embedded in her own story.

Coetzee, in fact, explicitly prepared us for this embedding at an earlier point in the novel. When, following that first lecture on realism and Kafka, John asks his mother why she chose that as the topic for her acceptance speech, and in particular why she selected Kafka, of all writers, as an entrée into realism, Elizabeth replies that even though Kafka's parable of the ape might not be realistic in any strict sense, it reveals a kind of foundational realism because "Kafka had time to wonder where and how his poor educated ape was going to find a mate. And what it was going to be like when he was left in the dark with the bewildered, half-tamed female that his keepers eventually produced for his use" (32). What is more, she continues, "Kafka's ape is embedded in life. It is the embeddedness that is important, not the life itself. His ape is embedded as we are embedded, you in me, I in you. That ape is followed through to the end, to the bitter, unsayable end, whether or not there are traces left on the page. Kafka stays awake during the gaps when we are sleeping. That is where Kafka fits in" (32).

Coetzee likely intends us to see the presence of the ape in Elizabeth's life more directly than even she implies or perhaps recognizes here. The ape's embeddedness is more than just a simile ("*as* we are embedded"), but rather a reality; in some ways Elizabeth has been transformed into the ape in this story (the poor figure granted no privacy, whose base urges and flights of brilliance are both on full display), even as she, in theory, plays the role of Kafka (the figure in the panopticon who never sleeps) in her own novels. That we are meant to see Elizabeth in the role of the ape becomes apparent when, in a brilliant conclusion to the opening section of the novel, Coetzee subjects her, as she sleeps on her return flight to Australia, to the kind of ethically suspect and perhaps gratuitous gazing that John finds objectionable in the most committed realistic fiction but that she seems to value in Kafka:

> She lies slumped in her seat. Her head is sideways, her mouth open. She is snoring faintly. Light flashes from the windows as they bank, the sun setting brilliantly over southern California. He can see up her nostrils, into her mouth, down the back of her throat. And what he cannot see he can imagine: the gullet, pink and ugly, contracting as it swallows, like a python, drawing things down to the pear-shaped belly-sac. He draws away, tightens his own belt, sits up, facing forward. No, he tells himself, that is not where I come from, that is not it. (33–34)

The remainder of the novel is ostensibly organized around the kind of monologues that Kafka's ape delivers, but it is also infused with this kind of access to the normally hidden animal reality of the speaker. And like Kafka, Coetzee follows his subject through to what would appear to be the bitter, unsayable end.

In *Elizabeth Costello* that end begins, fittingly, with Coetzee embedding Kafka's embedded allegory "Before the Law" in the allusively titled Lesson, "At the Gate." Coetzee is not trying to be clever here, not trying to create just enough resemblance between his text and Kafka's so that only the most astute readers will make the connection. Indeed, in case we have failed to pick up on the reference some fifteen pages into the chapter, Coetzee, using free indirect discourse to reveal Elizabeth's reckoning of her own situation, brings his indebtedness to Kafka out into the open: "The wall, the gate, the sentry, are straight out of Kafka. So is the demand for a confession, so is the courtroom with the dozing bailiff and the panel of old men in their crows' robes pretending to pay attention while she thrashes about in the toils of her own words. Kafka, only the superficies of Kafka; Kafka reduced and flattened to a parody" (209). So, there is never a question of somehow "not getting it"; the connections to Kafka are too strong to miss.

Yet both Elizabeth and the reader need to figure out why—why Kafka, and why these pieces of Kafka's work? "And why is it Kafka in particular that is trundled out for her?" muses Coetzee's narrator for Elizabeth. "She is no devotee of Kafka. Most of the time she cannot read him without impatience.

As he veers between helplessness and lust, between rage and obsequiousness, she too often finds him, or at least his K. selves, simply childish. So why is the *mise en scène* into which she has been hurled so—she dislikes the word but there is no other—so Kafkaesque?" (209).[27] The best response that Elizabeth can muster is irony: "One answer that occurs to her is that the show is put together this way *because* it is not her kind of show. *You do not like the Kafkaesque, so let us rub your nose in it*" (209). Clearly, Elizabeth sees this moment as the trial she must endure, as the test to which she must submit. And this test has two distinct facets.

The first aspect of Elizabeth's trial involves what she calls the "superficies of Kafka." In other words, someone has recreated the situation and the setting of *The Trial* and dropped her—unwittingly and unwillingly—into it. The resultant sense of confusion and disorientation leaves Elizabeth nonplussed, which does align her with a number of Kafka's protagonists, especially his various K.'s. As a novelist herself, one who has read even if she has not particularly enjoyed Kafka, Elizabeth recognizes the similarities between her story-world and the one created by Kafka almost immediately. After her first unsuccessful attempt to pass through the gate, for example, Elizabeth inquires of the sentry who mans the guardhouse whether she might be permitted to look through to the other side, "'Just to see if it is worth all this trouble'" (195). The sentry accedes and escorts Elizabeth up to the gate itself: "Past the soldier leaning on his rifle he takes her, till they stand before the gate itself, massive enough to hold back an army. From a pouch at his belt he takes a key nearly as long as his forearm. Will this be the point where he tells her the gate is meant for her and her alone, and moreover that she is destined never to pass through? Should she remind him she knows the score?" (196). She knows the score. She knows, in other words, the various parts assigned to the various players in this little embedded sketch because she knows Kafka. Like the reader, Elizabeth herself feels the embedded narrative—or, more accurately from her point of view, the narrative into which she has been embedded—exerting the prefigurative pressure that Honig identified, but this time the pressure is on her own situation. Acutely aware of her own situation and whence and from whom it derives, Elizabeth acts as the reader of her own narrative, and she interprets it largely through the lens of that other allegorical narrative.

And in many ways she actually gets it wrong. Coetzee's use of Kafka might appear parodic from her perspective, but from the reader's it is quite

---

27. Elizabeth's professed resistance to Kafka in this passage does not seem to square with her use of Kafka's "Report" in the opening section of the book. On the other hand, this apparent contradiction is in keeping with what we've seen of her and her ambivalence about convictions. Just because she does not like Kafka does not mean that she cannot use him.

serious. In some ways, the figures who occupy both texts (the sentries, judges, etc.) seem more credible—less reduced and flattened—in Coetzee's novel than they do in Kafka's. Indeed, whereas in Kafka's text the demands and the demeanor of the "Examining Magistrate" and his fellow judges appear unpredictable, erratic, and inappropriate (witness the mildly pornographic book *How Grete Was Plagued by Her Husband Hans* that K. finds lying on the Magistrate's table, for example [54]), the judges in Coetzee's novel, though stern and largely humorless with Elizabeth, act relatively reasonably. So, while the situation and the score seem uncanny (in the Freudian sense of the word, which emphasizes both repetition and helplessness) from Elizabeth's point of view, the reader of Coetzee's novel might interpret the effect of the embedding quite differently.

This difference arises from the fact that Elizabeth is too willing to accept a one-to-one correspondence between her situation and Kafka's weak allegory. Despite the fact that she finds Kafka's protagonists "childish," she steps easily and willingly into the shoes of Joseph K. from *The Trial*. As a result, she interprets her own experience at the gate as if it were identical to K.'s experience before the law, and this allows her to play the role occupied by K., the role of the lone sane person trying to make sense of a world without logic. And, just as K. initially refuses to take seriously the fact of his arrest and all that it entails for him (42), so too does Elizabeth deny the validity or legitimacy of the situation in which she finds herself. When she fails to gain passage through "what is evidently her gate and hers alone," she attributes this failure not to her inability to articulate to the judges what it is that she believes but rather to the vagaries of the court itself:

> Astonishing that a court which sets itself up as an interrogatory of belief should refuse to pass her. They must have heard other writers before, other disbelieving believers or believing disbelievers. Writers are not lawyers, surely they must allow for that, allow for eccentricities of presentation. But of course this is not a court of law. Not even a court of logic. Her first impression was right: a court out of Kafka or *Alice in Wonderland*, a court of paradox. (223)

But this conclusion is too facile, and it reflects a desire on Elizabeth's part to avoid the difficult, but ultimately quite reasonable, question that the judges put to her: what does she believe?

This requirement clearly puts her at a loss: "What if I am not a believer?" she asks. She is speaking to a guard at this point, and his response, unlike the responses that K. receives, must strike the reader as eminently reasonable: "The man shrugs. For the first time he looks directly at her. 'We all believe. We are not cattle. For each of us there is something we believe. Write it down, what you believe. Put it in the statement'" (194). Compared with those that K. receives regarding his situation, these instructions are blissfully clear, and they allow her to orient herself and to grasp the nature of her predicament. This is the point in the narrative, which I referenced earlier, when the narrator reveals Elizabeth's newfound certainty regarding her situation: "There is no more doubt in her mind about where she is, who she is. She is a petitioner before the gate. The journey that brought her here, to this country, to this town, that seemed to reach its end when the bus halted and its door opened on to the crowded square, was not the end of it all. Now commences a trial of a different kind. Some act is required of her, some prescribed yet undefined affirmation, before she will be found good and can pass through" (194). She clearly has an understanding of her predicament, and such an understanding Joseph K. never achieves.

Even though Elizabeth correctly picks up on the "score" of the narrative that has been embedded in her own story and recognizes the part assigned to her, the Kafka text does not exist within the confines of *Elizabeth Costello* as an *independent* embedded allegory. We recognize it, certainly, as a narrative that does exist autonomously elsewhere, but it is changed by the fact that it has become a part of and interdependent with Coetzee's story.[28] The most significant change results from Elizabeth's failure to recognize that her "first impression," that sense of the Kafkaesque, cannot serve as a final interpretation of her predicament. The epistemological uncertainties that the adjective Kafkaesque (particularly when it derives from *The Trial* as opposed to, say, *The Metamorphosis*) carries with it actually cover up—or perhaps allow Elizabeth to avoid—the more central problem for her: that abiding ontological problem of who she is. Elizabeth focuses on the strangeness of her circumstances and inaccurately reads her judges as the same characters that we find in Kafka's text, but she does not confront in a serious and satisfactory manner the question of what she believes.

After an ill-fated attempt to placate the judges by claiming that because she is a writer of fiction she should be granted an exemption from the rule requiring one to have beliefs (195), Elizabeth decides to tell the judges a

---

28. It is worth reiterating a general distinction between the independent embedded allegories and the interdependent embedded allegories that I have been discussing. In *The Trial* and in *Things Fall Apart,* the embedded allegorical narratives exist essentially as stories within, but distinct from, other stories. Connections between the embedded narratives and their hosts are exegetical in nature, and that exegesis may occur within the narrative or outside of it, by readers. In the interdependent embedded allegorical narratives under discussion, characters from the host narrative occupy roles in the embedded narrative, thus complicating the relationship between the two.

story, a narrative that she concedes "may sound allegorical" (217). The inspiration for the story comes from her childhood in Australia, more precisely, a childhood spent in a rural area "of climatic extremes: of scorching droughts followed by torrential rains that swelled the rivers with the carcasses of drowned animals" (216). The story she tells from this childhood of extreme weather involves frogs that, during the dry season, "go underground, burrowing further and further from the heat of the sun until each has created a little tomb for itself. And in those tombs they die, so to speak. Their heartbeat slows, their breathing stops, they turn the color of mud" (216). Then, when the rains return and the moisture begins to penetrate to the depths of the frog "tombs," "[i]n those coffins hearts begin to beat, limbs begin to twitch that for months have been lifeless. The dead awake. As the caked mud softens, the frogs begin to dig their way out, and soon their voices resound again in joyous exultation beneath the vault of the heavens" (216). Elizabeth offers this story as the answer to the question of what she believes: "I believe in those little frogs," she says, noting that they—and the situation that they inhabit—are real, "the Dulgannon [river] and its mudflats are real, the frogs are real. They exist whether or not I tell you about them, whether or not I believe in them. . . . [It] is because of their indifference to me that I believe in them" (217). This is a strange response, and one cannot be sure that it is made entirely in good faith, whether it is born primarily of the advice to show passion, or whether it is simply a desperate attempt to sway the judges.

Whatever the case, Elizabeth insists on a literal reading of her embedded narrative. "In my account," she explains, "for whose many failings I beg your pardon, the life cycle of the frog may sound allegorical, but to the frogs themselves it is no allegory, it is the thing itself, the only thing" (217). Elizabeth's desire to view this story from the perspective of the frogs, and therefore to downplay its allegorical potential, accords with her conception of art and her own literary production, which she views, in retrospect now as she seems to have reached the end of her professional (and possibly even actual) life, as defiantly and relentlessly mimetic. "Now that it is over and done with, that lifetime labour of writing, she is capable of casting a glance back over it that is cool enough, she believes, even cold enough, not to be deceived. Her books teach nothing, preach nothing; they merely spell out, as clearly as they can, how people lived in a certain time and place" (207). Such an approach to literature certainly runs counter to the kind of figuration required of allegory, and it also explains why she can see the life cycle of the frogs as simply the life cycle of the frogs. For her, those frogs simply are; it is their literal existence in which she believes, in which she places her faith. For readers, though, and equally for those to whom she makes her appeal, her emphasis on the literal aspect of her embedded narrative makes far less sense than does the allegorical interpretation.

Following her presentation of the story of the life cycle of the frogs, one of the judges asks a logical question, one that we might interpret as an opening for Elizabeth to acknowledge that her frog story has really been the transformation of the idea of the "spirit of life" into a figural narrative, thus resulting in an allegory: "You believe in life?" the judge asks (218). But Elizabeth does not take the bait, or the offer: "I believe," she reiterates, "in what does not bother to believe in me" (218). The questioner cannot accept this, as revealed by the "little gesture of impatience" she makes while she offers her follow-up comment: "A stone does not believe in you. A bush. But you choose to tell us not about stones or bushes but about frogs, to which you attribute a life story that is, as you concede, highly allegorical. These Australian frogs of yours embody the spirit of life, which is what you as a storyteller believe in" (218–19). This amounts to putting words in the author's mouth, for Elizabeth has said no such thing. She has admitted that the story she tells of the intrepid frogs "may sound allegorical," but she quickly minimizes this allegorical potential by focusing so relentlessly on the reality of the frogs and their particular and peculiar lives. She resists the notion, imposed on her by the judge, that she really means to transform the phenomenon of the frog's life into a figural narrative about the "spirit of [human] life." Without this turn, the turn that defines the use of tropes, Elizabeth's response seems sadly insufficient; it's really no wonder that this statement fails in its objective.

Coetzee might be using Elizabeth and her position—or perhaps her lack of a position is more apt here—to critique traditional notions of allegory. To recognize the story of the frogs as an allegory of the spirit of life is tantamount in some ways to committing an act of violence (to use Gordon Teskey's term) against the frogs. The experience of the frogs can only be validated if it can be anthropomorphized, or transformed into terms that have meaning for human beings. Elizabeth's immediate context (finding herself in a Kafkaesque embedded allegory, in other words) and the task required of her appear to demand this kind of turn; literal belief in frogs will not suffice, so allegory must turn the trick. Elizabeth's judges and the readers of Coetzee's novel all seem to expect this move, but Elizabeth stands firm against it.

If we return to one of the earlier "Lessons" in the novel, we can gain a better understanding of Elizabeth's intransigence on this point. Elizabeth makes it clear throughout the novel that she embodies what the philosopher Richard Rorty would call "liberal irony." A liberal ironist, according to Rorty, is someone who recognizes the necessary contingency of his or her own beliefs and sense of self and who wants to guarantee that others are respected and, above all, never humiliated.[29] When Rorty refers to "others" we can be relatively certain that he means other humans, but Elizabeth seems to want even broader application of liberal humility, extending it to the realm of animals. In a section titled "The Philosophers and the Animals," Elizabeth makes a strong and provocative argument in support of equating the fate of livestock animals to the treatment of the Jews at the hands of the Nazis; clearly, she is—at least in this section—a forceful advocate for animal rights, even animal equality, and she makes her case by attempting to deconstruct the binary opposition that philosophers typically use to differentiate humans from animals: reasoning beings versus unreasoning creatures. "Both reason and seven decades of life experience," Elizabeth contends, "tell me that reason is neither the being of the universe nor the being of God. On the contrary, reason looks to me suspiciously like the being of human thought. Reason is the being of a certain spectrum of human thinking. And if this is so, if that is what I believe, then why should I bow to reason this afternoon and content myself with embroidering on the discourse of the old philosophers?" (67). Here, Elizabeth seems to emphasize the stark limits of reason and thereby rejects the line of thinking that suggests reason should be used as the basis for distinguishing between humans and animals.

In the following section of Coetzee's novel, a section titled "The Poets and the Animals," Elizabeth extends her thinking to the artistic sphere, and she offers a certain kind of poetry as a means of transcending this problem of reason. Though we do not have access to her entire speech on this topic (this portion of the novel is again focalized through Elizabeth's son, John, and he arrives late to her talk, so we hear only what he does), Elizabeth seems to be drawing a distinction between poems that use animals figuratively or allegorically and those that use them for what, to Elizabeth, are more noble ends. As John walks into the room where his mother is speaking, he hears her proclaim that "In that kind of poetry [the figural kind] . . . animals stand for human qualities: the lion for courage, the owl for wisdom, and so forth. Even in Rilke's poem [she has apparently been discussing 'The Panther'] the panther is there as a stand in for something else" (94–95). Given what we know of Elizabeth's attitude toward animal rights, we can safely detect a note of ethical opprobrium in this description, a sense that the animals in this kind of poetry are simply being viewed through human eyes and used for human purposes.

Moving on from Rilke, Elizabeth finds an alternative in two poems by Ted Hughes, "The Jaguar" and "Second Glance at a Jaguar." In explicating

---

29. These notions permeate Rorty's writings, but they are most forcefully put forward in *Contingency, Irony, and Solidarity*.

these poems, Elizabeth arrives at an interpretation that foreshadows her frog story later in the novel. Hughes, Elizabeth argues, moves away from using the animal as a way to get at an idea and instead seeks to transmit in some direct way the experience of being the animal. "In these poems," she explains,

> we know the jaguar not from the way he seems but from the way he moves. The body is as the body moves, or as the currents of life move within it. The poems ask us to imagine our way into that way of moving, to inhabit that body.
> With Hughes it is a matter—I emphasize—not of inhabiting another mind but of inhabiting another body. That is the kind of poetry I bring to your attention today: poetry that does not try to find an idea in the animal, that is not about the animal, but is instead the record of an engagement with him.
> What is peculiar about poetic engagements of this kind is that, no matter with what intensity they take place, they remain a matter of complete indifference to their objects. In this respect they are different from love poems, where your intention is to move your object. (95–96)

The parallels between Elizabeth's reading of these poems and her own attitude toward literature and toward animals—an attitude that we might call "sympathetic"—in the novel is both striking and telling. When she describes what she has tried to do in the book that made her famous, for example, she notes that

> There are no bounds to the sympathetic imagination. If you [she is speaking in "The Philosophers and the Animals" section here] want proof, consider the following. Some years ago I wrote a book called *The House on Eccles Street*. To write that book I had to think my way into the existence of Marion Bloom. Either I succeeded or I did not. If I did not, I cannot imagine why you invited me here today. In any event, the point is, *Marion Bloom never existed*. Marion Bloom was a figment of James Joyce's imagination. If I can think my way into the existence of a being who has never existed, then I can think my way into the existence of a bat or a chimpanzee or an oyster, any being with whom I share the substrate of life. (80, emphasis in original)

When we hear Elizabeth speak about her own fiction in this way, we can perhaps understand better what she means when she professes to the judges in the "At the Gate" section that her role as an author amounts to being a "dictation secretary." "I am a writer," she insists, "and what I write is what I hear. I am a secretary of the invisible, one of the many secretaries over the ages. That is my calling: dictation secretary. It is not for me to interrogate, to judge what is given me. I merely write down the words and then test them, test their soundness, to make sure I have heard right" (199).[30] Transcribing, listening without judging, sympathizing with—these constitute Elizabeth's authorial imperatives and they also describe her version of animal rights. As both an author and an animal rights proponent, Elizabeth wants either to allow us—in the case of her fiction—or to compel us—in the case of her support of animals—to "imagine our way" into another being's existence.

That Elizabeth makes such frequent use of Red Peter, the ape from Kafka's "A Report to an Academy," makes perfect sense, then, because from her vantage point the ape presents us with an opportunity to sympathize with this compelling hybrid creature. And Elizabeth does take this story, despite its fantastic premise, quite seriously, and literally. She even goes so far as to acknowledge that on occasion she "feels like" this ape. When she speaks to the gathering of philosophers she concedes that the story might have allegorical possibilities—"an allegory of Kafka the Jew performing for Gentiles," for example (62)—but, as she does with the frog story, she quickly abjures this figural tack. Speaking of her remark that she feels like Red Peter, she says quite simply that "It means what it says. I say what I mean" (62), and the implication is that she believes as well that Kafka has said what he meant and that Red Peter really is an ape who has been thoroughly cleaned up and well trained, and who has something to say.[31]

Thus, Elizabeth implies strongly here that Kafka has done with Red Peter what Hughes has done with the jaguar and what she will do with the frogs, that is, construct narratives that facilitate the reader's sympathy, our fellow feeling, for another animal. Indeed, she even casts Kafka in the same role that she fancies for herself, that of dictation secretary, when she argues that Red Peter "wrote" his own life history and that Kafka functioned as his "amanuensis" (70). Though it strikes many in her audience, and probably the readers of Coetzee's novel as well, as somewhat incredible, Elizabeth suggests—admittedly without any confirming evidence—that Kafka might have been influenced when he wrote his "A Report to an Academy" by the work of Wolfgang Köhler, a German psychologist who published a monograph in 1917 in which he reveals the results of his largely unsuccessful attempts to

---

30. Elizabeth admits later on that the phrase "secretary of the invisible" originates not with her (or Coetzee) but with the Polish poet Czeslaw Milosz.

31. Again, we cannot realistically prove that Elizabeth is mistaken in this reading of Kafka; however, the number of allegorical animal parables that appear in Kafka's shorter works provides strong evidence to the contrary. Were "A Report to an Academy" an anomaly in Kafka's oeuvre, then her literal interpretation would be more tenable.

educate apes from the island of Tenerife (73). In making this assertion Elizabeth implies that Kafka might simply have imagined a different, more successful, outcome to Köhler's experiments and then—to borrow Elizabeth's own words—to have devised a way "to think his way into the existence" of the product (Red Peter) of those experiments.

Coetzee has embedded in this novel a narrative—"A Report to an Academy"—that most readers would recognize as a weak allegory but that his protagonist insists on reading literally. What are we to make of this, and what are we to make of that other embedded allegory, "Before the Law," that Coetzee embeds? I have not found an easy and entirely convincing answer to this question. I do, on the other hand, feel relatively confident in claiming that Coetzee himself is doing something similar to what he has Elizabeth do and what Elizabeth claims that Kafka has done in his story of the ape. In other words, the embedded allegories in *Elizabeth Costello* do not function as interpretive heuristics; Coetzee does not seem to intend them to encapsulate the meaning of the novel as a whole. We might better understand these embedded narratives as a means of inhabiting another body, as a way of *sympathizing*.

On one level, Elizabeth bears some obvious resemblance to Red Peter, and not simply because she acknowledges her own sympathy toward this figure. Perhaps more significantly, she occupies the same position and plays a similar role in Coetzee's narrative to those occupied and played by Red Peter in Kafka's, at least in Elizabeth's reading of Kafka. And if Kafka can be called Red Peter's amanuensis, then the same holds for the relationship between Elizabeth and Coetzee; the author of *Elizabeth Costello* dictates the experience of Elizabeth Costello. Elizabeth Costello sums up the connection nicely: "Red Peter [unlike Wolfgang Köhler] was not an investigator of primate behaviour but a branded, wounded animal presenting himself as speaking testimony to a gathering of scholars. I am not a philosopher of mind but an animal exhibiting, yet not exhibiting, to a gathering of scholars, a wound, which I cover up under my clothes but touch on in every word I speak" (71). The wound to which she refers here is a reference to one of the wounds that Red Peter suffered as he was being captured. In Red Peter's case, this wound also has some bearing on how he is perceived—as animal or human: "I read an article recently," he explains in his story, "by one of the ten thousand windbags who vent themselves concerning me in the newspapers, saying: my ape nature is not yet quite under control; the proof being that when visitors come to see me, I have a predilection for taking down my trousers to show them where the shot went in" ("A Report" 175). Elizabeth clearly ties herself to Red Peter by playing on the same issue of social decorum, and her explicit identification with Kafka's ape helps to form a metonymic rather than a metaphoric connection between the two narratives. So in this case, the embedded allegorical narrative is literalized by its relationship with the embedding narrative.

On a second, higher-order level, we can understand Elizabeth as the vehicle through which Coetzee inhabits not Kafka himself, but rather Kafka's corpus. Elizabeth argues, we should remember, that Ted Hughes has shown us through his jaguar poems not how to inhabit another mind but rather how to inhabit another body, and Coetzee's persistent now-explicit-now-allusive use of Kafka's work ("A Report to an Academy," "Before the Law," *The Trial,* "An Imperial Message," "A Hunger Artist") gives readers the sense that he is inhabiting the body of Kafka's work, if not quite the mind of its author. This novel stands as the "record of [Coetzee's] engagement" with Kafka without being a discourse on what he thinks Kafka was trying to say or what he thinks Kafka meant. One might of course argue that when Elizabeth expounds on "A Report to an Academy" she expresses Coetzee's sense of Kafka's meaning, but to do so rests on the assumption of identity between the author and his character; such an assumption is always dangerous, and in the case of this novel in particular, in which the implied Coetzee often comes across as severely critical of his protagonist, that strategy lacks credibility. So, if we eschew the temptation to regard Elizabeth as Coetzee's mouthpiece, we have, finally, a novel, *Elizabeth Costello,* in which the author, J. M. Coetzee, allows his protagonist, Elizabeth Costello, to take up residence in someone else's body of work, and this is a corpus, Elizabeth claims, that was produced by the one man among all others who "is the most insecure in his humanity" (75). Perhaps rather than any grand ideas, it is this *feeling* that Elizabeth and Kafka share.

Ultimately, I would suggest that Coetzee's engagement with Kafka and his use of the interdependent embedded allegories also results in a feeling, a sympathetic connection between the contemporary South African novelist and the early-twentieth-century Czech writer. By embedding Kafka's weak allegories in a narrative that rests primarily on a mimetic foundation, and by embedding his protagonist—herself a self-styled author of realistic fiction—in these narratives whose origins are allegorical, Coetzee has produced an odd hybrid of a novel, one that demonstrates both continuity with and departure from the kind of mimetic fare that Elizabeth has produced during her career. The use of Kafka gives the work an allegorical feel, but the interdependence of these embedded allegorical narratives makes a straightforward allegorical interpretation nearly impossible to manufacture. Kafka's weak allegories are weakened even further by their association with Coetzee's narrative, but they still lend a sense of the allegorical, a Kafkaesque feeling, to *Elizabeth Costello.*

Thematic Allegory

Roth

IN THE introduction I used Billy Collins's poem "The Death of Allegory" to illustrate the fact that according to many literary types (critics, theorists, and authors) allegory as it was once practiced in the West—especially in the medieval period and during the Renaissance—no longer exists. Collins writes:

> I am wondering what became of all those tall abstractions
> that used to pose, robed and statuesque, in paintings
> and parade about on the pages of the Renaissance
> displaying their capital letters like license plates.

Instead, Collins contends, we now have a stable of "real"—or at least realistic—objects standing in their place:

> Here on the table near the window is a vase of peonies
> and next to it black binoculars and a money clip,
> exactly the kind of thing we now prefer,
> objects that sit quietly on a line in lower case,
>
> themselves and nothing more, a wheelbarrow,
> an empty mailbox, a razor blade resting in a glass ashtray....

As I maintained in that introductory section, I think that Collins's speaker is at least partially correct: those "great ideas on horseback / and the longhaired virtues in embroidered gowns" seldom get cast in starring roles anymore, as the kind of fiction that once welcomed and depended on them drifts further and further toward the margins of literary consciousness.

As is the case with much of his poetry, however, Collins has colored "The Death of Allegory" with a tinge of irony, a tinge that has two hues. First, even if the "tall abstractions" have left the working world of literature and migrated to a "Florida for tropes" for the early-bird specials, lots of golf, and the final slow fade, it does not follow that their lower-case replacements—the vase of peonies, the black binoculars and the money clip, the wheelbarrow, the empty mailbox, and the razor blade resting in a glass ashtray—represent, as Collins claims they do, "themselves and nothing more." For example, the last supposedly merely self-referential item in his list (the razor blade in the ashtray) likely evokes in the reader of the poem images of drug use that belie the strict mimeticism that the speaker assigns to it. Though a razor blade is not an abstract concept in the same way that Valor and Chastity are, there is no reason that a razor blade could not be a leading figure in an allegorical transformation. The second ironic aspect of this poem, and the one that I want to focus on in this chapter, involves the intellectual tension produced by a narrative—and I do consider this poem to have a strong narrative component—that is about something that has ostensibly died. Collins's treatment of allegory has the effect of reviving it, at least in the reader's mind, even though the poem itself is not an allegory. This poem offers a clear example of what I want to call "thematic allegory."

The bulk of this chapter will be devoted to the explication of another narrative work of fiction—Philip Roth's *American Pastoral*—that has allegory as a prominent theme, but before I get to that novel, we need to consider the general and highly significant relationship that obtains between allegory and theme. To get at the nature of this relationship, we shall return to one of the basic tenets that supports my theorizing about allegory, namely that allegory depends on a narrative structure. If we accept this premise, then we will quickly realize that "theme" emerges as one of the most significant aspects of narrative for the study of allegory.

As I argued in the introduction, allegory and narrative are closely linked, and this is especially true in the case of narratives that are (also) allegories, such as those works that I addressed in my first two chapters. But, as I have tried to show, the connection between allegory and narrative runs even deeper than this kind of generic coincidence; *all* manifestations of allegory depend on a narrative structure.

Even approaching the concept of allegory from the reader's vantage point, rather than from the textual or authorial one, reveals the significant association of allegory with narrative. In *The Political Unconscious,* Fredric

Jameson argues that, as *readers* of literature, we might have a natural tendency toward allegory. Jameson intends his opening chapter, "On Interpretation," as a defense of his Marxist-inspired allegorical approach to hermeneutics. More broadly, however, he lays the groundwork for a theory of interpretation that depends on a narrative-based conception of allegory. Building on the work of both Marxists and myth critics (especially Northrop Frye), Jameson argues that we are predisposed to see our world in terms of "master narratives." These master narratives then serve as the framework through which we make sense of (interpret) the actual narratives that our culture produces. "The idea is," Jameson explains, "that if interpretation in terms of ... allegorical master narratives remains a constant temptation, this is because such master narratives have inscribed themselves in the texts as well as in our thinking about them; such allegorical narrative signifieds are a persistent dimension of literary and cultural texts precisely because they reflect a fundamental dimension of our collective thinking and our collective fantasies about history and reality" (34).

Even a reader skeptical of Jameson's claim that a collective political unconscious leaves evidence of itself in individual texts, which together form an uninterrupted historical-political master narrative ("the single great collective story" of Marxist struggle, in Jameson's take on things), might be convinced by his broader argument about the persistence of allegory and allegorical interpretation. In this regard, one of his most penetrating insights resides in his general claim about the centrality of the allegorical process to the hermeneutic endeavor. Equally illuminating from my perspective is his use of the term master *narrative* to describe what seems to be both the catalyst for and the product of the act of interpretation. As we have already seen, allegory has a narrative structure, and it seems, at least according to Jameson, as if readers have internalized this and recognize it as the natural state of affairs.

Despite the generally recognized connection between allegory and narrative, however, when we speak of allegory we tend to focus on the hermeneutic issues of meaning and interpretation, often to the exclusion of any in-depth analysis of the narratives that carry those meanings. I hope to have begun to offer a corrective to this oversight, and this chapter will continue that project. Before I get to the meat of this chapter (Philip Roth's *American Pastoral*), however, it might be instructive to try to understand why hermeneutics has trumped narratology when it comes to allegory. Toward this end, we can return to Northrop Frye's *Anatomy of Criticism*, which I discussed in chapter 1, "Strong Allegory."

The combination of Frye's idea that all commentary is allegorical interpretation and his claim that in actual allegory the poet has already provided all of the commentary we need goes a long way toward explaining why readers often abjure allegory: "The commenting critic is often prejudiced against allegory without knowing the real reason," Fry claims, "which is that continuous allegory prescribes the direction of his commentary, and so restricts its freedom" (90). For many readers, meaning is still the aim of interpretation; hence, these readers naturally shy away from anything that smacks of allegory because in allegory the author has often made his or her meaning clear, and an analysis of an allegory in this context might be seen as little more than a literary autopsy.

Frye does offer a second possible explanation for the lack of narratological attention paid to allegory, but in order to get at it, we will need to understand some of the terms he employs in his definition of actual and continuous allegory. We should first note that Frye uses the term "image" very broadly; an image in the context of this work can mean not only the "replica of a visual object," but also "symbol" and even "idea" (84). Furthermore, images often take on "thematic importance" in the context of a narrative (85). For Frye, allegory depends primarily on establishing a relationship between a literary work's "images" and the extraliterary concepts to which those images are meant to correspond. In actual allegory, that relationship is clear, (relatively) explicit, and stable.

In terms of reading allegory, Frye cautions that "even continuous allegory is still a structure of images, not of disguised ideas, and commentary has to proceed with it exactly as it does with all other literature, trying to see what precepts and examples are suggested by the imagery as a whole" (90). Frye is arguing, in other words, that reading allegory does not entail the identification of individual allegorical symbols, but rather the understanding of a larger "structure" that, in the case of allegory, points to some identifiable idea that exists outside of the text. The "structure of images," in Frye's anatomy, is the "form" of a work of literature, and that form, he says, "is the same whether it is studied as narrative or as meaning" (85). Frye contends that there is a general preference for the studying of meaning over narrative because of a "vague notion that the [former] method produces a simpler result, and may therefore be used as a commonsense corrective to the niggling subtleties of textual studies" (85).[1] Whether for this reason or for some other, Frye is correct when it comes to the reading of allegory. Even his own comments reveal more interest in examining allegory as meaning than as narrative, this despite his insistence that allegory must be approached as a

---

1. Frye's terminology is somewhat idiosyncratic. He claims that a work of literature's "narrative is its rhythm or movement of words" (78), and in this sense "narrative" seems to mean something close to style. Nevertheless, his use of the term still draws an important distinction between structure and meaning, a distinction that I will explore in more detail below.

structure, just like any other narrative.

My contention is that the way in which allegory manifests itself in many modern and contemporary narratives necessitates our approaching allegory from a more structural or narratological starting point; this is because many of our hoarier ideas about allegory and meaning often do not apply easily to these more current works. Taking the Collins poem as just one example, we can all recognize the presence of allegory as a part of the narrative structure, but I doubt that anyone would want to read the work as an allegory. The poem is about allegory, but it is not one. As we enter this realm of "aboutness," we perforce enter as well the narratological realm of "theme." Thus, I contend that Collins's poem stands as an example of thematic allegory but not as an example of allegory proper.

This raises the question of the relationship between allegory and theme in narratives that we do label allegories. Though we could certainly label "Soviet-style communism" a theme in *Animal Farm,* this move does not go far enough in capturing what happens in allegory. A narrative that we recognize as an allegory is not simply "about" some phenomenon (in the way that *The Iliad* is about war, for example) but is a rewriting of that phenomenon. The concept of theme simply does not satisfactorily capture what transpires in an allegorical work.

The reason for this failure lies in the fact that, as Gerald Prince argues, "a theme involves only general and abstract entities: ideas, thoughts, beliefs, and so on. When I speak of the theme of rain, the theme of Antigone, or the theme of Creon," Prince explains, "I merely use a kind of shorthand to evoke certain philosophical, ideological, or moral views or concepts . . ." (*Narrative* 5).[2] When we speak of allegory, on the other hand, we do not use the object

---

2. As an aspect of narrative, theme poses a number of problems, primarily because of the looseness with which we often use the term. In his *Narrative as Theme* Prince illustrates the impressive variety of ways in which we understand and use the term "theme":

> . . . theme is both intra- and extra-textual, immanent and transcendent, what the work speaks about and what allows one to speak about the work; theme is to plot as meaning is to form; theme is that which plot constitutes a temporal projection of; theme is what is made of a topic; theme is the main idea in a text, a central thread, a minimum generalization; theme is a highly abstract semantic category subsuming a set of motifs or minimal and concrete thematic units; theme is a frame, a macrostructure, a reality model, a system organizing knowledge about some phenomenon in the world; theme is what a text or part thereof is about; theme is a general thought unifying and summarizing a series of sentences. . . . (2)

Prince does not try to sift through all of these uses and identify the one true meaning of "theme"; instead, he takes a pragmatic approach and "[sketches] some of the elements entering into theming, into (re)organizing and grasping a text in terms of theme, into reading it for or according to theme" (3).

of the preposition "of" (an allegory of ___) as shorthand for anything; it is specifically what it is, only transformed into a narrative. At times, of course, the phenomenon transformed into a narrative happens to be the kind of abstract entity, even "a philosophical, ideological, or moral view or concept," that Prince describes as being characteristic of theme, but this occasional coincidence does not amount to identity.

Moreover, even when the phenomenon transformed in allegory is some abstract idea (say, the salvation of the human soul), the relationship between the transformational narrative and the phenomenon transformed differs from the relationship between a nonallegorical narrative and its theme(s). Prince points out that "theme is distinctive, if not unique, because of its relation to textual surface structure: it does not *consist of* textual units, and it is different from them in kind; rather, theme is *illustrated by* any number of textual units (or by other macrostructural categories, such as plot, or by other themes), just as a general law or rule or precept is illustrated by an example" (5, emphasis in original). In the case of allegory, the "textual units" function as constitutive elements of the transformed phenomenon because that phenomenon has been rendered as a narrative; in other words, the allegory—precisely because it is a narrative—consists of textual units rather than being illustrated by them. For example, the character "Envy" (a textual unit) in Langland's *Piers Plowman* has a role, literally, in the transformation of the idea of salvation into a narrative, and so it is an element of that allegory, not just an illustration of a theme. There are of course still themes in strong allegories such as this one, but the allegory itself is something differentiable from and superior to individual themes.

In works such as *Piers Plowman* or *Animal Farm* one can draw the distinction between allegory and theme relatively clearly. The allegory is the narrative transformation of some phenomenon, and separate themes might exist within that narrative. Thus, *Animal Farm* allegorizes Soviet-style communism while offering, say, "the corrupting influence of power" as a theme.[3] When we are dealing with what I have called weak allegories, the distinction becomes less obvious. If the phenomenon purportedly transformed cannot be identified with any real precision, then the textual units that would normally constitute an allegory do not work with such a concentrated purpose.

---

3. Prince draws distinctions between "theme" and several other related concepts, including one, "topic," that also seems to bear some relation to allegory. According to Prince, the primary difference between a topic and a theme is that the former can refer to concrete entities whereas the latter refers to abstract ideas (5). If this is so, then we might legitimately say that the topic of Animal Farm is Soviet-style communism. Though true on one level, this will not suffice because Prince's definition of topic cannot account for the transformative aspect of Orwell's novel. Only after we recognize the transformation can we identify the topic.

The standards for identifying a theme, I submit, are less rigorous than those for arguing for allegory because readers generally do not expect a theme to encompass all—or even most—of a narrative's textual units. As Prince makes clear, a prominent theme, or one that can be successfully argued for, subsumes a greater rather than a lesser number of textual units (9), but even the strongest theme does not require the same kind of unity of purpose that we see in strong allegories. In a weak allegory, on the other hand, some textual units fail to fit in with the majority of the other units that comprise the narrativized phenomenon; think back to my chapter on weak allegory and the monkey in *Coco the Carrot,* for example. Such outlying textual units often tend to undermine the reader's confidence in the implied author's intentions, and this lack of certainty might turn us away from allegory and toward theme.

But what then distinguishes a work that has a particularly strong theme and one that we might want to call a weak allegory? Could we reasonably argue, in other words, that women's equality is simply a theme in *Coco the Carrot* and that Kafka's *The Metamorphosis* offers us a choice among a number of potentially strong themes, including the sense of alienation experienced by modern humans or the difficulties of the writer's life? The short answer here is that we certainly could, and to do so would probably lower the standards in terms of the amount of textual evidence that we would need to produce in order to prove our hypothesis effectively. Yet in these particular examples I suspect that readers will always be pulled toward allegorical interpretations because of the respective narratives' emphasis on figuration.[4] When we have narratives that rely so heavily on figuration and that have such a pronounced thematic component, we likely and reasonably incline toward reading these texts in a certain way; the term "weak allegory" helps to classify both the texts and the way we read them.

Thus, the hermeneutic effect of strong figuration can mirror that produced by the presence of embedded allegories. It does not take much, it seems, to get many readers moving in the direction of allegorical interpretation, and once we start down that path, it can be difficult to change interpretive directions. This is why it can be so hard *not* to read Kafka allegorically and why a title such as Philip Roth's *Everyman*—an (intentional?) allusion to the medieval allegory of the same title—can catalyze allegorical interpretations even if the narrative itself fails to validate such an effort. Even as Roth's novella, for example, bears little resemblance to the late-fifteenth-

---

4. In Kafka's case, both the title of the story and the fact that Gregor undergoes a metamorphosis serve to nudge us even more forcefully toward allegory. For a historical overview of the tradition in which Kafka seems to be working, see Bruce Clarke's *Allegories of Writing: The Subject of Metamorphosis,* especially the second chapter, "History of Metamorphic Allegory."

century allegorical mystery-morality play, the shared and highly figurative title ensures that it is, in the words of the critic James Wood, "haunted by its near-namesake," if only "trivially" (28). Roth's title guarantees the presence of allegory—whether it be a trivial or a profound presence—in his novella, but it does not guarantee that the novella will *be* an allegory. In examples such as this one, we have, I submit, allegory present as a potential theme.

We see a similar phenomenon at play in the oeuvre of J. M. Coetzee, whose *Elizabeth Costello* served as one of my examples of embedded allegory but whose other narratives also play with allegory in interesting ways. As Derek Attridge notes, "It's hardly surprising that one of the terms in the critical lexicon most frequently applied to Coetzee's novels and novellas is *allegory*" (32). Attridge points to the "often enigmatic characters," "the scrupulous avoidance of any sense of an authorial presence," and "the frequently exiguous plots" of Coetzee's fiction as markers that "encourage the reader to look for meanings beyond the literal, in a realm of significance which [a number of his novels] may be said to imply without ever directly naming" (32).

While acknowledging the large body of critical ink devoted to allegorical interpretations of Coetzee's work,[5] Attridge wants to pursue a different path: "With the encouragement of the fiction itself," he explains, "I want to ask what happens if we *resist* the allegorical reading that the novels seem half to solicit, half to problematize, and take them, as it were, at their word" (35). Attridge's path of interpretive resistance has been blazed by Susan Sontag's "Against Interpretation" and Donald Davidson's "What Metaphors Mean." Both of these essays, according to Attridge, eschew the notion that literary works of art intend to "say" something and are instead animated and motivated "by the same impulse: for Sontag what is important about art-works, and for Davidson what is important about metaphors, is not what they *mean* but what they *do*" (37). Thus, Attridge turns a blind eye to the temptation to read allegorically and, recognizing that "we are dealing [in Coetzee's work] with novels which, to a greater degree than most, concern themselves with the acts of writing and reading, including allegorical writing and reading," decides to ask, as his primary research question, "how allegory is thematized in the fiction, and whether this staging of allegory as an *issue* provides any guidance in talking about Coetzee's *use* of allegory" (33–34).

Attridge, therefore, recognizes the presence of the idea of allegory in much of Coetzee's fiction (his focus is on *Waiting for the Barbarians* and *Life & Times of Michael K*), but he responds to this presence with what he calls a literal reading, a reading that "occurs as an event, a living-through

---

5. Among these works are essays by Peter McDonald, David Atwell, and books by Atwell, Dominic Head, Teresa Dovey, and Sue Kossew.

or performing of the text that responds simultaneously to what is said, the way in which it is said, and the inventiveness and singularity (if there is any) of the saying" (60). This kind of reading, which approximates the point I was trying to make about Coetzee's use of embedded allegory in *Elizabeth Costello,* stands in contrast to readings that tend toward allegoresis because these, Attridge contends, "arise less . . . from the actual experience of works of literature than from the imperatives that drive literary commentary" (61). Attridge helps us to see that the presence of allegory as an idea in a narrative text does not necessarily mean that the author intends the entire narrative to be an allegory and, consequently, to be read only as such.

The abstract *idea of allegory* fits Prince's description of a theme quite well, and there is no reason that a narrative could not be about allegory on some level without actually being one. Indeed, I see a great deal of potential in allegory as a theme because the ways in which we think about allegory can reveal much about how we think about literature, aesthetics, culture, and meaning. And we can turn to Philip Roth to witness one author who apparently shares this interest in the idea of allegory. Even more than is the case with *Everyman,* Roth's *American Pastoral* is a narrative haunted by allegory, a haunting that makes allegory one of the novel's central themes.

The first chapter of *American Pastoral* is a historically contextualized discourse on allegoresis and the problems of interpretation that inhere in this process of constructing allegories and allegorical figures. This early chapter is an intradiegetic narrative insofar as it serves as the prelude to the primary narrative that will follow it. As the novel opens, Roth's narrator is reminiscing about his past, and in particular about a boy several years older than himself who had come to embody the hope of a community of immigrant Jewish families in New Jersey, a handsome and athletically gifted youth who had been transformed into a "household Apollo" by his working-class neighbors (4). This is the intradiegetic narrative, the story of how this figure comes to represent what he does, the story of how, in other words, he has been constructed and interpreted as a character by his community. The primary narrative that follows this early allegorical narrative, however, is essentially a corrective one, one in which the narrator abandons the allegorized version of the protagonist for something more mimetic, something more real. Clearly, the relationship between the two narratives is problematic, but understanding the source of the problems and how they are handled can be enlightening with regard both to the novel itself and to allegory more generally.

At the center of Roth's story is the novel's Jewish protagonist, Seymour Irving Levov, a star athlete at a Newark high school whose Nordic good looks beget the nickname "the Swede." Coming of age in the 1940s, the Swede becomes a mythic, if somewhat unlikely, hero figure for the local Jews, a population that typically "venerated academic achievement above all else" (3), including athletic exploits. In the context of the Second World War, however, the Swede's physical gifts take on special significance. Nathan Zuckerman, Roth's narrator for this and several other novels, notes that "through the Swede, the neighborhood entered into a fantasy about itself and about the world, the fantasy of sports fans everywhere: almost like Gentiles (as they imagined Gentiles), our families could forget the way things actually work and make an athletic performance the repository of all their hopes. Primarily, they could forget the war" (3–4). Yet the Swede seems to offer more than the possibility of temporarily forgetting what is happening to American soldiers and to the European Jews; he also facilitates a more active fantasy. For this neighborhood, at this time, Zuckerman remarks, the Swede stands "as a symbol of hope," as "the embodiment of the strength, the resolve, the emboldened valor that would prevail to return our high school's servicemen home unscathed" (5).

The Swede functions on two figurative levels here. First, he is clearly a symbol, someone who represents or stands for a multitude of abstract positive ideas (hope, strength, innocence, purity) at a time when a particular group needs him to do so. In the eyes of his community, the Swede coincides perfectly with what he purports—is even required—to represent: "there appeared to be not a drop of wit or irony to interfere with his golden gift for responsibility" (5). Second, the Swede is also part of a complex of allegories. Once the Swede's symbolic qualities find their way into a narrative structure, even a hypothetical one such as the safe return of local soldiers or the ultimate defeat of the Nazis, his nature becomes allegorical. As an allegorical figure, the Swede plays the leading role in several public narratives, even if he remains unaware of his own significance.

The Swede's first allegorical role is as the protagonist of several war-related scenarios. As Zuckerman notes, "The elevation of Swede Levov into the household Apollo of the Weequahic Jews can best be explained, I think, by the war against the Germans and the Japanese and the fears that it fostered" (4). Out of these fears, the Swede emerges as a figure who represents the potential for American victory and Jewish survival. In this case, the hope that the Swede represents is translated into a narrative that has a happy ending. This was a period, Zuckerman remarks, "when our entire neighborhood's wartime hope seemed to converge in the marvelous body of the Swede" (20).

Perhaps more interesting, however, is the Swede's role in an even more particularly Jewish narrative. In this scenario, the protagonist represents the potential for overcoming a kind of Jewish angst. Zuckerman describes this angst, and how the Swede is seen to resolve it, in a paragraph that is worth quoting entirely:

> The Jewishness that [the Swede] wore so lightly as one of the tall, blond athletic winners must have spoken to us too—in our idolizing the Swede and his unconscious oneness with America, I suppose there was a tinge of shame and self-rejection. Conflicting Jewish desires awakened by the sight of him were simultaneously becalmed by him; the contradiction in Jews who want to fit in and want to stand out, who insist they are different and insist they are no different, resolved itself in the triumphant spectacle of this Swede who was actually only another of our neighborhood Seymours whose forebears had been Solomons and Sauls and who would themselves beget Stephens who would in turn beget Shawns. Where was the Jew in him? You couldn't find it and yet you knew it was there. Where was the irrationality in him? Where was the crybaby in him? Where were the wayward temptations? No guile. No artifice. No mischief. All that had been eliminated to achieve his perfection. No striving, no ambivalence, no doubleness—just the style, the natural physical refinement of a star. (20)

The Swede is seen here, again, as the happy resolution to a plot that has the potential for disaster. He is the Jew who can be but not seem Jewish, the Jew who has achieved a "oneness with America" that has consistently proved elusive and illusory to many other Jews. The Swede personifies what Zuckerman identifies as the hypothetical teleological apotheosis of Jewish-American assimilation, the product of "each new generation's breaking away from the parochialism a little further, out of the desire to go the limit in America with your rights, forming yourself as an ideal person who gets rid of the traditional Jewish habits and attitudes, who frees himself of the pre-America insecurities and the old, constraining obsessions so as to live unapologetically as an equal among equals" (85). The price of this freedom seems to be Jewishness itself, but it also seems to be a price that many would have been willing to pay.

The means by which the Swede realizes his apparent success in this area both underscores his differences with other Jews and explains his ability to forge his "unconscious" connection with America. As a star athlete, the Swede is simultaneously an atypical Jew and the prototypical American icon. The Swede's athletic prowess, in fact, enables him to participate in one of American culture's great collective figures: sport as a metaphor for life, and the sports star as one for whom life in general comes easily. As a boy five years younger than his neighborhood idol, Zuckerman is dazzled by the Swede's physical gifts, his grace, and his natural style, all of which characterize the Swede not only as an athlete but also as a kind of ideal human. Reflecting on one incident during which the sixteen-year-old Swede calls the narrator by his nickname ("Skip") in front of a group of his friends, Zuckerman acknowledges that this recognition from one whom he already considered a "god" transformed, in his mind, the sports hero into something even larger and more significant:

> The mock jock self-pity, the manly generosity, the princely graciousness, the athlete's self-pleasure so abundant that a portion can be freely given to the crowd—this munificence not only overwhelmed me and wafted through me because it had come wrapped in my nickname but became fixed in my mind as an embodiment of something grander even than his talent for sports: the talent for "being himself," the capacity to be this strange engulfing force and yet to have a voice and a smile unsullied by even a flicker of superiority—the natural modesty of someone for whom there were no obstacles, who appeared never to have to struggle to clear a space for himself. (19)

This is a powerful and persistent act of allegorical figuration, or allegoresis, one that even today we find tempting, especially with our sports heroes.

We can see that the Swede functions as the protagonist in a variety of related allegories. In just the first chapter of *American Pastoral*, the Swede is the central figure in allegories of the overcoming of the Germans and the Japanese, the overcoming of the difficulty of Jewish assimilation into American cultural and social life, and the overcoming of the difficulties associated with life in general. In all three cases, the literal narrative facilitates a movement toward anagogy (interpretation in spiritual terms) on the part of the interpreters. Success on the basketball court or baseball field, or a simple act of kindness, for example, is endowed with near-mystical meaning as it is reread in allegorical terms. The agents behind the allegorizing in this early section of the novel are Roth's characters—including his first-person narrator—and this is important to keep in mind because Roth sets out in *American Pastoral* not to write an allegory, but rather to write a novel largely about allegory.

The fact that we have Roth's narrator acting as a commentator, helping us to interpret and assign meaning to these narratives, further strengthens the claim that we are in fact dealing with allegoresis here, even if it is as a theme rather than as a genre.[6] Zuckerman's narration includes his explication of the Swede's figurative significance and the ways in which that allegorized figure functioned within his particular "interpretive community." Roth's intention is not to be allegorical in writing this section of *American Pastoral*; rather, he takes as one of his themes the allegorization of the Swede. Through Zuckerman, Roth is looking back on and representing realistically several fictional acts of allegoresis.

This representation of allegory (or of allegoresis) is what I am calling thematic allegory. In *American Pastoral* Roth uses the early representation of allegory as the impetus to construct a counternarrative, one that will ultimately allow his narrator to rewrite a story that risks leading to a failed allegory. In order to understand how Roth's thematization of allegory leads to this rewriting, however, we need to examine the effect that the presence of allegory in this work has on three important and closely related narratological issues that bear heavily on the concept of allegory: characterization, plot, and focalization.

Since the object of an allegorical narrative is to transform some phenomenon into a figural narrative, the primary allegorical narrative depends on the careful coordination of character, plot, and focalization. All of these aspects of narrative must work together to facilitate the transmission of the author's intended meaning. In such works, the author would ostensibly begin with the idea and construct a narrative—including characters and a plot—that facilitates its reception by the reader. When allegory appears thematically in the context of a realistic narrative, however, we tend to see a case of reverse engineering. The author's representation of the process of allegoresis reveals the artificiality that remains behind the scenes and uncovers certain instabilities that seem paradoxical to the nature of allegory. Roth's depiction of the Swede, for example, allows the reader to see that an act of allegoresis necessarily occurs in a determinative context—a nexus of historical, political, and personal forces that facilitates various interpretations of Seymour Irving Levov—and that any allegory that results from a particular act of allegoresis is dynamic rather than stable. In thematic allegory, in other words, the progression of the narrative continually changes the landscape in which

---

6. The opening chapter of *American Pastoral* comes close to being what Frye calls an actual allegory—or at least the re-presentation of an actual allegory—because Zuckerman fairly "explicitly indicates the relationship of his images to examples and precepts" (Frye 90). Indeed, Zuckerman tells us quite clearly what the Swede meant to those in his community.

interpretation takes place, thereby putting constant pressure on the resultant allegory, pressure that it may not always be able to bear.[7]

This state of affairs is in keeping with Prince's general conception of how we read for themes: we identify them as possibilities, and then verify as we progress through the narrative. Like any narrative, a primary allegorical narrative is kinetic, but the phenomenon transformed by that narrative tends to be stable, oftentimes resembling one of a culture's recognizable master plots.[8] In strong allegories, the primary narrative always seems to build easily toward this secondary narrative; any difficulties in constructing characters and a plot that work seamlessly with the intended secondary narrative have been "edited out," as it were, of the final draft. Thematic allegory, on the other hand, lays bare all of the inner workings of allegoresis because the narrative depicts the process of constructing the allegorical narrative. As the primary narrative progresses, the meaning that the act of allegoresis was meant to capture is repeatedly assailed by new events, new developments, new revelations, and new interpretations. The passage of chronological time in *American Pastoral* has precisely this effect on the meaning of the Swede. As Zuckerman takes the reader from the 1950s into the 1990s, the Swede's allegorical significance is questioned, denied, and ultimately radically revised.

If Zuckerman's commentary serves to clarify the allegorical nature of the Swede, as I claim above, its unfolding as the narrative progresses also allows the readers to recognize that we are not intended to accept this allegorical representation as a sufficient or final interpretation of this character. Although we are not meant to question the fact that the Swede did function allegorically, we are meant to think critically about the process of allegoresis that led to the Swede's embodying all that he did for his community and to question whether our understanding the Swede as a figure in a series of related allegorical narratives is sufficient or even accurate. Indeed, Zuckerman himself is skeptical as he remembers and reconstructs the past—the Swede's, his own, and his community's.

The impetus to remember the Swede, and then to reinterpret him, comes in the mid-1990s in the form of a letter that Zuckerman receives from the protagonist himself, a letter that invites the narrator to meet in order to discuss the Swede's recently deceased father, for whom the son is supposedly struggling to write a memorial tribute. The letter and the subsequent

---

7. In retrospect, Zuckerman acknowledges the inherent instability of the allegory his community has created around the Swede: "Even as boys," he avers, "we must have known that it couldn't have been as easy for him as it looked, that a part of it was a mystique" (83).

8. Abbot defines master plots as "Recurrent skeletal stories, belonging to cultures and individuals that play a powerful role in questions of identity, values, and the understanding of life" (192). He points to Cinderella and the Horatio Alger story, among others, as examples (42–43).

meeting have the effect of forcing Zuckerman to revisit the idealized image of the Swede that both he and his entire neighborhood held and to come to a new understanding of who the Swede is and what he represents. Looking back as an adult, Zuckerman is skeptical of the allegories that he and his community had constructed around the Swede, and he begins to question, to dig beneath the surface, figuratively speaking. Zuckerman recognizes and celebrates the smooth surface that facilitated the various allegories about the Swede, but he begins, in retrospect, to wonder about the reality beneath that surface: "Only . . . what did he do for subjectivity? What was the Swede's subjectivity? There had to be a substratum, but its composition was unimaginable" (20).

That substratum is unimaginable to Zuckerman because he is, at this point, still blinded by the narrative of the Swede that dominated his youth. In anticipation of their meeting as adults, Zuckerman wonders "What, if anything, had ever threatened to destabilize the Swede's trajectory" (20). That upward trajectory, however, is the one imposed on the Swede; it is the natural playing-out of his allegory's narrative plot. Zuckerman knows intuitively that no real life could unfold in the ideal, obstacle-less manner that the Swede's seemed to, and that his allegory would more or less require, but he cannot imagine the alternative, the counternarrative that would serve as the corrective to the naïve allegory: "No one," Zuckerman muses, "gets through [life] unmarked by brooding, grief, confusion, and loss. Even those who had it all as kids sooner or later get the average share of misery, if not sometimes more. There had to have been consciousness and there had to have been blight. Yet I could not picture the form taken by either, could not desimplify him even now: in the residuum of adolescent imagination I was still convinced that for the Swede it had to have been pain-free all the way" (20). Our narrator, as he admits, is unable to provide a point of view other than that of his youth; he can only focalize the Swede and his story in one way. This conflicts, however, with his sense of reality. He realizes that his vision of the Swede is simplified, naïve, and, in a word, allegorized, but "the residuum of adolescent imagination" does not allow him to see the Swede in a more complicated, realistic way.

Although the Swede is not, strictly speaking, an example of a personified abstraction (such as Hope or Charity, for example), Zuckerman's difficulty in imagining him leading a life narrative that has a complicated, convoluted, or circuitous plot is in keeping with Gordon Teskey's claim that "in allegory narrative and personification are inversely prominent" (23). Allegories that rely heavily on personification tend, in other words, to have simple plots. "In Johnson's allegories, for example," Teskey explains, "the thought represented by a series of personified abstractions is carefully worked out so that only the most rudimentary narrative is required to link the elements of the series together" (23). Zuckerman's simplification of the Swede is actually more a simplification of plot than of character; given his conception of this figure, Zuckerman cannot imagine him in a complicated plot.

As we get to the end of the first chapter of the novel, however, we see Zuckerman actively beginning to reexamine this simplified vision of the Swede; he is recounting the allegorical aspects of the Swede in order to reevaluate those allegories and to reread the figure at the center of them. Indeed, the narrative moves through the first chapter of the novel from the point where "the Swede" was a "magical name" attached to a mythlike figure who is the hero of several allegorized narratives, to a moment when Zuckerman, after a meeting with the Swede in 1995, decides that "This guy is the embodiment of nothing" (39). Even in characterizing him as "the embodiment of nothing," however, Zuckerman continues to see the Swede in figurative terms, as a vessel that carries significant meaning at one point, but who, when viewed from a different vantage point at a different time, embodies the concept of nothingness; he becomes the representation of the vacuous sports hero or Hollywood star. "There's nothing here but what you're looking at," Zuckerman tells himself. "He's all about being looked at. He always was" (39).

At this point it has become clear to both Zuckerman and the reader that we do not know the real Swede, if such a thing can be said to exist. Zuckerman's dual role of narrator and participant in the past events of his narration seem to preclude any objective or mimetic representation of the main figure of the narrative. As a writer, Zuckerman recognizes and accepts—even embraces—the difficulty of accurately portraying a human figure. When trying to understand others, he laments, "You get them wrong before you meet them, while you're anticipating meeting them; you get them wrong while you're with them; and then you go home to tell somebody else about the meeting and you get them all wrong again. Since the same generally goes for them with you, the whole thing is really a dazzling illusion empty of all perception, an astonishing farce of misperception" (35). The first chapter of *American Pastoral* is the chronicling of Zuckerman's misreadings of the Swede, of the various ways in which he gets or has gotten him wrong. But it is also Zuckerman's recognition and confession of the fact that this has been the case. Indeed, his difficulty reading the Swede serves as a kind of perverse reminder that he is alive: "The fact remains that getting people right is not what living is all about anyway. It's getting them wrong that is living, getting them wrong and wrong and wrong and then, on careful reconsideration, getting them wrong again. That's how we know we're alive: we're wrong" (35). It is with this pronouncement that Zuckerman begins the process of deconstructing the allegory that for so many years had stood as his conception of the Swede. In order to do so, he must refocalize the narrative.

We have in this novel a clear and significant shift in focalization. I'm using the term focalization here to refer exclusively to the perspective—as opposed to voice—through which the narrative is represented. The narrative voice remains relatively consistent throughout the novel; it is that of Zuckerman the narrator. Zuckerman, however, has a kind of epiphany at his fiftieth high school reunion and decides to alter the way in which he has been focalizing the Swede and his story. In the opening, allegorical section, Zuckerman's status as a homodiegetic narrator (he participated in the narrative he recounts and was profoundly influenced by the figure at the center of his story) makes it difficult for him to view the Swede realistically.[9] At the reunion, however, he learns more about the fate of the Swede after Zuckerman was no longer a consistent character in the narrative. It is here, as Zuckerman dances with a former classmate, that he admits to a kind of focal shift, admits to having

> lifted onto my stage the boy we were all going to follow into America, our point man into the next immersion, at home here the way the Wasps were at home here, an American not by sheer striving, not by being a Jew who invents a famous vaccine or a Jew on the Supreme Court, not by being the most brilliant or the most eminent or the best. Instead—by virtue of his isomorphism to the Wasp world—he does it the ordinary way, the natural way, the regular American-guy way. To the honeysweet strains of "Dream," I pulled away from myself, pulled away from the reunion, and I dreamed.... I dreamed a realistic chronicle. I began gazing into his life—not his life as a god or demigod in whose triumphs one could exult as a boy but his life as another assailable man. (89)

From here, Zuckerman recedes from the diegesis and becomes a more traditional heterodiegetic narrator. He pulls away from himself, as he says, and attempts to see the Swede more objectively so as to portray him more realistically. The voice is still unmistakably Zuckerman's, but the vision we get of the Swede is no longer determined by the allegorical version of the character that dominates the first chapter.

The shift from homo- to heterodiegesis entails a similar shift from internal to zero or free focalization. At the beginning, the story is obviously

---

9. The focalization in the first chapter is admittedly somewhat more complicated than this. Zuckerman is relating the events of this chapter retrospectively, and so he is not literally a participant in those events. Nevertheless, he was an actor in the events that compose that narrative's plot, and this fact is significant because it has unmistakably limited how he has been able to view the Swede.

focused through Zuckerman the character and, by association, his Jewish community. This focalization makes the maintenance of the allegorical reading of the Swede understandable in an ethnocentric context. It also reveals a kind of childlike naïveté, which Zuckerman recognizes in retrospect by acknowledging that he was still under the sway of that "residuum of adolescent imagination." It is only in shedding this limited perspective that Zuckerman is able to portray the Swede from a more realistic, "desimplified" vantage point, even if the story that comes out of that perspective is largely imagined or "dreamed."

Roth's shift in focalization allows him to allow his narrator to tell a story that would not be possible to tell if the early allegorized version of the Swede remained intact. The initial characterization of the Swede effectively limits the direction of any plot that Zuckerman can conceive, given his pre-understanding of the central figure. When he removes the filter through which he has seen the Swede, new narrative possibilities present themselves. And when Zuckerman learns that the Swede had a daughter from his first marriage who killed a man when she exploded a bomb in protest of the war in Vietnam, he realizes that the Swede's "pastoral" narrative has exploded as well; this daughter has transported the Swede "out of the longed-for American pastoral and into everything that is its antithesis and its enemy, into the fury, the violence, and the desperation of the counterpastoral—into the indigenous American berserk" (86). At this point, Zuckerman seems to realize that his initial conception of the character of the Swede coupled with the new plot twist has exploded, so to speak, the allegorical narrative established early on. This development then necessitates a re-vision of the primary narrative.

This reworking takes the form of a less idealistic reading of the Swede that Zuckerman produces after his epiphany on the dance floor. Interestingly, Zuckerman uses the "dream," which is a traditional marker of allegory, to signify entrance into a mimetic narrative that will serve as a counternarrative to the allegorical, but "real," narrative that we have had so far concerning our protagonist. The reference to dreams and dream worlds is usually indicative not of "realistic chronicles" but rather of allegories. In this case, though, what was ostensibly the real narrative—the one Zuckerman "participated in" as a youth—seems less plausible than the fictionalized account of the Swede that he eventually endeavors to create.

The primary difference between the two competing narratives is Zuckerman's evolved understanding of the plot, the events of the Swede's life. The first chapter is dominated by a seemingly immutable character, and the perceived ontology of the Swede limits plot possibilities.[10] As Zuckerman

---

10. I would hold that this limitation is prevalent in all traditional or strong allegories. If a

begins to realize the complex nature of his character's life, he also realizes that his allegorical narrative has become insufficient and untenable. His eventual move to free focalization allows for the interplay between character and plot to become much more complicated because the narrator is ready to "desimplify" his subject. In Zuckerman's own words, he sets out to "chart [the Swede's] collapse" and "to make of him, as time wore on, the most important figure of my life" (74). As he does so, plot becomes a stronger force than character, shattering the original allegories constructed around the Swede and forcing both narrator and reader to resituate this figure in a revised master narrative that is, given both its juxtaposition with the early allegorical reading of the Swede and Roth's title, ironic.

Zuckerman's dualistic approach to the Swede and his story brings us back to a question that was raised in the introduction: is all interpretation—even of characters—somehow allegorical? This possibility certainly presents itself in this novel, for even the "realistic chronicle" that is meant to override the simplified notion of the Swede presented in the first chapter leads to an allegorical interpretation. When he is no longer able to see the Swede's story as the story of (Jewish) American success, Zuckerman instead sees it as the story of modern American calamity: "His great looks, his larger-than-lifeness, his glory, our sense of his having been exempted from all self-doubt by his heroic role—that all these manly properties had precipitated a political murder made me think of the compelling story . . . of Kennedy, John F. Kennedy, only a decade the Swede's senior and another privileged son of fortune, another man of glamour exuding American meaning, assassinated while still in his mid-forties just five years before the Swede's daughter violently protested the Kennedy-Johnson war and blew up her father's life. I thought, But of course. He is our Kennedy" (83). Thus, we witness here the process by which Zuckerman adapts his reading of the Swede to the allegorical exigencies made manifest by the progression of the plot. Zuckerman reweaves his early version of the Swede into an allegorical narrative that tracks along a downward, tragic trajectory rather than an upward, pastoral, and anagogic one.

Nevertheless, the recasting of the Swede in an alternative allegorical plot (the one meant to correspond with or call to mind the rise and fall of Kennedy) does not lead to the conclusion that all interpretation is allegory or that all reading is allegoresis, particularly given the way in which I am using "allegory" here. Indeed, my claim is that although Zuckerman's narrative is allegorical, Roth's narrative is not. Roth uses Zuckerman's narrative to thematize allegory, to highlight Zuckerman's allegorizing of the Swede and to invite us to think about the habit of reading others' lives in allegorical terms.

---

character is going to hold as an allegorical figure, the range both of what can and cannot happen to him or her and of what he or she can do is necessarily limited.

If all interpretation were allegory, then I would have to say that there's something allegorical about Roth's thematizing. But since one of Roth's thematic points is that allegory is often reductive, allegorizing his narrative would undermine his thematizing—and do so in a way that I don't believe the novel invites. To put these points another way, I claim—using *American Pastoral* as an example—that an interpretation of a narrative can uncover the representation of allegory as a theme within a narrative that is not (necessarily) allegorical. Unlike many other themes, allegory is inherently narrative; consequently, the representation of this theme allows readers to glimpse the narrative structure that underlies allegory more generally. Ultimately, I hope to have demonstrated that a careful analysis of that intradiegetic narrative structure—an analysis that highlights what Frye calls those "niggling subtleties of textual studies" (plot, character, and focalization, in this case)—can go a long way toward helping us to understand how allegory works and, on occasion, why it fails to do so.

Ironic Allegory

Dante and Mann

THE KIND of treatment that Roth gives allegory in *American Pastoral* has a peculiarly modern stamp on it; it takes a modern, cynical disposition to call into question the very possibility of the kind of uplifting and redemptive allegory that the Swede's story starts out to be. We are perhaps too jaded now for this kind of artificial transformation, and so we can accept allegory only as an idea or a theme—and a quaint one at that—to be dissected and analyzed. When we look to the past, and to allegory's past in particular, we see something far removed from our current climate and that of our recent past, something that in many respects strikes us—as it did Nathan Zuckerman—as barely plausible anymore. Ironically, we have arrived at a collective decision that allegory (or a particular kind of allegory, anyway) is no longer realistic.

When we do not believe in allegory anymore, it becomes increasingly rare that we see entire allegorical narratives and more likely that when we do see allegory present in a narrative it will be in one of the more limited ways that I have tried to describe in this book.[1] In this chapter, I want to explore one additional modern manifestation of allegory, a complicated one that depends on our modern skeptical attitude toward allegorical figuration but that also reveals its enduring appeal. I call this manifestation "ironic

---

1. When we do encounter contemporary strong allegories—such as John Barth's "Click," which I discuss in the following chapter—they tend to be very self-aware and self-conscious of their status as such.

allegory." Ironic allegory, like all allegory according to my definition, entails a transformation of some phenomenon into a figural narrative; in the case of ironic allegory, however, the authorial audience is not meant to take this transformation at face value or seriously. I will use Thomas Mann's *Death in Venice* as my case study in ironic allegory, but it will be helpful to begin this chapter with a look further back historically for some context and for a text that I can use as a "straight" foil for Mann's highly ironic text. I will start, therefore, with a brief discussion of Dante and allegory before moving on to discuss *Death in Venice*. This preliminary work will serve two purposes: first, it will provide a background against which to read Mann's modernist work, thus allowing me to highlight certain rhetorical and aesthetic facets that are central to his text; and, second, it will allow me to demonstrate how we can read one particular twentieth-century narrative as an instance of ironic allegory.

Dante is a logical introduction to any discussion of allegory, because he was both an allegorical writer and one of the earliest and most insightful theorists of allegory. He was, simply put, a man driven by the metaliterary, and he was constantly trying to explain all that literature could be and all that one could say with it. Dante used the idea of allegory to free himself from both the limitations and the potential incriminations of the literal. As he explains it in the *Banquet*, a postexile[2] commentary on his own poetry, the allegorical is the sense that is concealed by a beautiful lie.[3] Such an explanation was intended to protect literature from the charge that it was a genre that dealt only in lies, and was thus a dangerous enterprise. Unlike theology, which is true on every level, literature speaks the truth only once the reader has gotten beyond the literal. The object of the reader, then, is to unveil the truth through his or her understanding of the poem. As this proves a difficult task, Dante often reads his poetry for us, telling us explicitly how to work through the literal to the allegorical, and even beyond that to the moral and the anagogic. Despite his facility with them, however, words frustrate Dante,[4] and he seems to sense that once he has committed himself to paper, the work of controlling his meaning is just beginning. Because Dante wants to maintain that truth underlies the literal, he finds himself in the somewhat

---

2. As a result of his being on the "wrong side" of a political struggle, Dante, at about thirty-six years of age, was exiled from his native Florence, and he never returned.

3. Dante defines these terms at the outset of the second book of the *Banquet*. Here he argues that beyond the literal sense of a work of fiction, there is a second sense, the allegorical, which is "a truth hidden under a beautiful fiction" (73).

4. Dante's *De Vulgari Eloquentia* (*On the Eloquence of the Vernacular*) is essentially the search for a language that works better for expressing meaning than either Latin or any one particular Italian vernacular. Significantly, this work is unfinished.

awkward and undoubtedly exhausting position of continually playing Virgil to the lost pilgrims reading his works, always pointing us toward an extraliteral significance. In Dante in particular there is always a personal imperative behind his project; indeed, one often feels while reading Dante that Dante's own existence, or at least its significance, depends on his defense and interpretation of allegory.

There is, in fact, an interesting connection between Dante's allegorical construction of literary character and the way in which he deconstructs and reconstructs his own self. This relationship is particularly apparent in the pre-exile *libello The New Life*, a work in which Dante, in his mid-to-late twenties, looks back at what he considers the most formative experience of his life: his peculiarly one-sided relationship with Beatrice, the young woman whom he first sees when both are about nine years old and who continues to absorb his thoughts and dominate both the substance and the tenor of his work throughout his life. As *The New Life* has no real plot—the "action" is essentially confined to Dante's musings about his beloved and the effect that she has on him—character takes center stage. And central to Dante's project is allegorical figuration.

Prosopopeia is Dante's trope of choice in this endeavor, as he makes Love one of the principal characters in his narrative. Although confined to Dante's dreams and imagination, Love assumes a prominent role in this story; so much so, in fact, that Dante, just after seeing Beatrice for the first time, confesses that "Love ruled over my soul, which was so early espoused to him, and he began to assume over me such assurance and such mastery, through the power that my imagination gave him, that I was obliged to do all his bidding fully" (49). Yet Dante does not limit his personification of Love to the rhetorical realm—speaking or writing of Love as if it had human qualities—but rather undertakes the complete anthropomorphism of this figure. Love, as an emotion, does not simply rule over Dante, but *really* appears to him, and through him to the reader, as "a figure of a master, of an aspect frightening to whoever might behold him" (49), or, later, as "a young man dressed in whitest garments; and with the aspect of one deep in thought . . ." (63).[5] That Dante ascribes to Love such human physical traits conforms to

---

5. Dante is concerned about how his readers might react to his use of an allegorical figure such as this one, and he addresses the issue directly in this work. Following one of his sonnets in *The New Life*, a sonnet in which he characterizes Love as a personified abstraction, Dante undertakes a complicated argument in support of the propriety of his using such an allegorical figure in his versification. His "proof" ends as follows:

> Consequently, because to poets is granted greater license of expression than to prose writers, and these writers in rhyme are none other than poets of the vernacular, worthy and reasonable it is that to them is granted a greater license to speak than is

the original meaning of *prosopopeia,* which derives from the Greek *prosopon* (person or face) and *poiia* (to make), and makes this figure a good example of the trope.⁶

Just as important as the visage is Dante's attribution of a voice to this figure, for it is through Love's speech that the protagonist-narrator establishes and maintains a separation between himself and his figure.⁷ To a certain extent, this work depends on the readers' understanding Love as an example of *prosopopeia* rather than as a synecdoche, rather, that is, than a part of the narrator which, at the time of the events narrated, has become the dominant aspect of his own personality and, as a result, seems to speak for the whole. Indeed, as in all of his writings, Dante strives here to maintain a rather carefully conceived sense of order and proportion. Thus, he does not allow his love for Beatrice to manifest itself as a temporary infatuation that forces him to lose perspective (as what we call love often tends to do), but rather abstracts love from himself, gives it an aspect and a voice, and makes of it a rational figure to which one may logically submit oneself. As Dante concedes near the opening of the narrative, "although [Beatrice's] image . . . gave Love its strength to rule over me, it was nevertheless of such noble power that at no time did it allow Love to rule me without the faithful counsel of reason, in those things where such counsel was useful to heed" (49).

In ceding power and control to Love, Dante has, in a sense, made this figure the allegorical hero of the tale, for it is Love that, or perhaps who, ultimately calls the shots for Dante. In his influential work on allegory, Angus Fletcher argues that "A systematically complicated character will generate a large number of other protagonists who react against or with him in a syllogistic manner. I say 'generate,'" Fletcher continues, "because the heroes

---

granted to the other writers in the vernacular; hence if a certain figure or rhetorical color is granted poets, it is granted to vernacular versifiers. Therefore, if we see that poets have addressed inanimate things as if they had sense and reason, and have made them speak to each other: and not only of true things but of things not true: that is, they have said of things non-existent that they speak, and said that many accidents speak as if they were substances and human beings; worthy is the vernacular writer in rhyme to do the same, but not without a reason, rather with a reason that is then possible to disclose in prose. (109)

Dante wants to make room for his treating Love allegorically, as a personified abstraction that rules his thoughts and actions. If he can do so, then his motives can be seen as pure; if Love is indeed his master, then his approach to Beatrice must be validated, if not entirely beyond reproach. He might not always have been good, but he had good intentions.

  6. Prosopagnosia, interestingly, is the term for the rare condition of being unable to recognize others by their faces. Sufferers often have experienced trauma to the cerebral cortex.

  7. In *The Poetics of Personification,* James Paxon claims that "the speaking aspect of a *prosopopeia* is essential in describing a personification character's essential status" (3).

in Dante and Spenser and Bunyan seem to create the worlds about them" (35). While this claim seems particularly valid in reference to a work such as Dante's *The Divine Comedy,* where the pilgrim does in some sense generate the allegorical figures he encounters during his travels, *The New Life* is not a perfectly analogous case. Dante, in this earlier work, goes to great lengths to assure himself and his reader that he has not generated the figure of Love, but rather that the figure of Love has somehow generated him, has given him, both literally and figuratively, a new life. Although we readers intuitively know that Love, Beatrice, and even the figure we know as Dante in this work are *really* generated by the author Dante, the text itself asks us to participate in the fiction's narrative audience by allowing the separation that the author wants to effect between what would seem to be the inseparable pair of a person and one of his emotions. If Dante can successfully negotiate for the autonomy of Love, then he will have ultimately succeeded in relegating himself to a secondary role in his own story. "The allegorical hero," as Fletcher explains, "is not so much a real person as he is a generator of other secondary personalities, which are partial aspects of himself" (35). And Dante, more than anything else, wants to be recognized as *participating* in a Love that is noble and transcendent, not as simply and obsessively *being* in love, in the sense that he is characterized by that particular, and particularly human, emotional state.

To convey this complicated relationship between himself and Love, Dante represents his allegorical protagonist as, not unlike the monster in Shelley's *Frankenstein,* quickly becoming independent of the mind that begot him. One of the ways that Dante accomplishes this is by representing Love as, at times, incomprehensible, both insofar as Love transcends the limits of the human protagonist and insofar as what Love actually says to Dante often proves indecipherable. Love's occasional obscurity furthers Dante's allegorical ends because it forces both him and the reader to question the literal and to look for "deeper" meanings.

When, for example, Love appears to Dante in the twelfth chapter and confronts the protagonist with the Latin metaphor "Ego tanquam centrum circuli, cui simili modo se habent circumferentie partes; tu autem non sic" ["I am like the center of a circle, to which all the points of the circumference bear the same relation; you, however, are not"] (65), I suspect that the reader, like the protagonist, is not supposed to understand. That neither he nor the reader does understand effectively releases Love from the confines of the literal and intimates that its real meaning is figural, and perhaps somehow beyond our ken. It is—significantly—at this point in the narrative that Love becomes an active and guiding force, relegating the young Dante to the role of a minor character. "Ask no more than may be useful to you," Love replies to Dante's question about the obscurity of the Latin circle metaphor, after which he proceeds—in a style remarkably similar to that of a hostage-taker—to instruct the poet to compose for Beatrice "certain words in rhyme, in which you make clear the power that I hold over you through her. . . . Let these words be like an intermediary, so that you do not speak to her directly, which is not fitting; and do not send them without me to any place where she might hear them, but let them be adorned with sweet harmony, in which I will be present whenever it is necessary" (65).

Love's counsel serves as the intended *modus operandi* for the duration of the work; essentially, Dante will write courtly love poems for Beatrice. As the story moves forward, however, Dante's point of emphasis often shifts from Beatrice to his own emotional state, a shift that leads to his being upbraided by a group of female acquaintances and subsequently to an important moment of self-criticism. The crucial passage occurs after Dante has composed a sonnet that reveals some of the suffering caused by his unrequited love:

> Oftentimes there come to mind
> the dark qualities that Love bestows upon me,
> and there comes to me pity, so that often
> I say: "Ah! can this happen to someone?";
> for Love assails me suddenly,
> so that life almost abandons me:
> there survives in me but one live spirit,
> and that remains because it speaks of you.
> Then I struggle, seeking to help myself;
> and all pale, of all valor empty,
> I come to see you, thinking to be healed:
> and if I raise my eyes to look,
> in my heart arises a tremor
> that from my pulses causes the soul to part. (77, 79)

Stepping back to review his work, Dante senses that his poetry—including this sonnet and two that have immediately preceded it—has become too personal, and perhaps too maudlin, because, he confesses, "After I wrote these three sonnets in which I spoke to this lady, for they were the narrators of almost everything about my condition, I believed I should keep silent and write no more, for I seemed to have revealed much about myself . . ." (79). A chance meeting with several "gentle ladies" reinforces this feeling, as one of them asks Dante to what end or purpose he loves Beatrice, when it seems as though he cannot even bear to be in her presence. Dante responds that

Beatrice's mere greeting "was the end of all my desires. But because it pleased her to deny it to me,[8] my Lord Love, in his mercy, has placed all my beatitude in that which cannot fail me" (81), which he reveals to be the words that he uses to praise Beatrice. In a sharp rebuttal, however, one of the women replies to Dante: "If you were speaking the truth to us, those words that you have said to us in making known your condition you would have used with another purpose" (81). This comment serves as a catalyst for Dante's decision to focus all of his literary efforts on offering "words in praise of this most gentle one" (81).

Dante's subsequent praise of Beatrice brings to mind the kind of hyperbolic rhetoric that we often associate with being in love, or just loving more generally. And this rhetoric has a storied history in literary works. As examples, Romeo's often over-the-top claims about Juliet ("She doth teach the torches to burn bright")[9] or even Hamlet's praise of his murdered father ("so loving to my mother / That he might not beteem the winds of heaven / Visit her face too roughly" [I.ii. 10–12]) can serve nicely. But as readers, we need to evaluate these claims, to decide what intention prompts their utterance and to decide whether we should take them at face value, or not. So, do we accept Dante's claims regarding Beatrice's perfection as being made in good faith and as being true; do we accept that he believes these claims but recognize his words of praise as the rhetorical manifestations of a youthful obsession; or do we dismiss the claims altogether because we sense that Dante has some ulterior motive in making them?

While we can obviously never know with complete certainty, most readers tend to believe that Dante acts and speaks in good faith in this work, even as we remain skeptical about his "reading" of Beatrice. We trust Dante's sincerity for several reasons; these include our ability to empathize with the condition of loving someone; our historical understanding of the traditions of the European troubadours and the concept of courtly love; the fact that Dante does not appear averse to self-criticism (in fact, at times he is almost too critical of himself); and, finally, the fact that Dante's feelings for and treatment of Beatrice remain constant long past her death, despite the opportunities he has to "move on with his life," to use a phrase in the current vernacular.

---

8. Earlier in the narrative Dante has feigned interest in another woman as a kind of screen. This relationship becomes the source of some gossip within Dante's circle, and he is spoken of in terms that go "beyond the bounds of courtesy" (63). Consequently, Beatrice once fails to greet him when they encounter each other; this snub has a profound impact on Dante.

9. For an interesting interpretation of Romeo's feelings for Juliet and of the reader's willingness to credit these feelings, see the chapter titled "Love Stories" in Tzachi Zamir's *Double Vision: Moral Philosophy and Shakespearean Drama*.

The death of Beatrice, as one would expect, has a profound influence on Dante, and the poetry that issues immediately from it naturally returns to the theme of his "condition," which can only be characterized as pitiable. A full year later, still depressed by Beatrice's passing and still plagued by "painful thoughts to such an extent that they gave [his] outward appearance a look of dreadful dismay" (131), Dante notices a young and very beautiful woman whom he perceives to have noticed his own anguish and who seems to empathize with him. Reasoning that one who evinces such compassion for someone else's suffering must possess in herself "a most noble love" (131), Dante resolves to write a sonnet in which he describes this event and his interpretation of it. This leads to his paying a visit to this lady and to what appears to be a growing attraction to her. "I came to such a point," he confesses, "through the sight of this lady that my eyes began to delight excessively in seeing her" (133). This strikes me as a pivotal point in the narrative because it offers up the possibility of Dante's "getting over" Beatrice and moving on to a new love interest. And if we were dealing with contemporary notions of romantic love, this plot turn is indeed what we might expect. Even Dante senses this possibility, revealing that he found this new gentle lady to be "beautiful, young, and wise" and thinking that, perhaps, "she has appeared . . . through the will of Love, so that [his] life might find some rest" (135).

Dante, however, does not allow himself to pursue this line of thinking, choosing instead to reinterpret his interest in the new lady as a failure to remain true to Beatrice. He works out his conflicted feelings in an allegorical sonnet in which he casts his "appetite" for the enticing living woman as his heart and his fidelity to Beatrice as his soul or reason. Reason, not surprisingly, carries the day and Dante, following a vision of Beatrice dressed in the same crimson clothes she wore when he first saw her, begins to refocus his attention on the true source of his beatitude: "I then began to think about her; and remembering her according to the order of time past, my heart began painfully to repent the desire by which it had so basely allowed itself to be possessed for several days against the constancy of reason: and after casting out this malicious desire, all my thoughts began to revert to their most gentle Beatrice" (137). Several sonnets follow this recommitment to Beatrice, but the narrative ends rather abruptly with Dante's decision—one catalyzed by "a wonderful vision," the contents of which he never describes—to "write no more of this blessed one until I could more worthily treat of her" (145).

We do not know why Dante ultimately found his treatment of Beatrice in the sonnets and *canzone* of *The New Life* to be unworthy, but it seems clear that we readers are being prepared for Dante's masterpiece, *The Divine*

Comedy, and we might assume that the vision that Dante experiences contains the germ of that larger work. If this is so, then we might also attribute some part of Dante's disappointment with his work to the fact that Beatrice, in *The New Life*, remains too human. To be treated in the manner that truly befits her, she must become completely transcendent and she must serve some larger purpose; she must, in other words, become a figure in a strong allegory, a figure who can extend the significance of Dante's work to the anagogical level.

Even though *The New Life* contains descriptions of Beatrice that exalt her in such a way that she sounds more perfect than any human could be and that imply her close connection with the divine—"She is no earthly woman, but one of those most beautiful angels of heaven" (111)—we cannot overlook the fact that we hear such hyperbolic language from real people as well as fictional characters with some regularity. And while Dante does his best to render Beatrice as something extraordinary, readers are left with the sense that this side of her belongs exclusively to the poet. She is *his* beatitude, perhaps, but this could also just be love speaking. One of the most perceptive readers of *The New Life*, Charles S. Singleton, argues, in fact, for a strictly human interpretation of Dante's love, at least in this work: ". . . Beatrice is a creature, a wonderfully beautiful individual of flesh and blood who lived once in a time. In *The New Life* we see her die. Beatrice will not happen again. Let us for the moment forget the allegories of the *Convivio*, and let us forget Beatrice as she is in the *Comedy*. For there Beatrice unquestionably becomes an allegory, though she does not, for that, cease to be the person she was in *The New Life*" (111). Beatrice, then, exists between two worlds in this text; Singleton is correct to emphasize her humanity, but Dante clearly wants this "glorious lady of [his] mind" to be and to represent more (47). The reader senses throughout this text that the young Dante never fully articulates the significance of the figure he sees, worships, and eulogizes. Despite his persistent attempts, Dante cannot decide what Beatrice means, and his writing, in some ways, represents an unsuccessful attempt to determine how he should read and then represent this enigmatic figure.

For me, the "failure" of *The New Life* results from Dante's inability to have the various elements of his narrative coalesce into the kind of allegory he wanted—a strong one. Dante has, in other words, allegorical elements (most notably Love), but he lacks the narrative thread that can hold them together in a meaningful way; the phenomenon that he wants to transform into his narrative never clearly materializes from the narrative that he does construct, and this produces a work that is weak, allegorically speaking. I need to reiterate here that I do not mean to imply that strong allegories are always somehow qualitatively superior to weak ones, or that weak allegories cannot by their very nature be cohesive works of literary art (the weakly allegorical but extraordinarily coherent *The Metamorphosis* demonstrates that this is not so), but in this case Dante clearly recognizes that his work fails to achieve the rhetorical end he seeks, and we know that the next work in which Beatrice figures is the strongly allegorical *Commedia*. We may deduce, therefore, that even Dante saw the earlier work as something of a prelude to what was to come, and what was to become his greatest creation.

Yet even as Dante struggles with the question of how to speak about Beatrice, readers, as I have argued, generally do not call into question his motives. Dante's love for Beatrice seems genuine, and so his struggle involves how to convey the phenomenon that she is to him in a narrative form rather than simply to win her love. In other words, Dante's attempt to weave Beatrice into a strong allegory—an effort that he begins in *The New Life* but that he fully accomplishes only in the *Commedia*—strikes us as legitimate, or genuine, or straight, or whatever term we might want to use as an antonym for ironic. Dante has constructed an ethos through his narrative that warrants our good faith.

Such is not the case with Aschenbach in Thomas Mann's *Death in Venice*, a novella that gives us access to the psyche of a man who, like Dante, is both a man of letters and a man obsessed by a figure in his text. As we will see below, Dante and Aschenbach have much in common, but while we readers are willing to credit Dante's attempt to allegorize his relationship with Beatrice, even if he fails to transform her effect on him into a strong allegorical narrative, Aschenbach's similar design relating to Tadzio is depicted in a highly ironic way. We can use the tools of a rhetorical approach to narrative and to allegory to account for this significant divergence.

Although rarely the subject of comparative study, there are some striking structural and thematic similarities between Mann's narrative and Dante's *The New Life*, similarities that belie the seven centuries that separate them. Indeed, the central relationship in both works is a tenuous one in which there is little or no direct contact between a lover and the object of his affection. Moreover, the relationship that does evolve in each work is a triadic one that depends on an intermediate figure for authorization and validation. In *The New Life* that figure is (Christian) Love, while in *Death in Venice* it is (Classical) Eros. In both stories the lover uses his intermediary as a way of triangulating his position relative to the object he desires, and thus attempts to define or characterize that object according to the conventions and ideals embodied by the intermediary. This figure, therefore, functions as a legitimizing and normalizing force for a character whose motives and actions might otherwise seem deranged and illicit. Within each narrative, then, we see that one character's desire for another character results in a rhetorical process whereby the desired object (ostensibly a "fellow" human being) undergoes a process of allegoresis.[10] The apparent goal for both Dante and Aschenbach is to make Beatrice and Tadzio signify Love and Eros, respectively; or, to put it another way, to overcome the differences that separate Beatrice and Tadzio from the ideals of Christian love and Classical love, *as Dante and Aschenbach understand those ideals.*

Mann's *Death in Venice* takes place in the early part of the twentieth century, first in Germany and then in Venice. The protagonist is Gustav von Aschenbach, a middle-aged, respected, and well-known author in his home country. While on vacation in Venice, Aschenbach becomes obsessed by a young Polish boy, Tadzio, and this obsession becomes the focus of Aschenbach's efforts and of Mann's novella. My interpretation of this novella rests on the premise that Mann's intention is to represent his character's efforts at transforming his (Aschenbach's) sexual desire for the young boy into a historically informed aesthetic allegory in which Tadzio plays the part of a classical work of art and Aschenbach acts as a passionate but disinterested art critic. By the end of the narrative, however, Mann has made it impossible to accept the validity of Aschenbach's allegorical transformation, thereby creating an ironic allegory.

I want to begin this reading by pointing out two major differences between *The New Life* and *Death in Venice*: Dante, because he acts as author, narrator, and character, has near-total control over his text, and the love that dominates his work is the love of a man for a female, albeit a very young one at the outset. Aschenbach, conversely, is a character, a character with no "real" authority over his own story and a character who, from all appearances, is gay. We must resist the tendency to confuse Aschenbach with the author of *Death in Venice,* despite the apparent similarities between them, and recognize that the former, as a character, represents *more* than a man, a gay man, a gay artist, or a repressed gay artist at the beginning of the twentieth century. Although interpretations that have characterized Aschenbach in these terms have been provocative and instructive, we should not feel as though we have understood *Death in Venice* when we decide that this novella is about such a man. I believe, in fact, that critics who read this work as the depiction of the psychological struggle and eventual downfall of a man trying to deal with his sexuality in an intolerant society do the text a

---

10. I recognize that Dante acts as both character and author in his work, while Aschenbach is just a character. I discuss the significance of this difference below.

disservice. Such an approach relies too heavily on a mimetic and literal conception of character and ignores aesthetic and rhetorical considerations that are crucial to our interpretation of the text and its characters.

In general, the homoerotic nature of the novel did not receive in the first fifty or sixty years following its publication the kind of attention it does today. One explanation for this, T. J. Reed contends, can be found in the novel's style. The work's form, insofar as it maintains an "elevated style and noble tone" and insofar as the narrator grows increasingly critical of his subject, who finishes rather badly, seems to support the argument for Mann as moralist and, consequently, to give the work a conservative feel. As Reed correctly notes, however, few critics "have come to terms with the trenchant irony associated with the high style and what might lie beneath it" (*Death* 16), an irony so pervasive and so corrosive that it leaves *any* interpretation of the novel on shaky ground. Be that as it may, the style of *Death in Venice*, if one overlooks the irony beneath it, might have given, as Reed contends, critics and reviewers something other than the taboo idea of homosexuality to focus on and to write about.

Yet things have changed rather dramatically during the last thirty years or so. The issue of the protagonist's sexual orientation, in fact, has now assumed center stage. This is due partly to changing social mores in the West, partly to a relatively more tolerant political and professional (within the academy, that is) environment, partly to a more powerful and focused homosexual community, and partly to the publication of Mann's diaries, in which he confirms his own semirepressed homosexuality. In an essay written from the perspective of a gender studies critic, Robert Tobin notes the importance of such firsthand confirmation of Mann's sexual leanings for gay readers and critics: "Although it has always been obvious that male–male desire plays a prominent role in Mann's writings, and gay readers have often leaped to the conclusion that only another gay person could write so fluently about such topics, it has only been in the last twenty years, with the posthumous publication of Mann's diaries, that readers have become aware of just how homosexual Mann was" (227).

Why does it matter that we now know definitively that Mann was, in his own estimation and despite a heterosexual marriage that produced children, gay? Tobin, for one, suggests that our awareness and acceptance of "just how homosexual Mann was" can lead to a fuller appreciation of *Death in Venice* because the reader can finally allow and encourage the text to be what it naturally is: "Rather than suppressing the story's homosexual tones, as generations of previous critics have done, the reader can augment them, bring them out. Such a search for the homosexual signifiers of the story will put Aschenbach into a clearer context and provide for a much richer reading of the novella and its understanding of society" (229). And on this point Tobin is correct: gay criticism has contributed immeasurably to our interpretation of Mann and his works and, as regards *Death in Venice* in particular, has illuminated one aspect of the novel that previously received scant attention.

In some ways, however, readings that adhere to a particular perspective or that come out of a particular ideology can transform literary texts from aesthetic objects into evidence in support of a critical approach or stance. And there is often a reluctance today to deal with the notion of the aesthetic, a reluctance that stems not only from a feeling of unease with the subjective nature of aesthetics and the value judgments it engenders but also from a desire to construct an interpretation that is politically and socially applicable. Thus, many contemporary critics approach a text with a predetermined agenda and a desire (and too often a professional need) to produce a relevant interpretation. In doing so, however, they often lose, or discard, the aesthetic character of texts, something that Hans-Robert Jauss argues is "a hermeneutic bridge ... which makes possible the historical understanding of art across the distance in time in the first place, and which therefore must be integrated into the execution of the interpretation as a hermeneutic premise" (146). When we rush past the aesthetic moment of interpretation in our attempt to find something applicable or relevant to say we often fail to recognize the text's determinate horizon of understanding, and a full appreciation of literary character is often the first casualty of this failure.

The centrality of aesthetic issues in *Death in Venice* demands that we pay closer attention to them in our interpretations, particularly as regards character. Critics have always recognized the aesthetic elements in the novella—Aschenbach's status as an author, the wondrous prose that Tadzio inspires, references to classical beauty and to Plato's *Phaedrus* and *Symposium*—but have treated aesthetics thematically, rather than constitutively.[11] We have recognized, in other words, that the book is, on one level, about aesthetics, but have failed either to recognize or to articulate how aesthetics has made the text and its characters signify what and as they do.[12] For my purposes, aesthetic history actually plays a central role in the allegory that Aschenbach wants to construct, an allegory that will be the transformation of his illicit desire into a narrative of art appreciation.

Turning to a typical, but important, passage from *Death in Venice*, we can begin to understand how aesthetic considerations not only reveal something

---

11. See, for example, Alice van Buren Kelley's "Von Aschenbach's Phaedrus: Platonic Allusion in 'Death in Venice.'"

12. On the literal level, critics have talked about aesthetic issues—particularly style—as a constitutive element of this work. See, for example, Frederic Amory's "The Classical Style of 'Death in Venice.'"

of Aschenbach's character (psychology, if we want to call it that), but are also absolutely crucial in producing Aschenbach as a character. In the fourth chapter, where Aschenbach's apotheosizing of Tadzio culminates in a burst of aesthetic productivity and, finally, in "that page-and-a-half of choice prose that soon would amaze many a reader with its purity, nobility, and surging depth of feeling" (39), Aschenbach takes shape for us not only as an artist but also as a historically determined, aesthetic figure. Indeed, more important than the five hundred words or so that Aschenbach purportedly produces here is the narrator's ironic undercutting of that achievement, a rhetorical act that thrusts issues of hermeneutics to the fore.

Immediately after informing the reader of Aschenbach's production, the narrator remarks that it is good that the world knows only that work, and neither its origin (*Ursprünge*) nor its context (*Entstehungsbedingungen*), for to understand these would confuse readers and thus compromise the text's purity and nobility, if not its depth of feeling. I say that this is an ironic move on the narrator's part because the readers of *Death in Venice* know *only* the origins and context of Aschenbach's work, and nothing of the text itself. Whereas the narrative audience of Mann's novella might well take the narrator at his word here, the authorial audience picks up on the irony and understands full well that any sense of "purity" or "nobility" regarding what Tadzio inspires in Aschenbach has already been compromised. Yet even if we cannot read the text that Tadzio inspires, we can nevertheless read or interpret that inspiration. In doing so, we must submit Aschenbach's interpretation of Tadzio to a hermeneutic analysis in order to determine how the former responds to the latter. Once we understand Aschenbach's response to Tadzio, we can better understand what and how Tadzio signifies in the context of the novella. The origins and context of Aschenbach's reading of Tadzio will prove more telling than the page-and-a-half of narrative that we never see.

Aschenbach's response to Tadzio is predominately aesthetic, in both senses of that term: Tadzio is an object of beauty and the cause of a sensual response on the part of a perceiving subject. In *Death in Venice,* these two aspects of aesthetics are intimately related and often indistinguishable because Aschenbach functions as both the artist behind Tadzio and the observer facing and responding to him. This novella depicts Aschenbach's often desperate attempt to create a Tadzio (as an aesthetic object) that can accommodate and validate the visceral response occasioned by his beauty. Aschenbach's goal in this endeavor resembles Dante's aim in *The New Life*: he wants to find a way to transform a love object into an allegory, one that will therefore acquire a meaning that transcends the literal, the immediate, and the mundane. Tadzio represents the same kind of challenge that Beatrice represents for Dante—a surfeit of significance that must somehow be represented rhetorically. The successful allegorization of Tadzio would represent the ultimate artistic achievement for the intellectual Aschenbach, for Tadzio seems to represent the kind of life force that stands in opposition to the relatively staid and intellectual artist we meet in the second chapter, the artist who labors for years to create a single work.

Until Tadzio's appearance, Aschenbach resembles an intellectual *Schriftsteller*—or author—more than he does a *Dichter*—or poet, in its most classical and laudatory sense; and this is an important distinction. Indeed, Mann himself struggled with these terms, primarily because few of his contemporaries would recognize him as the kind of Goethean artist who merited the title "*Dichter.*" T. J. Reed explains that "Within the cultural scene [Mann's] notes recreate, the honorific term *Dichter,* always an arbitrary judgment, was accorded only to writers whose work offered some analogy with the visual beauty, sensuousness, unintellectual immediacy of the plastic arts and could be given the accolade *plastich*" (*Thomas Mann* 127). Like that of his creator, most of Aschenbach's works—or what we know of them—sound like *Literatur,* not *Dictung;* they are the compositions of a knowledgeable and often cynical intellect. Yet near the close of chapter 2, readers learn of a shift in Aschenbach's approach that prepares both us and him for his encounter with Tadzio. We learn, in fact, that Aschenbach has relatively recently turned away from the intellectual approach of his youth, an approach that betrays a "moral skepticism" and a "sympathy with the abyss," and has instead experienced the "miracle of ingenuousness reborn" (11).

Together, this information concerning Aschenbach's changed approach to his craft, our knowledge of the "classical" quality that ultimately results from this change, and Aschenbach's classical characterization of Tadzio (which I will discuss in more detail below) all function as a kind of aesthetic (as opposed to objective) correlative that can help the reader understand the tortured writer's emotional state and his character more generally. According to T. S. Eliot in his famous essay on *Hamlet,* "The only way of expressing emotion in the form of art is by finding an *objective correlative;* in other words, a set of objects, a situation, a chain of events which shall be the formula of that *particular* emotion; such that when the external facts, which must terminate in sensory experience, are given, the emotion is immediately evoked" (124–25). Eliot goes on to argue that *Hamlet* is a flawed play because, in fact, there is no objective correlative for Hamlet's emotion, that, in other words, "Hamlet (the man) is dominated by an emotion which is inexpressible, because it is in *excess* of the facts as they appear" (125).

Although this concept has generated much provocative discussion, it has not been widely accepted. One of the most trenchant critiques of it comes in W. K. Wimsatt and Monroe Beardsley's "The Affective Fallacy," wherein they point out that Hamlet's "emotion must be expressible, . . . and actually expressed too (by something) in the play; otherwise Eliot would not know it is there—in excess of the facts" (35). Wimsatt and Beardsley are correct to alert us to the logical inconsistencies in Eliot's reasoning, but their objections do not necessarily succeed in discrediting the idea of the correlative itself. Eliot's concept, which depends on a kind of aesthetic symmetry, in that a character's emotions must refer to or stem from a reasonable (objective) cause, maintains its interest despite its philosophical shortcomings. Like the rest of us, Eliot wrestles with what makes characters convincing, interesting, and successful. Hamlet is an interesting character, but not a successful one, because he "is up against the difficulty that his disgust is occasioned by his mother, but that his mother is not an adequate equivalent for it; his disgust envelops and exceeds her" (125). Wimsatt and Beardsley's critique notwithstanding, I find Eliot's inclination to assess the relative success of an author's attempt at characterization to be worth pursuing, and the idea of the objective correlative does have some value as a way of linking a character's actions to the larger context of the work.

The objective correlative, however, does not exhaust the list of such potential linkages, and I want to suggest another—the aesthetic correlative. This concept seeks to address in the realm of *emotion* the same issues that Eliot wants to cover in the realm of *actions*. Strictly applying Eliot's criteria for the objective correlative, we would have to call not only *Hamlet* but also *The New Life* and *Death in Venice* artistic failures because the objects, situations, or events that we find in these narratives never effectively express or justify the emotions of the respective protagonists. If Eliot desired a verisimilar and proportionate correspondence in the relationship between emotion and its cause, he would not find it in either *The New Life* or *Death in Venice*, where the figures of Beatrice and Tadzio—*if we read them as representations of real people*—strike us, when we look at the situations from a rational and disinterested perspective, as absurdly inadequate to elicit from their texts' protagonists the type and depth of emotion that they apparently do. But this aporia between emotion and expression is precisely what these works are about. In order to understand them, we must shift our attention to the nature of the characters (particularly the protagonists) and try to find an aesthetic correlative to their feelings, responses, and emotions, as they are represented in the text. Ultimately, we will find that the characters themselves function allegorically, as figures that occupy a role in the transformation of some phenomenon into a narrative.

In the case of Aschenbach, one of our first and most important clues to his aesthetic correlative is his relatively recent experience with "ingenuousness reborn." Given that Aschenbach is a cultured and learned German artist with a classical bent, this reference to ingenuousness should recall for the reader the ingenuousness, or *naïveté*, described by Friedrich Schiller at the end of the eighteenth century.[13] All poets, according to Schiller, can be classified as either naïve or sentimental, depending on their general temperament. The naïve/sentimental distinction effectively corresponds with Schiller's distinction between the classical and the modern, and rests on the very issues that Aschenbach faces in his own work. His move away from intellectualism and moral skepticism toward ingenuousness and classicism, in fact, not only describes a move from *Schriftsteller* to *Dichter* but also brings into play the crucial distinction between the sentimental (modern) poet and the naïve (classical) one.

The naïve poet, who appears rarely and almost miraculously in the guise of genius in the modern, civilized world of ideas, is characterized by a childlike innocence and naturalness. Those with a childlike temperament, according to Schiller, "often act and think naively in the midst of the artificial circumstances of fashionable society; they forget in their own beautiful humanity that they have to do with a depraved world, and comport themselves even at the courts of kings with the same ingenuousness and innocence that one would find only in a pastoral society" (93). In general, however, modern society, Schiller argues, has lost its connection with nature, and modern man suffers from this disconnect. When we encounter objects in nature, objects such as streams and birds singing, we appreciate them because they represent for us a unity of being, a oneness with their own nature, that we have lost: "*They are what we were; they are what we should once again become*" (85, emphasis in original). This too describes our attitude toward the ancient Greeks, who, unlike modern European society, "had not lost nature in [their] humanity" (85), and who had remained naively naïve. "They felt naturally," Schiller explains; "we feel the natural.... Our feeling for nature is like the feeling of an invalid for health" (105). This longing for lost nature ultimately manifests itself in modern sentimental art, and particularly in poetry, through the nostalgic treatment of nature as idea or object.

The sentimental poet seeks nature. More specifically, he or she points to an idealized image of nature as a figure for the unity of self that has been lost. "The correspondence between his [modern man's] feeling and

---

13. Mann himself was clearly familiar with and influenced by Schiller. In 1905, in fact, he wrote a piece, *Schwere Stunde*, to commemorate Schiller on the one-hundredth anniversary of his death. Indeed, as T. J. Reed points out, Mann's work on this essay enabled him "to create an impression of total familiarity with Schiller and his situation" (Thomas Mann 323), a familiarity that clearly manifests itself in *Death in Venice*. We should also note that Mann's uncompleted essay on art and culture ("Geist und Kunst") owes much to Schiller's philosophy. See Reed's chapter titled "Art and Intellect" in *Thomas Mann: The Uses of Tradition*.

thought," Schiller explains, "which in his first condition *actually* took place, exists now only *ideally*; it is no longer within him, but outside him, as an idea still to be realized, no longer as a fact in his life" (111). When we meet Aschenbach as he begins to develop his plans for a vacation to the South, we sense, I think, something of this self-alienation, and his recent discovery of ingenuousness reborn suggests the type of nostalgia for the naïve and the natural that Schiller describes. If we understand the figure of Aschenbach in these terms, then we are better prepared to understand how he finds in Tadzio precisely what he has been seeking and, moreover, how what he finds becomes his own sentimental creation.

Aschenbach's first encounter with his object of desire occurs in a setting that dramatizes Schiller's naïve/sentimental dichotomy and that serves as a cultural and aesthetic backdrop against which Tadzio takes shape as a figure. In the lobby of the Lido's Hotel des Bains, where Aschenbach will be staying, "A broad horizon, tolerant and comprehensive" unfolds before Aschenbach, revealing a scene in which "All the great languages of Europe melded together in subdued tones," and in which "Evening dress, the uniform of cultured society, provided a decorous external unity to the variety of humanity assembled here" (21). This is humanity in its most cultured, and perhaps least natural state: thoroughly adult, restrained, dressed, and proper. Not surprisingly, Aschenbach feels quite at home—even content—here, as he looks on from a somewhat detached vantage point and with a newspaper, gleaned from a nearby table, as a kind of buffer between himself and the rest of humanity.

As he scans the room before him, Aschenbach finds his attention drawn to a group of young people who are speaking Polish. Up to and including this point in the description of the scene, Mann's narrative has been a model of realism, a controlled and ostensibly objective description from a third-person narrator that both matches and helps to establish the tone and the mood of the lobby tableau. Indeed, the narrator provides us with a series of details—the names of actual hotels, the fabric (leather) of the chair Aschenbach selects in which to await the dinner hour, the color (green) of the elevator operator's uniform, the nationalities represented in the lobby (American, German, French, Slavic)—that allows the reader to participate in Aschenbach's careful and keen observation of his surroundings; like the protagonist whose eyes we are borrowing, we miss nothing and are rather pleased with our ability to notice and interpret the minutiae of the environment.[14] Ours is a scholarly and

---

14. In "The 'Second Author' of *Death in Venice*," Dorrit Cohn notes that "the narrator steadfastly adheres to his protagonist's perspective on the outside world; from the initial moment when he observes the strange wanderer standing on the steps of the funeral chapel to the final moment when he watches Tadzio standing on the sandbar we see the events and figures of the outside world through Aschenbach's eyes" (*Distinction* 134). She correctly goes on to note,

intellectual detachment, and so a thoroughly "modern" one.

Yet the time we have spent with Aschenbach, as he reclines in his leather chair and intermittently and distractedly reads his newspaper, amounts to only a brief interlude of subjective control and order in the midst of an otherwise strange journey. Just hours before he descends to the hotel lobby, in fact, our narrator tells us that Aschenbach has been troubled by the rather odd events—including his encounters with the repugnant old man on the boat to Italy and with the mysterious and illegitimate gondolier who brought him to his hotel—that have preceded his arrival. Though these events, we are told, were not necessarily incongruous with reason, they were nevertheless troubling because they struck Aschenbach as odd, perhaps even portentous, and thus produced in him a feeling of unease. After washing his face, instructing the maid, taking afternoon tea, walking along the boardwalk, and dressing himself in his customarily deliberate and fastidious manner for dinner (21), however, Aschenbach has effectively exercised his demons and seems to be himself once again, a fact that is reflected in and reinforced by the carefully controlled narrative portrait of refinement and culture in the hotel lobby.

And it is of course here, while taking inventory of the group of youths speaking Polish, and while in relative control of his faculties, that Aschenbach's gaze alights, finally, on that longhaired youth who will become his Tadzio. Given what we already know about Aschenbach's interest in the ingenuous or naïve, it should not surprise us that his initial reaction to Tadzio results in a classical aesthetic characterization. After informing the reader that Aschenbach noted with amazement Tadzio's perfect beauty, the narrator seems to step back, and the successive description of Tadzio takes the form of an essay or lecture on a work of art, in this case one that recalls "Greek statues from the noblest period of antiquity" (21). For almost a page, "Aschenbach" is replaced by general pronouns ("onlooker," for example), and our introduction to Tadzio amounts to an academic reading of him as a classical aesthetic figure. Although we know that the point of view in this passage is Aschenbach's, his nominal absence from this initial description is meant to betray a kind of critical—and Kantian—disinterestedness. At this point, Aschenbach has engaged Tadzio, but he has done so from a safe distance and from behind a buffer of aesthetic differentiation.

As we see him through Aschenbach's eyes, Tadzio appears to us as a posed figure, like one of the statues to which our narrator has just referred: "He sat so that the observer [Aschenbach] saw him in profile. His feet were clad in black patent leather and arranged one in front of the other; one elbow was propped on the arm of his wicker chair with his cheek resting on his

---

however, that in contrast to the empirical solidarity he maintains with Aschenbach, the narrator becomes increasingly distanced "on the ideological level" as the novel advances (134).

closed hand; his demeanor was one of careless refinement, quite without the almost submissive stiffness that seemed to be the norm for his sisters" (22). Moreover, Tadzio's long, curly hair recalls for the observer the Greco-Roman statue of the young boy removing a thorn from his foot. The combined effect of this early aesthetic description of Tadzio is twofold. First, it reinforces the roles of the novella's two principal characters; Aschenbach continues as the observant, intellectual artist and critic, and Tadzio emerges as his object of study. Yet the description also provides the reader with material that will allow us to characterize Aschenbach, who is, in turn, characterizing Tadzio, and thus laying the foundation for his intended allegorical transformation.[15]

It is clear from the beginning of the story that the mature Aschenbach sees himself as an important part of a larger German cultural heritage. His oeuvre, in fact, includes both a prose epic about Frederick the Great, the eighteenth-century King of Prussia, and an essay, "Geist und Kunst," whose "power of organization and antithetical eloquence had prompted serious observers to rank it alongside Schiller's 'On Naïve and Sentimental Poetry'" (7). Moreover, we know through the narrator of the story that from early on Aschenbach had been bent on achieving public notoriety through his art, that as his career and work evolved he became anthologized in school textbooks, and that "he did not refuse" when a German prince awarded him an honorary title on his fiftieth birthday (12).

With this in mind, we can pursue a reading of *Death in Venice* that will allow us to see Aschenbach as an aesthetic and cultural composite, a figure whose responses, emotions, and language derive from and point us to an earlier aesthetic context. Having already pointed out the methodological and philosophical affinities between Aschenbach and Schiller, I will now turn more specifically to Aschenbach's interpretation of Tadzio in order to demonstrate that Aschenbach's character signifies more than a self.

Three principal aspects of his characterization of Tadzio allow the reader

15. We should also note that Aschenbach's initial description of Tadzio has undertones of decadence, which seem to work against the classical, aesthetic description of this figure. It is telling that Aschenbach wonders at the end of this first encounter whether, given his pale complexion, Tadzio might be sick. Although he decides that the boy is probably just coddled, the seeds of death and decline have been sown, and this theme—or threat—will oppose the "healthier" aesthetic descriptions of Tadzio throughout the novella. Interestingly, it is not Tadzio who declines during the course of the story, but Aschenbach. For a provocative discussion of the decadent elements of this work, see Edward S. Brinkley's "Fear of Form: Thomas Mann's *Death in Venice*." Brinkley's main point is that "Death in Venice signals a decisive break with decadent modernism by refusing any transseminal link between Aschenbach and Tadzio, by transferring the decay from adolescent male to adult male, and thus by returning the trope of interior disintegration back to its 'author'" (4). For a more general discussion of decadence in relation to Mann's novella, see Naomi Ritter's "Death in Venice and the Tradition of European Decadence." This article also suggests further reading on the subject.

to identify Aschenbach's aesthetic correlative and, consequently, to understand how he responds to the figure of the boy and why it is a boy who attracts his attention in the first place. Indeed, the fact that the object of Aschenbach's desire is a boy is one of these telling aspects, the others being Tadzio's purported statuelike and classical qualities. Combined with the allusions to Aschenbach's move toward a naïve approach to his art, these elements collectively recall an eighteenth-century German neoclassicism and, in particular, the figures of Schiller (as already noted), Goethe, Gotthold Lessing, and Johann Winckelmann.[16] Once we see Tadzio in this light, we can begin to understand how his existence in the text depends on Aschenbach's interpretation and description of him, and also how our understanding of him as a rhetorical figure—as an element in an allegory that seeks to transform an aesthetic phenomenon into a figural narrative—allows us to understand Aschenbach. Our experience in reading these characters takes the form of an interpretive (hermeneutical) circle: we can understand Aschenbach only by interpreting Tadzio, and we know Tadzio only through Aschenbach's perception and interpretation of him.

When we recognize the influence of eighteenth-century aesthetic theory on Aschenbach's character, the hermeneutic circle becomes a productive interpretive tool and the text as a whole—as well as the characters in it—begins to make more sense. Even the initial descriptions of Tadzio in sculptural terms, for example, which might at first seem to be merely the hyperbolic reactions of a smitten man, ultimately help to reveal the nature of Aschenbach's character. We cannot, in other words, afford to dismiss the significance of Aschenbach's characterization of Tadzio as being like a Greek statue because to do so will prevent us from fully understanding Aschenbach's own character.

Given what we already know about Aschenbach and his relationship to German aesthetic culture, we must read his response to the figure of Tadzio from within a particular aesthetic context. In this regard, the remarks concerning the similarity between Tadzio and Greek sculpture are particularly informative and resonant. Indeed, the reference to the plastic arts at this point reinforces the neoclassical motif that has already been established by the allusions to Schiller and his distinction between naïve and sentimental poetry. Here, though, we are reminded of the importance of painting and

---

16. In her article on *Death in Venice,* Lida Kirchberger touches on Mann's use of eighteenth-century aesthetic theory—and particularly how it transmits ideas of Greek antiquity—in this novella. However, she limits herself to "explicit references in the Novelle to eighteenth-century phenomena" (324), all of which she finds in the second chapter, and which only deal with Frederick the Great and Schiller. I believe that we need to pursue this issue further, and to look for its resonances throughout the text.

sculpture in the aesthetic theories of German critics such as Winckelmann and Lessing. These eighteenth-century critics were concerned with the nature of beauty and with its representation in the arts, both the plastic arts and poetry writ large. The historical figures that these formidable critics became, as well as the issues they struggled with, are unmistakably present in *Death in Venice*.

The figure of Winckelmann, in particular, seems to haunt, and in a way to determine, Aschenbach's reception of Tadzio. Like Schiller, Winckelmann believed that the ancient Greeks were intimately in touch with and blessed by a naturalness or naïveté that modern humans have somehow lost. And it was Winckelmann's work in art criticism and art history that ushered in the era of German neoclassicism that was to be one of the most important and productive in the history of aesthetics. That the Greeks were simply more beautiful than modern humans is a key assumption of Winckelmann's work. He claims, for example, that "everything that was instilled and taught from birth to adulthood about the culture of their bodies and the preservation, development, and refinement of this culture through nature and art was done to enhance the natural beauty of the ancient Greeks. Thus we can say that in all probability their physical beauty excelled ours by far" (11). Moreover, Winckelmann continues, "The probability is that in the beautiful bodily forms of the Greeks as well as in the works of their masters there was a greater unity of the entire structure, a nobler connection of parts, and a greater fullness of form, without the emaciated tensions and depressions of our bodies" (19).

Tadzio's body brings to Aschenbach's mind images quite similar to those evoked by Winckelmann; or perhaps we should say that Aschenbach's rhetoric characterizes Tadzio in a way that recalls Winckelmann. In a scene in which Aschenbach watches Tadzio swim toward the beach, for example, the narrator relates Aschenbach's classically inspired reading of the event: "The sight of this lively adolescent figure, seductive and chaste, lovely as a tender young god, emerging from the depths of the sky and sea with dripping locks and escaping the clutches of the elements—it all gave rise to mythic images. It was a sight belonging to poetic legends from the beginning of time that tell of the origins of form and of the birth of the gods" (28). The references here to myth, the origins of form, and the birth of the gods clearly associate Tadzio with the classical tradition, but with the classical tradition *as it was interpreted and understood by eighteenth-century aesthetic critics*. In characterizing Tadzio as a tender young god and in casting him as a living example of a Greek statue (much like the Pygmalion story, if Pygmalion had never spoken with Galatea), Aschenbach allows himself to participate in a kind of idol worship that has both cultural antecedents and, thus, some amount of intellectual credibility.

Aschenbach uses the aesthetic tradition that has influenced him as an artist to characterize Tadzio allegorically, thereby giving his figure an aesthetic significance that might justify and validate the protagonist's questionable visceral reaction to the boy. It is not surprising, then, that Tadzio's face, which reminds Aschenbach of Greek statues, causes "the onlooker" to doubt his having ever witnessed anything of equal perfection either in nature or in art (28). This description of Tadzio as being somehow beyond both nature and art should recall for us Schiller's description of modern humanity's encounter with naïve objects. When we encounter such objects, he contends, we appreciate in them their "existence in accordance with their own laws, [their] inner necessity, [and their] eternal unity with themselves" (181). Effectively, naïve objects *remind* us of what we have lost and can never truly regain through art or through nature herself. "In them . . . we see eternally that which escapes us, but for which we are challenged to strive, and which, even if we never attain to it, we may still hope to approach in endless progress" (181). As an artist, Aschenbach recognizes in Tadzio a naïve aesthetic ideal that he has not captured in his own work; as a man, Aschenbach recognizes in Tadzio the promise of a physical fulfillment that is equally inaccessible, but equally compelling. Aschenbach is careful, however, to try to describe his attraction to Tadzio in acceptable aesthetic and cultural terms, just as Dante has tried to do with his Beatrice.

We see another example of this later in the third chapter, when Aschenbach watches Tadzio enter the hotel's dining area. Here again we witness the transformation of Aschenbach into an "observer," and follow along as our protagonist receives, describes, and appreciates the figure of the boy as he enters the scene:

> Smiling, he murmured a word in his soft, indistinct speech and took his place, showing his full profile to the observer. The latter was once more, and now especially, struck with amazement, indeed even alarm, at the truly god-like beauty possessed by this mortal child. . . . It was the face of Eros, with the yellowish glaze of Parian marble, with delicate and serious brows, the temples and ears richly and rectangularly framed by soft, dusky curls. (24–25)

Like Dante, Aschenbach attempts to mitigate the mundane reality of his object by casting him allegorically. In this case the allegory is an aesthetic one that points back to the eighteenth century and that is meant to lend significance and integrity to Tadzio, to Aschenbach's appreciation of him, and to Aschenbach, who still—at this point in the narrative—fashions himself as a respectable and respected intellect. As the narrator tells us, in fact, Aschenbach, after recognizing Tadzio's as the face of Eros, sits back and simply admires the figure with "that professional, cool air of appraisal artists sometimes use to cover their delight, their enthusiasm when they encounter a masterpiece" (25).

Looking carefully at the figure that Aschenbach sees and describes in this scene, the reader of Mann's novella should be struck by the complexity and significance of the image described. Tadzio emerges here as a gestalt of allegorical references that at once "characterize" him and dehumanize him: He is mortal but godlike, alive but like a work of art, modern but classical. Aschenbach works quite diligently to describe Tadzio in such a way that the resultant image will, like Dante's Beatrice, be sufficient to carry the meaning he wants to ascribe to the figure. For Aschenbach, classical aesthetics offers the most resonant material with which to construct Tadzio's exterior because it provides him (Aschenbach) with a set of pre-established cultural meanings conducive to the propagation of an image of himself that he has worked for years to construct.

At the heart of Aschenbach's emerging allegory lies the close association that many eighteenth-century critics claimed existed between classical aesthetics and morality. For Winckelmann in particular, the beauty of the Greek figures represented not simply a superficial perfection available to be copied but also an idealized conception of beauty and, perhaps more importantly, a sense that outer beauty coincided with a noble (inner) nature. In one of the most famous passages from his study of Greek painting and sculpture, Winckelmann makes the provocative claim that the most telling characteristics of the greatest Greek works of art are the "noble simplicity and quiet grandeur" revealed in both the posture and the expression of the figures represented. "Just as the depths of the sea always remain calm however much the surface may rage," Winckelmann explains, "so does the expression of the figures of the Greeks reveal a great and composed soul even in the midst of passion" (33). The Laocoön, according to Winckelmann, is the greatest example of this phenomenon because the pain that he must be experiencing while in the grip of the serpents "expresses itself with no sign of rage in his face or in his entire bearing. He emits no terrible screams such as Virgil's Laocoön, for the opening of the mouth does not permit it. . . . The physical pain and the nobility of soul are distributed with equal strength over the entire body and are, as it were, held in balance with one another" (33–35).[17] For Winckelmann, then, the figures in Greek art represent a correspondence between aesthetic and moral perfection, between inner and outer beauty. In the process of reading these figures, he finds a sublime integrity and a rare state of signification—that state that eluded, at least temporarily, Dante in his

---

17. Laocoön, as depicted in the *Aeneid*, is the priest of Apollo who tries to warn the Trojans not to trust the Greeks and their apparent gift of the wooden horse. As punishment, Aethena sends two large serpents to crush Laocoön and his two sons.

The New Life—wherein form exactly expresses content.

Equally important for our purposes, is Winckelmann's belief that the artists of these works had to share in this dignified nature in order to be capable of producing such art: "The expression of such nobility of soul goes far beyond the depiction of beautiful nature. The artist had to feel the strength of this spirit in himself and then impart it to his marble" (35). Thus, the relationship between artist and art is a symbiotic one in which the artist must participate in the beauty and the nobility of his subject. A similar philosophy underlies Aschenbach's peculiar relationship with Tadzio, and we sense this more acutely as the narrative progresses. In the fourth chapter, in fact, Aschenbach begins to mingle his classical interpretation or characterization of Tadzio with his "other" work as an artist in an apparent attempt to participate in the general beauty and nobility of his object. Watching the youthful figure at play on the beach, Aschenbach describes Tadzio in terms meant to evoke a sentiment akin to Winckelmann's belief in the mutually reinforcing relationship among beauty, intellect, and morality in art and artist:

> His honey-colored hair clung in circles to his temples and his neck; the sun made the down shine on his upper back; the subtle definition of the ribs and the symmetry of his chest stood out through the tight-fitting material covering his torso; his armpits were still as smooth as those of a statue, the hollows behind his knees shone likewise, and the blue veins showing through made his body seem to be made of translucent material. What discipline, what precision of thought was expressed in the stretch of his youthfully perfect body! But was not the rigorous and pure will that had been darkly active in bringing this divine form into the clear light of day entirely familiar to the artist in him? Was this same will not active in him, too, when he, full of sober passion, freed a slender form from the marble mass of language, a form he had seen with his spiritual eye and that he presented to mortal men as image and mirror of spiritual beauty? (37)

Here again Aschenbach casts Tadzio as being both "classically" beautiful and statuelike, but the professional and disinterested demeanor that he has heretofore maintained as an "observer" now gives way to a more active, participatory role as he makes the connection between what he wants Tadzio to represent and what he (Aschenbach) does—as well as who he is—as an artist. Like Winckelmann's description of the Greek artists who must have felt and shared in the spiritual beauty of the figures they represented, Aschenbach's representation of himself as a rhetorical sculptor whose medium is an aesthetic and spiritual beauty implies that he must be a good man to participate in such a beautiful aesthetic project.

This particular encounter with Tadzio on the beach culminates in Aschenbach's ultimate work—that page and a half of pure and noble prose whose origins, ironically, are better left obscure. As the narrator tells us, Aschenbach wants to work with Tadzio in view, to use—like a painter or sculptor—"the boy's physical frame as the model for his writing, to let his style follow the lines of that body that seemed to him divine, to carry his beauty into the realm of the intellect as once the eagle carried the Trojan shepherd into the ethereal heavens" (39). Informed as we are of the events that have led to this moment, however, readers of the narrative should by now suspect that Aschenbach's classical rhetoric serves as a veil behind which to hide his lascivious desires and that his participation in eighteenth-century aesthetic tradition has become something of a self-delusional cover-up. At this point, everyone involved in the narrative knows that Aschenbach's motives are neither pure, noble, nor principally aesthetic, a fact reinforced by the feeling he experiences after this episode with Tadzio: "Strange hours! Strangely enervating effort! Strangely fertile intercourse between a mind and a body! When Aschenbach folded up his work and left the beach, he felt exhausted, even unhinged, as if his conscience were indicting him after a debauch" (39). This unhinging marks the beginning of the end for Aschenbach, for he now abjures "self-criticism" and devotes himself to the pursuit of Tadzio. In a sense, Aschenbach has abandoned his original character—the one described as leading a tense but controlled existence, like a tightly balled fist—and has relaxed into a licentious old man.

To borrow a phrase from the plastic arts, Aschenbach has failed to hold his pose. Although he has generally managed to maintain the image of Tadzio as a Greek-like figure (and all that that means), he loses control of his own image, or character, as the narrative unfolds. Aschenbach's aesthetic ideal amounts to a composite of the depictions of Saint Sebastian and Laocoön, both of whom are depicted as showing dignity, calmness, and modesty while enduring great pain. Indeed, until the very climax of his story Aschenbach has attempted to appear publicly in a "refined and respectable bearing" that would reveal nothing of his "inner tumult" (42). This pose is in keeping with Winckelmann's conception of beauty, one in which the subject's noble nature triumphs over his pain and silences the unaesthetic scream that might otherwise result. Like Winckelmann, Aschenbach seems to believe that "The more tranquil the state of the body the more capable it is of portraying the true character of the soul. . . . A soul is more apparent and distinctive when seen in violent passion, but it is great and noble when seen in a state of unity and calm" (Winckelmann 35).[18] And it is this state of unity and calm so

---

18. It is interesting to note that—in "reality" as well as in aesthetics—Aschenbach and

carefully cultivated throughout his career that Aschenbach cannot maintain when faced with Tadzio.

Aschenbach's most pressing problems in *Death in Venice* are narrative progression and character development, both of which arise because he does not have control of this story. As readers, we know that Aschenbach has created a character and an image for himself *outside* of the narrative we are reading, but in this story he cannot control, or stop, the rather unaesthetic climax that undermines his self-characterization. Unlike Dante, Aschenbach does not have the option of simply writing no more until he feels ready and worthy to continue, but rather must struggle to redescribe people, events, and himself as the narrative unfolds. The sculptural metaphor that Aschenbach adopts is revealing—particularly since he is a writer—but not altogether surprising. In sculpture, Aschenbach can allude to the same sense of permanence and stasis that critics such as Winckelmann found so appealing in classical works. Unlike traditional narrative, sculpture—as interpreted by the eighteenth-century neoclassical Germans—allows the artist to render and isolate a beautiful figure in such a way that it transcends both time and the physical world while also reflecting the nobility and purity of its creator. Aschenbach would clearly like for Tadzio to stand as such a monument.

Not all of the eighteenth-century critics, however, agreed with Winckelmann's assertion that the calmness and serenity of the embattled figures of Greek art directly conveyed the nobility of the Greek soul. Gotthold Lessing, for example, argues in his own essay on the Laocoön that the Greek, in general, actually "felt and feared, and he expressed his pain and grief. He was not ashamed of any human weakness, but it must not prevent him from attaining honor nor from fulfilling his duty" (9). If, therefore, Lessing reasons, "crying aloud when in physical pain is compatible with nobility of soul, then the desire to express such nobility could not have prevented the artist from representing the scream in his marble" (11). According to Lessing, the figures of Greek art—and particularly the Laocoön—look as they do because of purely

---

Winckelmann might have been working toward similar ends. Kevin Parker claims—in a provocative attempt to read Winckelmann's project as one of controlling, repressing, or redirecting his own (Winckelmann's) homosexual desires—that "as an historian, rather than a philosopher, . . . Winckelmann can . . . take up his relationship to the object of his desire, which is Greek art, in the conviction that he will be able to master it by mastering himself" (543). That is to say, in essence, that Winckelmann is able to take the life and, thus, the danger, out of the forms he studies by bracketing them historically. As a result, Parker argues, "The seductive spell of the others' lived body . . . has been broken. The absence of the Greek body, guaranteed by Winckelmann's institution of historical difference as a relation of presence to absence, is now the unapproachable object of our gaze" (543). This historical distance is what Aschenbach needs in order to sustain his allegorical reading of himself and Tadzio, and their relationship, but it is also precisely that which he does not have and which finally proves to be his undoing.

aesthetic considerations, and his essay establishes that "among the ancients beauty was the supreme law of the visual arts" and that "whatever these arts may include must give way completely if not compatible with beauty, and, if compatible, must at least be subordinate to it" (15). Regarding the Laocoön, Lessing maintains that the artist "strove to attain the highest beauty possible under the given condition of physical pain" (17). Thus, while Winckelmann reads the visage of the figure as a perfect representation of the nobility of the Greek soul, Lessing attributes the pose to an aesthetic decision: "The demands of beauty could not be reconciled with his pain in all its disfiguring violence, so it had to be reduced. The scream had to be softened to a sigh, not because screaming betrays an ignoble soul, but because it distorts the features in a disgusting manner" (17).

Lessing makes some important generic distinctions in this essay, which first appeared in 1766, two years before Winckelmann's death. He claims, for example, that Laocoön's expression is determined by the fact that it is represented in one of the visual arts and is, therefore, constrained by the aesthetic laws that govern it. When he turns his attention to poetry, Lessing argues that the concern with physical beauty or perfection that we see in the Laocoön statue would be misplaced in narrative or verse. What Lessing calls the "external form" can, he argues,

> at best be only one of the least significant means by which he is able to awaken our interest in his characters. Often he ignores it entirely, being convinced that once his hero has won our favor his other qualities will either occupy us to such a point that we do not think of his physical form or, if we do think of it, we will be so captivated that we give him of our own accord if not a beautiful form, at least an ordinary one. (23)

As an example, Lessing cites Virgil's depiction of Laocoön in the *Aeneid*, pointing out that although the Roman poet's Laocoön does cry out in pain, his character is not diminished in the eyes of the reader because "we already know and love him as a prudent patriot and loving father" (24).

In reading *Death in Venice*, however, we are never quite as convinced of our main character's character as readers of Virgil are of Laocoön's. Moreover, and perhaps more importantly, we sense through the narrator's trenchant irony that even Aschenbach himself has doubts about the character that underlies the image he has created. In a troubling and foreboding passage following Aschenbach's initial sighting of Tadzio, the narrator informs us that in the nature of the artist "is inborn . . . an indulgent and treacherous tendency to accept injustice when it produces beauty and to respond with complicity and even admiration when the aristocrats of this world get preferential treatment" (22). Indeed, the feeling from the beginning of the novella is, as many critics have pointed out, portentous, and we sense somehow that there is more to the disciplined and controlled Aschenbach than meets the eye. The narrator's early reflections on Aschenbach's artistic "rebirth" and his increased "rigor" and "discipline" (at least prior to leaving for Venice) prepare us for the impending difficulties. Musing about the new, formally classical bent of Aschenbach's work, the narrator wonders, provocatively, whether the idea of form itself might not be Janus-faced, at once moral and amoral, "moral insofar as form is the product of expression of discipline, but amoral and indeed immoral insofar as it harbors within itself by nature a certain moral indifference and indeed is essentially bent on forcing the moral realm to stoop under its proud and absolute scepter" (11).

The relationship between form and morality, or more generally between aesthetics and morality, is apparently a more complicated one for our narrator, for Aschenbach, and for the contemporary reader than it was for eighteenth-century interpreters of the Greeks, or for Dante for that matter. These latter critics generally maintained that a beautiful form bespeaks a noble nature and would concur with Dante's definition of allegory as truth cloaked in a beautiful lie or fiction. Thus, Beatrice's incomparable beauty in Dante's *The New Life* fittingly conceals a beatific soul; the challenge for Dante is not to justify his belief in what Beatrice represents but rather to figure out how best to express that belief in words. As an artist, Dante wants to participate in what Beatrice represents. In *Death in Venice,* however, the prevailing ironic mood of the narrative constantly reminds us that the beautiful fiction on the surface or literal level might actually belie a rather ignoble, amoral, or even immoral nature. In contrast to Dante, Aschenbach's biggest challenge in this twentieth-century story is to convince himself that there might in fact be some connection between formal beauty and spiritual or moral nobility and that he, as an artist, can benefit from this connection.

It is not surprising, then, that Aschenbach refers to and reminds us of figures such as Schiller, Winckelmann, and Lessing, because these are the figures who believed what Aschenbach wants to signify. By borrowing the rhetoric of these critics for his characterization of Tadzio, Aschenbach hopes to characterize *himself* in a way that comports with the public image he has so carefully cultivated. He is the artist who, in his own words, sculpts images of spiritual beauty from the mass of language, who wants to recognize Tadzio's form as the manifestation of a noble and naïve spirit, and who embraces the classical stance—or at least what has been interpreted as the classical stance—that beauty is "the sensitive man's way to the spirit" (39).[19]

---

19. Here, Aschenbach draws from Plato's *Phaedrus.*

Aschenbach's choice of a sculptural metaphor is meant to anchor his characterization of both Tadzio and himself and to reinforce the idea that beauty of form can represent an unwavering nobility of character. Aschenbach senses that a relationship with Tadzio, seen through to its logical conclusion in the context of this narrative, will not have a particularly beautiful ending, and so he works as an artist to forestall that ending by invoking the plastic arts. As Lessing claims, the painter and sculptor must "never present an action at its climax" because the climax, once depicted, leaves nothing more to the imagination (19). Regarding Laocoön, Lessing contends that if he sighs, "the imagination can hear him cry out; but if he cries out, it can neither go one step higher nor one step lower than this representation without seeing him in a more tolerable and hence less interesting condition. One either hears him merely moaning or else sees him dead" (20). Aschenbach wants to avoid rendering himself in either of these two states, and thus seeks that moment of pregnant equilibrium that the master of Laocoön managed to depict.

In this context, *Death in Venice* would have a more aesthetically fitting ending were it to reach its climax and its conclusion at the end of the third chapter. Here, we see Aschenbach posed, literally, in such a way that reminds us of Laocoön's calm and dignified manner of meeting his supreme challenge. For Aschenbach, however, the threat does not manifest itself in an encounter with serpents, but rather in the possibility of a physical encounter with Tadzio:

> He sat quite still, quite unseen in his elevated location and looked into himself. His features were active; his brows rose; an alert, curious, witty smile crossed his lips. Then he raised his head and with both his arms, which were hanging limp over the arms of his chair, he made a slow circling and lifting movement that turned his palms forward, as if to signify an opening and extending of his embrace. It was a gesture of readiness, of welcome, and of relaxed acceptance. (34)

At this point, Aschenbach has not yet abandoned self-criticism, and he seems acutely aware of the image he presents as he looks at himself and the pose he strikes from his observer's vantage point. He portrays himself as active, alert, curious, and still in control as he readies himself—with a feeling of both joy and pain in his soul—for the inevitable encounter with Tadzio. Like Winckelmann's interpretation of the Laocoön sculpture, Aschenbach seems to want to convey a sense of calm resignation here and to cast himself in the role of the Trojan hero who, Winckelmann attests, clearly suffers, but does so in a dignified and noble manner: "his pain touches our very souls, but we wish that we could bear misery like this great man" (35).

In keeping with the pervasive ironic mode of *Death in Venice*, however, the story continues forward, forcing Aschenbach down from his pedestal. Ultimately, the passage of narrative time erodes Aschenbach's classical facade and moves him and the reader toward an inexorable and decidedly unaesthetic climax.[20] In the fifth chapter, Aschenbach's pose of relaxed acceptance becomes active lechery as he abandons his reason in favor of his senses. Following a disturbing dream in which Aschenbach sees himself merging with the figure of Dionysus, the protagonist begins a downward moral spiral that is mirrored by his physical decline.[21] Quickly, Aschenbach's once active features and solid brow become haggard and wan, giving him the modern, emaciated, and unhealthy look that Winckelmann laments in his essay. Finding his own image suddenly disgusting in comparison to that of Tadzio, Aschenbach increases his visits to a barber who not only colors his hair but also applies various cosmetics to give the impression of vibrancy and health to our degenerating protagonist. This made-up but sickly Aschenbach stands in stark contrast to the image we had at the end of chapter 3, but he can maintain even this weak and pathetic pose only briefly. Indeed, we will shortly have our last view of Aschenbach, one that has him collapsed and dying beside his beach chair, his features slack and sunken. This is the climax we were never meant, at least from Aschenbach's perspective, to see.

Stepping back and looking at *Death in Venice* as a whole, the problem for our protagonist can be read as an interesting rhetorical one. On one level, Aschenbach functions as a successful allegory; that is to say, he appears as a figure that points to, but never exactly coincides with, an aesthetic correlative that is anterior to his own existence. In this regard, the character of Aschenbach is a highly suggestive rhetorical figure, one that clearly refers—in my particular reading—to something beyond a single, autonomous individual and to a particular aesthetic philosophy. At least in his own mind, Aschenbach has transformed his encounter with a boy into a narrative in which he (Aschenbach) represents an eighteenth-century aesthetic ideal and the boy

20. We should note again that Tadzio's continued presence in some ways undoes Aschenbach. Like Dante, Aschenbach undertakes a poetic project of transforming his desire into some kind of aesthetic allegory. But Beatrice's death allows for "Dante," as Robert Pogue Harrison claims, to bring his "subject to rest in aesthetic stasis. [In death] Beatrice no longer initiates desire but placates it" (44). This possibility never presents itself to Aschenbach, who must always deal with a living and continually tempting Tadzio.

21. The figure of Dionysus reminds us of the centrality of Nietzsche both to Mann's protagonist and to his work as a whole. While I have been arguing for an eighteenth-century aesthetic correlative, I would be remiss not to note that Nietzsche looms as a nineteenth-century aesthetic correlative. In fact, the work that Nietzsche did on classical art—particularly in his *Birth of Tragedy*—seems to be one of the impediments to Aschenbach's successful construction of his intended allegory. Dionysus constantly threatens the Apollonian image that Aschenbach wants to proffer.

represents the object of aesthetic contemplation. Ironically, however, it is precisely this allegorical aspect of Aschenbach, and particularly his inability to coincide with the figures to which he refers, that leads to his downfall. He has created a flawed allegory of himself—an ironic allegory in which there is ultimately no correspondence between the beautiful lie on the outside and the truth on the inside.

Aschenbach ultimately fails because the story he tries to tell himself—his attempt, in other words, to transform his obsession with Tadzio into a palatable figural narrative—diverges markedly from the narrative that the reader of Mann's text receives. In her "The Second Author of *Death in Venice*," Dorrit Cohn notes that "the relationship of the narrator to his protagonist . . . may be described as one of increasing distance. In the early phases of the story it is essentially sympathetic, respectful, even reverent; in the later phases a deepening rift develops, building an increasingly ironic narratorial stance" (180). While this distance and the irony it engenders do not lead to Aschenbach's fall (that seems to be his own doing), they do facilitate our ability to know (of) it and to interpret it. The importance of the narrator to our exegetical effort is obvious: without the narrator we would have no story; we would not even know of that page and a half of magnificent prose, much less of its sordid origins.[22] Yet as Cohn points out, the distance that increasingly characterizes the relationship between narrator and protagonist proves to be just as crucial to our understanding of the text. The cracks in this relationship allow for irony to seep in and to undermine the aesthetic foundation that Aschenbach is trying to lay (in not wanting to appear as though he wants to "lay" Tadzio). Aschenbach's allegory is ironized and therefore undercut by the moralizing narrator; this is not something that Dante—as a first-person narrator—had to face.[23]

All of this leaves unresolved, of course, the question of the implied author in *Death in Venice*, a question that does not trouble us in regard to

22. In an interesting article devoted to that page and a half of prose, Scott Consigny argues that we should interpret the passage in which we learn of its production ironically. We should read it "as a distorted and self-deceptive act" rather than as the one point in Aschenbach's artistic life where he successfully reconciles his passion and his craft.

23. Cohn goes on to argue that the narrator himself becomes ironized, and that at the end we are left with the sense that "the author behind the work is communicating a message that escapes the narrator he placed within the work" (145, emphasis in original). She never fully explains, however, what that message is. Whether Mann's narrator is wholly reliable or not is, in one sense, irrelevant. We do not need him to be infallible or infallibly objective to see that Aschenbach's allegorical endeavor is a farce. If the narrator does not speak for Mann and if he is, as Cohn suggests, limited by irony, then we might have more sympathy for the pathetic Aschenbach, but we are no more likely to believe in his allegory. The narrator would have to be completely unreliable to alter drastically our interpretations of Aschenbach, and that does not seem to be the case.

The New Life, where Dante, the author, both speaks for himself and has the authority to *stop narrating* when he feels as though he has lost control of his story. Mann has placed Aschenbach—himself an author—at two removes from real authorial control (author → narrator → character) to convey his powerlessness over the unfolding narrative that becomes the culmination of his own life. Aschenbach cannot control what happens to him, how he responds, or—significantly—whether anyone ever hears the story of what does transpire in Venice. That such powerlessness and lack of control stand in stark contrast to the manner in which he has tried to construct his life up to this point only exacerbates the prevailing irony of this short novel. Mann wants us to recognize the potential for humiliation when forces beyond our control—whether those forces be our emotions, our sexuality, other people, or society more generally—make it impossible to construct our own narratives, or allegories, out of whatever fabric we have at hand. Aschenbach is, in some ways, a pitiful character at the end, but he is not one for whom we have no sympathy, and I believe that that is as Mann intended it.

The Presence of Allegory

Barth Revisited

AS I recognized in the introduction, not all instances of allegory serve as clear-cut examples of the categories that I have devised. I do not see the potential uncertainty that this entails as a threat to my schema. My theory gives us the concepts and the vocabulary necessary to talk productively about some of these challenging cases in ways that we would not otherwise be able to do. Indeed, without the ideas that I have put forward, we might well encounter narrative texts whose allegorical nature or aspect we completely, but wrongly, overlook simply because we would have lacked the critical tools—the concepts and vocabulary—necessary to address or even recognize it. John Barth's short story "Click" will serve as an example of one such work.

I am tempted to call Barth's work a postmodern treatment of allegory, a treatment that is playful, allusive, and ultimately difficult to define. It is a hybrid case that contains an embedded allegory in the service of a strong thematic allegory. Ultimately, Barth transforms the phenomenon of narration itself into a figural narrative for the rhetorical purpose of promoting a particular view of the self. Barth accomplishes this transformation by constructing three intersecting levels of allegory—the first about a couple called Fred and Irma, the first second about a couple called Mark and Val, and the third about the author–reader relations enacted in the telling of the first two. Each of these levels is foregrounded at particular points in the narrative, and each helps to facilitate the transmission of Barth's dominant theme.

The Theme

In this case, it will help us to start with the main thematic claim that Barth wants to put forward, and then to see how his deployment of several types of allegory helps him to convey and illustrate that theme. The point toward which Barth works throughout his story is this: that the "self" is what he calls a "center of narrative gravity," an entity, in other words,

> that, in order to function in and not be overwhelmed by the chaotically instreaming flood of sense-data, continuously notices, ignores, associates, distinguishes, categorizes, prioritizes, hypothesizes, and selectively remembers and forgets; that continuously spins trial scenarios, telling itself stories about who it is and what it's up to, who others are and what they're up to, that finally *is,* if it is anything, those continuously revised, continuously edited stories. (259)

Barth has adopted a position regarding the nature of the self similar to that espoused by a number of contemporary intellectuals from different academic disciplines, including Jerome Bruner, Oliver Sacks, and some within the field of literary studies: that the idea of the human self is best understood through the concept of narrative; we are the stories we tell about ourselves. Barth is not a cognitive psychologist like Jerome Bruner, or a neuroscientist like Oliver Sacks, or even (primarily) a literary theorist; he is a writer of fiction, so his way of conveying his message differs significantly from that of these other thinkers. Barth seeks to make his case about the importance of narrative through that very medium, and, as we shall see, he makes extensive use of allegory in its various manifestations in order to do so.

Embedded Allegory

"Click" is a story with a complex narrative structure (the story in some ways represents the effort to mimic hypertext fiction on the printed page), and this complicates efforts to summarize it effectively or efficiently.[1] Fittingly, the form of the narrative reflects its content: the story begins as a representation of what Barth calls E-fiction, created by a figure called CNG ("Center of Narrative Gravity") and located at the fictional Web site http://www.epiphs.

---

1. For those readers who want the full impact of Barth's story, I have reprinted it as an appendix.

art. This site, we are told, is the "homepage of an anonymous oddball (Net-named 'CNG') who offered a shifting menu of what he/she called 'electronic epiphanies,' or 'e-piphs.'" (240). "Click" opens with two characters—"Fred" and "Irma"—perusing the Web offerings of CNG.[2] Fred and Irma find their way to this site because, as they go to the computer to check e-mail messages, the imperative "Click" is the only item displayed on their monitor. Obediently, they do as bidden and are directed to one of CNG's e-piphs, titled *The Hypertextuality of Everyday Life*. The underscoring indicates that one may click on any of those words and follow the links wherever they lead; it is, in other words, an example of hypertext, albeit an inoperative one for the reader of "Click." The menu of scenarios on the Web site purportedly changes, but Barth's narration, determined as it is by its more traditional medium, focuses on *The Hypertextuality of Everyday Life*, under which we find the second-level link "Fred and Irma *Go Shopping*," a link that takes us into what is a dependent embedded allegory.

The story of Fred and Irma is a figural narrative whose rhetorical purpose is to convince its readers of the veracity of the epiphanic metaphorical expression "The hypertextuality of everyday life." Fred and Irma, it turns out, are a fictionalized version of a couple named Mark and Val whom CNG, who is also the narrator of the short story we are reading, had observed the day before he posted "Fred and Irma *Go Shopping*" on his e-piphs Web site.

Mark and Val are a romantically involved and cohabitating couple who get into an argument during a weekend visit to Baltimore's Inner Harbor. Ostensibly, the narrator of "Click" witnessed the climactic scene of their argument near the *USS Constellation*, which was, at one time, moored in the harbor. Mark and Val's argument stems from a disagreement concerning their visit to the harbor's attractions. They spend a considerable amount of

---

2. Fred and Irma appear in slightly altered form in an essay—"Ad Lib Libraries and the Coastline Measurement Problem: A Reminiscence"—that Barth published several years before "Click" first appeared in the *Atlantic Monthly*. In the essay, Fred and Irma were married but are now estranged. Irma functions as an example of a narrative conundrum: how much detail should a narrator spend on any given incident or character? "How long does it take Irma to answer the telephone, once she hears it ring?" Barth asks rhetorically. "In real life," he answers for us, "anywhere from a few seconds up to maybe half a minute, if the caller persists and the answering machine doesn't intervene; in narrated life, however, whether factual or fictional, the answer depends on the author's verbal/narrative waypoints" (241). Barth finds an analogy for this narrative problem in cartography, pointing out that different measurements of the same coastline can vary greatly depending on how much detail the one doing the measuring wants to include: "Measuring 'as the crow flies' gives us a rough-and-ready though not very realistic lower limit; but as soon as that crow . . . begins to deviate from its course to follow the contours of reality, the coast of Portugal or the shoreline of the Chesapeake is as long as you want it to be. . . ." (240–41). Along with Irma, this coastline-measurement "problem" makes its way into "Click" as one of CNG's electronic epiphanies.

time doing various shopping errands (hence the main action [shopping] of the embedded Fred and Irma story) on their way, and once they reach their destination they are left facing the prospect of a long line and just a short time to visit the aquarium, which had been the focus of their plans. As they continue to hem and haw about what to do, Mark gets increasingly upset for at least three reasons, the first proximate, the second underlying, and the third unrevealed. As the narrator describes it,

> The problem, in Mark's ever-warmer opinion, was—rather, the problems were—that (a) this constant sidetracking, this what's-the-rush digression, can take the edge off the main event by the time one gets to it, the way some restaurants lay on so many introductory courses and side dishes that one has no appetite for the entrée, or the way foreplay can sometimes be so protracted that (etc.). Having no timetable or deadlines doesn't mean having no agenda or priorities, wouldn't she agree? And (b) it wasn't as if this were just something that happened to happen today, or he'd have no grounds to grouse; it was the way certain people went at *everything*, from leaving for work in the morning to telling an anecdote.... (247)

Val, however, interrupts Mark in mid-rant; as the narrator explains: "he never reached (c) *(click on it if you're curious)*, because by this time V was giving as good as she got..." (247). In short, Val accuses Mark of erring too far in the opposite extreme—calling him "a bullheaded whambamthankyouma'amer of a Taurus whose idea of foreplay was three minutes of heavyweight humping to ejaculation instead of two" (248)—and, essentially, of being so focused on a specific goal that he loses the ability to see or do anything not directly related to the achievement of that goal. This quality is especially troubling in Mark's case because he is an aspiring, but as yet unsuccessful, novelist; his stories, Val contends, have no middles (257). Thus, we see the nature of the disagreement, one that essentially boils down to two different, and at times seemingly incompatible, ways of being in the world. Everyday life, then, is hypertextual in the sense that one must choose how to maneuver through the Web: go straight to the desired location, or allow oneself to explore to whatever extent one prefers the "links" that are perhaps related to one's goal, or perhaps not. This insight regarding Mark and Val lies at the heart of "Click," for it serves as the source of the narrator's epiphany—which he will convert to an "e-piph," which takes the form of the dependent embedded allegory in which Fred-the-expeditor and Irma-the-enhancer represent Mark and Val and their respective ways of being in the world.

As Barth transforms Mark and Val into Fred and Irma within an allegory about the suitability of the concept of hypertext to characterize "everyday life," he reifies the vehicle (hypertextuality) of that metaphor by feigning the use of hypertext as the medium through which to transmit the allegory. Barth's reification of the vehicle is a characteristic effort to have his cake and eat it too: on the one hand, he takes an abstract concept (the hypertextuality of everyday life) and gives it a concrete representation in the formal features of his text, while, on the other hand, his use of print rather than digital hypertext underlines his ultimate interest in the metaphorical dimension of this concept (it is not hypertext itself but the hypertextuality of everyday life that he is thematizing). Unlike Orwell's *Animal Farm*, for example, a narrative that takes real historical phenomena and transforms them into figures that convey abstract concepts, Barth has taken an abstract concept and transformed it into a narrative that makes that concept real (because it is represented through hypertext) and, at the same time, figural.

In the context of his larger narrative (the story "Click"), this embedded allegory about Fred and Irma serves three primary functions. On the most basic level, as I have already mentioned, it stands as evidence in support of the veracity of the metaphor "the hypertextuality of everyday life." Beyond this, the embedded allegory also opens the door for Barth to discourse on the process and the rationale for allegorizing the Mark and Val experience, which pushes the story into the realm of thematic allegory; this discussion both depends on and subsumes the embedded allegory. Finally, the embedded allegory allows Barth to introduce another *figure* into his narrative and, in doing so, to draw readers' attention to the relationship between author and narrator. This figure is the purported author of the embedded allegory and the proprietor of the Web site that purportedly hosts that narrative: that "anonymous oddball" CNG. Ultimately, Barth will need this figure, as we will see below, to help him make his central claim about the self-as-narrator, and this explains why he (Barth) needs an embedded allegory that reifies the concept of hypertextuality. The embedded allegory in this case has little hermeneutic potential in its own right, even as it does illustrate an important concept; rather, it performs the crucial narrative task of providing Barth with a believable—that is, realistic—way of talking about narrating and about narrators in an age in which hypertext is a reality.

Thematic Allegory

We can safely say, then, that the embedded allegory in "Click" does not exhaust the allegorical potential of this story; Barth, I suspect, has more ambitious aims when it comes to the figural aspect of his narrative. Thus, while he has constructed a clever, self-reflexive story, one that his own narrator opposes to "proper" (i.e., conventional) stories (253), it becomes quite clear by the end that Barth does not intend this work only to display his formal innovativeness. Rather, the story's conclusion foregrounds issues of meaning and significance to such an extent that the reader cannot help but see the formal qualities of the work as part of a vehicle rather than as self-sufficient ends. The central question that emerges over the last third of the story is "so what?" (258): what, in other words, is the point, the value, of narrating this story? Indeed, the literal level of this story entails primarily the "set-to" between Mark and Val, and the value—or lack of value—of narrating or even thinking about this rather pedestrian argument is an issue addressed directly by the narrator, and by Mark himself as he reflects on what has happened between him and Val: "If this were fiction (the wannabe writer asked himself), a made-up story, why should anyone give a damn?" (253).

This question has two levels of significance for Mark. On one hand, it results from his attempts to put his argument with Val into some kind of global perspective. The future of his relationship is in doubt, at least at this moment, but "*So what?* He has asked himself before any of us can ask him. The world comprises approximately 4.7 zillion more mattersome matters, from saving the tropical rainforests to finding money enough in the chaotic post-Soviet Russian economy to bring their fiscally stranded cosmonauts back to earth. Not that love and loss, or commitment and (potential) estrangement, aren't serious even among Volvo-driving yuppies, but really, what of real consequence is at stake here?" (252–53). The second level of significance for Mark emerges out of his interest, as a "wannabe" writer, in storytelling. If the argument he has just had with Val were to have happened to two literary characters, why should the reader care, and what might he or she ultimately take from that episode? How, in other words, does one give meaning to such a seemingly mundane incident?

While Mark never arrives at his own answers, Barth's CNG clearly sees the argument between Mark and Val as the key in transforming his metaphor (the hypertextuality of everyday life) into the embedded allegory featuring Fred and Irma. The argument and the events that lead up to it may not ultimately be particularly meaningful on the surface level—as Mark intuits—but as the raw material for a narrative (characters and incidents) they offer great promise as the means for transforming that metaphor into something that conveys meaning, in this case an allegory. Thus, the narrator of "Click" makes it abundantly clear to the reader that the Mark and Val story has a level of significance that transcends the apparent insignificance of its literal existence; it is not just a fight between two random people, it is a means to allegorize and thereby to invite the audience to realize and to participate in the significance of "the hypertextuality of everyday life."

But Barth does not stop here. After working to convince readers that the episode that occurs between Mark and Val has meaning that transcends that particular incident, he seeks to extend that point to the realm of narration more generally:

> ... as to the aforedemonstrated essential difference between Ms. Valerie's sensibility and Mr. Mark's, it is nowhere more manifest than in the way each, in the other's opinion, tells a story. "Anna train squish" is how Val claims Mark would render Leo Tolstoy's *Anna Karenina*; indeed, given the man's Middle-challengedness, she suspects he might skip the train. She, on the other hand (claims he, whether teasingly or in their Sunday Set-To mode), would never get beyond Count Tolstoy's famous opening sentence—"Happy families are all alike," etc.—indeed, would never get through, much less past it, inasmuch as she would need to pause to explore such counter-evidence as that her family and Mark's, for example, while both prevailingly quite "happy," are as different in nearly every other respect as aardvarks and zebras; and once having clicked on Mark's family, or equally on hers (or, for that matter, on aardvarks or zebras), she would most likely never get *back* to Tolstoy's proposition, not to mention on to its second half and the eight-part novel therebeyond.
>
> • Myself, I'm on both their sides in this matter, not only because M and V seem equally reasonable, decent, harmless souls, but also because their tendencies represent contrary narrative impulses of equal validity and importance. A satisfyingly told story requires enough "Valerie"—that is, enough detail, amplification, and analysis—to give it clarity, texture, solidity, verisimilitude, and empathetic effect. It requires equally enough "Mark"—i.e., efficiently directed forward motion, "profluence," on-with-the-storyness—for coherence, anti-tedium, and dramatic effect. In successful instances, a right balance is found for the purpose (and adjusted for alternative purposes). (257–58)

Thus, a figural rendering of the trouble between Mark and Val becomes a lesson in creative writing. And this is why Barth needs to have the embedded allegory in which Mark becomes Fred-the-expediter and Val becomes Irma-the-enhancer. Barth is not aiming exclusively for a realistic representation of the intricacies of Mark and Val's relationship problems and how their respective dispositions contribute to them. He also wants to tell a story about telling the story of Mark and Val, and to convince us that this is a worthwhile enterprise.

Barth's approach to thematic allegory is procedural rather than conceptual; he focuses, in other words, on how one tells a story that has significance beyond or other than its literal meaning and not on the kinds of ontological questions (can allegory exist in the modern world?) that Roth and Collins have made central to their respective works. As a result, Barth's embedded allegory functions in an important way as the "workshopping" (to borrow a pedagogical term from the discipline of Creative Writing) of the theme that plays out in the Mark–Val relationship. Given this dynamic, it is not surprising that "Click" moves back and forth between the embedded allegory and its "real world" antecedent, foregrounding now one, now the other, and using each to comment on or underscore some point relating to the other. The interplay between the dependent embedded allegory (Fred and Irma) and the larger thematic issues that emerge in the telling of the Mark and Val saga serves as a good example of the "amorphous borders" that might obtain in contemporary or postmodern fiction that makes use of allegory.

The procedural nature of Barth's approach to allegory also allows for the enhancement of the thematic allegory with an ongoing discussion about hermeneutics, and in particular about the levels of interpretation that critics beginning with Dante (especially in the *Banquet*) have argued characterize the allegorical process. According to Dante, an allegorical work might make four levels of significance available to a good reader: the literal, the allegorical, the moral, and the anagogic. Barth, who is well read in the medieval period (references in his work to Dante, Boccaccio, Scheherazade, etc. abound), makes use of all of these: on the literal level, the story of Mark and Val is simply the story of a frustrating day-trip; it is then refashioned as an allegory (the Fred–Irma story); and it is later ascribed moral significance (in the form of a "lesson" on narrative fiction) as Barth reflects on and thereby thematizes the allegory.

Strong Allegory

Beyond the moral level, according to Dante, lies the anagogic or spiritual level of allegorical significance, and Barth extends the meaning of his work to this level as well, a move that propels Barth toward his major claim about the self as a center of narrative gravity. Why, the narrator asks, should the reader not interested in the strategy of successful narration care that a good story requires the right proportions of both Mark and Val, so to speak? Having explained the connection between the enhancer (Val)–expediter (Mark) dichotomy and the challenge of telling stories, the narrator offers another "hot link" (*So What*), that we readers ostensibly can choose or not, a link that will take us to the anagogical level of the allegory.

> So what? you ask, unless one happens to take some professional interest in storytelling, which you for one do not? Thanks for clicking on that Frequently Asked Question, reply CNG and I: The "so what" is that that same right-balance-for-the purpose finding applies to the measurement of coastlines, the appropriate scaling of maps, and—hold that clicker—not only interpersonal relations, Q.E.D., but *intra*personal ones as well.
> Intrapersonal relations?
> Thanks again, and yes indeed. For what is Valerie, finally, what is Mark, what are you, and what am I—in short, what is the self itself—if not what has been aptly called a "posited center of narrative gravity" . . . . (258–59)

At this stage, the reader of "Click" recognizes that Barth has used Mark, Val, and their argument as the textual elements for the narrative transformation of his epiphany about the hypertextuality of everyday life. The larger narrative—the one we are reading—then becomes a narrative whose main theme is the decoding of the significance buried within that allegorized epiphany.

The form of Barth's story allows the author to guide the reader through the process of arriving at the same multilayered allegorical epiphany that his narrator experiences and narrates. Ultimately, we see that it is a rhetorical exchange between author and reader—mediated of course by the text—that produces this allegorical epiphany. In short, the author–reader exchange that occurs as the story progresses enacts the relation between Expediter and Enhancer that occupies the thematic center of the story. Even if the form of Barth's story is not typical, or not "proper," what it appears to reveal about the transmission of the allegorical effect does, I think, accurately reflect the nature of typical allegorical narratives.

Furthermore, the fact that "Click" reaches its climax at what Dante considers the apex of the allegorical enterprise (the anagogic level) might well justify the claim that the story itself is a strong allegory whose purpose is to make the argument that calling the self a center of narrative gravity is a valid way to conceive of human nature, the argument toward which the embedded allegory and the thematic allegory have been working. Barth takes a very different route toward strong allegory than does either Orwell or Jackson, but he seems to end up in a similar spot. The strength of Barth's allegory depends as much on the layering of allegorical elements (Fred–Irma, Mark–Val, and author–reader) to guide the audience to the successive levels of figuration (expediter v. enhancer; hypertextuality of everyday life; self as collection of stories) as it does on figuration itself. This highly self-conscious and transparent approach to constructing a strong allegory would be in keeping with a general postmodern literary ethos.

Given that Barth seems to be weaving together a medieval conception of the allegorical process with a postmodern literary style, the end of the story is fitting as it represents the successful outcome, the lesson learned, so common in medieval and Renaissance allegory. The final lines of *Everyman*, for example, leave the audience with a pithy summary of the play's primary message, a message delivered by the respected and learned theologian:

> And he that hath his account whole and sound,
> High in heaven he shall be crowned,
> Unto which place God bring us all thither,
> That we may live body and soul togither.

The dénouement of "Click" does not share in the religious spirituality of *Everyman* but it does echo the theme of unification that the morality play emphasizes. Barth's conclusion contrives to have Mark and Val put their argument behind them, profess their love for each other, and "recouple" (259) in an act of lovemaking that brings the story to a conclusion that works for them on a personal level but that also works on the allegorical level, as the narrator/CNG "encourages them from the hyperspatial wings": "*Not too fast there, Mark. Not too slow there, Val. That's got it, guys; that's got it . . .*" (260). This recoupling represents the (at least temporary) reconciliation of Mark and Val while it also figuratively represents success in achieving the right balance between the "enhancer" and the "expediter" that Val and Mark have come to represent, respectively. This balance allows Barth's narrator to bring his own narrative to a successful conclusion, and in so doing it allows the reader of the print narrative to recognize narrative itself as the prime exemplar of the hypertextuality of everyday life, the place wherein one always has the possibility of striking the perfect balance and "writing" a pleasing self.

In what is an interesting twist for a supposedly postmodern story and a postmodern writer, the author plays a very prominent role in coaching or conducting both his characters (*Not too fast . . . not too slow . . . that's it . . .*) and his readers (*So what, you ask . . .*) toward resolution and significance; this fact reinforces my sense that the very old-fashioned idea of allegory and the host of hermeneutic issues that it carries with it lie at the heart of this most current and cutting-edge narrative. Marjorie Worthington has argued that "instead of challenging the primacy of authorship, Barth's metafictional experiments serve to cement the author into a position of authority over the text" (114). Worthington does not claim that the term "author" in her construction means the real John Barth, but asserts rather that it refers to "the narrator who is ostensibly also the author of the text he narrates" (116), a dynamic that applies equally well to *Lost in the Funhouse*—the focus of Worthington's essay—and to "Click." In both of these cases, the narrator plays the role of an author (and this is crucial for the allegories in "Click"), which draws attention to the important questions of authorial intent and narrative control, questions that are central to the concept of allegory that I have put forth in this book. I still maintain that we need to recognize a distinction between the implied Barth and his narrator, even if that narrator is also an author, because it is the implied Barth who has placed that figure in his story-world so that he, the narrator, is also a component of the narrative shaped in the service of the implied author's rhetorical purpose. Nevertheless, the composition of that figure as an authorial voice makes a significant contribution to the allegoricalness of the text.

Looking at "Click" through the lens of allegory as I have defined it allows us to understand why the author figure remains such a critical player in Barth's fiction. That fiction is often about conveying and finding meaning in figures, and that, at its heart, is the stuff of allegory. "So what?" Barth asks. What, in other words, is the point of fiction? What's the use of telling stories, of making things and people up? The answer that "Click" invites us to extrapolate from its figuration is the same one that we can give—and that has been given for centuries—to defend allegory: fictional narrative can carry important messages about both everyday life and life beyond its everyday concerns from authors who are worth listening to. Barth just reminds us how strangely fun and surprising the process of finding those messages can be.

Conclusion

MY PRIMARY aim in this book has been to offer a new conception of a very old literary and rhetorical concept. In so doing, I hope that I have encouraged my readers to rethink allegory from the perspective of their own reading experience. During the course of the many discussions that I have had with friends, family, and colleagues about the nature of my research, one thing has struck me repeatedly—once they know what I am trying to do, almost everyone can come up with a good example, often one with which I am completely unfamiliar, that fits well within at least one of my main categories of allegory—strong, weak, dependent, independent, interdependent, thematic, or ironic. This heartens me, as it indicates that the terms and concepts that I have introduced here might have relevance beyond the set of texts that I have used to illustrate them.

As opposed to producing the definitive treatise on allegory, my intention has been to provide a framework and a vocabulary to use when a reader encounters a narrative text that seems purposively figural or a text that has allegorical elements that need to be explained. I hope, therefore, that what I have presented has some practical value as readers confront allegorical texts. In addition to its heuristic value, I hope that readers of this book will find themselves better equipped to answer some of those difficult conceptual questions—some of which have dogged allegory forever—that I posed in my introductory chapter. I will use this concluding chapter as a venue for reflecting back on what I've done in the preceding pages and tackling these questions head-on.

Can a text still be an allegory if the author did not have a particular phenomenon or purpose in mind when he or she composed the work?

Some theorists of allegory would answer yes, definitively. Those, for example, who believe that readers ultimately determine whether a narrative is allegorical or not would not concern themselves much with this issue of authorial intention. But even E. D. Hirsch, a critic who built the early part of his career around the issue of authorial intention, would answer this question affirmatively. In a 1994 essay from *New Literary History,* Hirsch argues that writers, in many cases, want their work to "apply across time," and so that work "typically intends to convey meaning beyond its immediate occasion into a future context which is very different from that of its production" ("Transhistorical" 552). Thus, Hirsch can make the case that "original intentions are not, as a matter of empirical fact, limited to original meanings" because authors often "*intend* their writings to have meanings that go unforeseeably beyond their original, literal contents" (555, emphasis in original).[1] If Hirsch is correct, then a writer can intend for his or her work to be an allegory of something, but that something does not need to be predetermined.

From my rhetorical perspective, I would argue that Hirsch might be right about this, but the end result would more than likely tend toward weak rather than strong allegory. Indeed, the kind of allegorical intentions that Hirsch imagines here would almost certainly produce the kind of figural indeterminacy that evokes allegory without a commitment to some specific phenomenon or purpose. A reader would likely pick up on the author's allegorical intentions, but the allegorical effect would be dampened by the lack of specificity. The feedback loop of interpretation would provide resistance to a strong allegorical reading. As Hirsch postulates, though, the possibility certainly exists that an author would have a strong intention to write a work that would be read as a weak allegory, as I tried to show was the case with Kafka.

In a hypothetical situation in which the author had no allegorical intentions at all but some reader or readers of that text interpret the work allegorically, we would find ourselves in a similar situation. We might demonstrate

---

1. Hirsch's line of thinking here comes out of a later turn in his work where he attempts to grapple with the issue of the effect of the passage of time on textual meaning. In addition to the essay on transhistorical intentions cited here, readers might be interested in his "Meaning and Significance Reinterpreted." In "Meaning as Concept and Extension: Some Problems," James Battersby and James Phelan take issue with Hirsch's revisions to his earlier claims about meaning and significance, arguing that the direction Hirsch takes in his later work—including this essay on allegory—muddles the helpful distinction he made earlier between these two concepts.

that the narrative can support a weak allegorical interpretation, but strong allegory would, again, be very unlikely. If an author did not intend for his or her readers to arrive at such an interpretation, then the textual elements would almost assuredly not fit together as coherently as they do in a work such as *Animal Farm* or "The Lottery."

Does a reader have to know the phenomenon that is to be transformed prior to reading the narrative in order to "get" allegory?

No.

In many respects, the process of allegorical interpretation takes us back to the apparent paradox of the hermeneutical circle. That paradox, as Friedrich Ast describes it, arises from the presumption that "the particular can be understood only through the whole, and conversely, the whole, only through the particular" and that "the perception or concept precedes cognition of the particular, even though perception and concept seem to develop only through these" (45). Ast formulates the problem of the hermeneutical circle (or the problem of understanding more generally) as an interpersonal one, as something that describes the relationship between two beings—an author and a reader—separated by time. This formulation places him in the company of other theorists who, according to David Couzens Hoy, conceive of understanding as "a process of psychological reconstruction. The object of understanding is the original meaning of a text handed down to the present from a past that is no longer immediately accessible. Reconstruction—which can take place only when there is a bridge between past and present, between text and interpreter—is psychological when this bridge consists of a relation between two persons: the author and the reader" (11).

Although Ast uses terminology that gives the interpretive process a more metaphysical feeling than I would prefer to do, Ast's resolution of the apparent paradox comes close to the view of reading that I am promoting here. "In the explication of a work or of a particular part," Ast asserts,

> the idea of the whole is not generated by the combination of all its individual parts, but is rather evoked in the person who is capable of comprehending the idea in the first place with the comprehension of the first particular, and becomes ever clearer and livelier, the further the explication of the particular progresses. The first comprehension of the idea of the whole through the particular is conjecture, i.e., as yet still indefinite and undeveloped foreknowledge of the spirit, which turns into vivid and clear cogni-

tion through growing comprehension of the particular. Upon exploration of the sphere of the particular, the idea, which was still conjecture at the point of first comprehension, emerges now as a clear and conscious unity of the manifold presented in the individual. Understanding and explication are now complete. (46)

A rhetorical approach to narrative—and to allegory specifically—is largely consonant with this view of understanding insofar as it presumes that an author intends to convey something to a reader; there is an important communicative function to the literary act. The question is: how does the reader reach an understanding of the author's intended meaning?

The idea of "narrative as rhetoric" rests on the premise that readers make judgments about texts—and revise those judgments—as the narrative unfolds temporally. In *Narrative as Rhetoric* James Phelan puts forward a view of narrative that "focuses on the text as an invitation to an experience that is dynamic in at least two ways. First, the experience is crucially influenced by the movement of the narrative through time. Second, the experience is multilayered, one that engages a reader's intellect, emotions, judgments, and ethics simultaneously" (90). Phelan employs the term "progression" to capture the dynamic nature of a reader's experience with narrative. "Progression," he explains, "refers to the way in which a narrative establishes its own logic of forward movement . . . and it refers to the way that movement carries with it invitations to different kinds of responses in the reader . . ." (90). In allegorical texts, the forward movement of the narrative will generally serve to invite some very specific responses from the reader; collectively these responses will result in a recognition on the part of the reader that the author has figural and transformative intentions.

"Click," the story by John Barth that I discussed in the previous chapter, provides an excellent example of the progressive nature of the allegorical experience. In this story, Barth's narrator walks the reader through the dynamic process that Phelan has identified. As the discourse moves forward through time, characters and events become thickened with thematic importance. A reader's initial inklings of allegorical potential are corroborated by the positive feedback of textual phenomena and the interjections of Barth's narrator. The *dénouement* of this narrative depends less on a plot revelation or resolution than it does on the final unfolding of the story's allegorical significance.

When we move out of the realm of strong or weak allegories, then the question of whether a reader has to know the phenomenon or rhetorical purpose that is to be transformed becomes largely meaningless because, as we consider dependent, independent, interdependent, thematic, or ironic allegory, we should no longer think of the narrative as a unified transformation. The text is no longer an allegory *of something;* instead, it includes allegory or the idea of allegory as a textual element or a theme.

Does allegory depend on "elite" readers?

I offer a qualified "yes." But by "elite" readers I simply mean good readers, those who are attentive, generally well informed, and willing to play according to conventional literary rules. (And this is the same answer that rhetorical theorists would give for any literary genre.) In *Before Reading* Peter J. Rabinowitz claims that "Every literary theoretician these days needs a governing metaphor about texts" (37); for his, Rabinowitz takes the idea of the unassembled swing set, and this metaphor can help explain what the kind of reader I refer to here as "elite" needs to be able to do. The swing set, Rabinowitz explains, is

> a concrete thing that, when completed, offers opportunities (more or less restricted depending on the particular swing set involved) for free play, but you have to assemble it first. It comes with rudimentary directions, but you have to know what directions *are,* as well as how to perform basic tasks. It comes with its own materials, but you must have certain tools of your own at hand. Most important, the instructions are virtually meaningless unless you know, beforehand, what sort of object you are aiming at. If you have never seen a swing set before, your chances of riding on the trapeze without cracking open your head are slight. (38)

As I argued in the chapter devoted to strong allegory, authors of allegorical works generally intend them for a sophisticated audience, an audience that does have the tools and the prior experience required to assemble the metaphorical swing set. This "authorial audience" stands in contrast to, and in some ways above, the "narrative audience," a far more credulous and less astute group of readers.

In the realm of allegory in narrative or allegories of narrative (as opposed to allegories as narrative), the need for something like an ideal reader is just as pronounced. Coetzee's *Elizabeth Costello,* for example, almost demands a reader with some knowledge of Kafka, or at least a willingness to learn something about Kafka. Without this, an individual reader cannot hope to participate in Coetzee's authorial audience. This audience-related shortcoming does not change the author's intention, nor does it vitiate the allegorical aspect of the narrative, but it does change the experience of reading that narrative for a reader or a group of readers.

I hope that this book has raised more questions about allegory than I could possibly answer in this short conclusion; indeed, if we do ever reach the point where all of the questions have been answered, then we might truly be able to say that allegory has died. I doubt that that will be the case, however, because, as with many other literary genres or devices, authors will certainly continue to find new ways of manipulating allegory and incorporating it into their narratives. As I have shown, the term "allegory" can effectively describe a class of works that achieves an author's rhetorical purpose through the transformation of some phenomenon into a figural narrative. As long as we readers are willing to recognize the myriad ways that this transformation can happen, and as long as we recognize that this transformation can happen in a number of different contexts, then I believe that we will see critical work on this concept that matches the creativity with which authors continue to employ it.

Appendix

CLICK

❖

"CLICK?"

So reads their computer monitor when, in time, "Fred" and "Irma" haul themselves out of bed, wash up a bit, slip back into their undies, and—still nuzzling, patting, chuckling, sighing— go to check their e-mail on Fred's already booted-up machine. Just that single uppercase imperative verb or sound-noun floating mid-screen, where normally the "desktop" would appear with its icons of their several files: HERS, HIS, SYSTEM, APPLICATIONS, FINANCES, HOUSE STUFF, INTERNET, ETC (their catch-all file). Surprised Irma, having pressed a key to disperse the screen-saver program and repeated aloud the word that oddly then appeared, calls Fred over to check it out, but the house cybercoach is as puzzled thereby as she. Since the thing's onscreen, however, and framed moreover in a bordered box, they take it to be a command or an invitation—anyhow an option button, like SAVE or CANCEL, not merely the name of the sound that their computer mouse makes when . . . well, when clicked.

So they click (Irm does) on CLICK, and up comes a familiar title, or in this case maybe subtitle—<u>The Hypertextuality of Everyday Life</u>—followed this time by a parenthesized and italicized instruction: *(Click on any word of the above).*

"Your turn," declares our Irma. That's not the woman's real

name, any more than the man's is Fred; those are their "online" names, in a manner of speaking, for reasons presently to be made clear. Never mind, just now, their "real" names: They would involve us in too much background, personal history, all the stuff that real names import; we would never get on with the story. Sufficient to say that although these two are unmarried, they're coupled housemates of some years' standing, a pair of Baby-Boomer TINKs (Two Incomes, No Kids) of some ethnicity or other, not necessarily the same, and profession ditto—but never mind those, either. Sufficient to say that what they've just rolled out of the sack from (one of them perhaps more reluctantly than the other) is an extended session of makeup sex after an extended lovers' quarrel, the most serious of their coupleship: a quarrel currently truced but by no means yet resolved and maybe inherently unresolvable, although they're really working on it, fingers crossed.

A bit of background here, perhaps? That's Fred's uncharacteristic suggestion, to which Irma, uncharacteristically, forces herself to reply "Nope: Your turn is your turn. On with the story."

And so her friend—partner, mate, whatever—reaches from behind her to the mouse and, kissing her (glossy auburn) hair, clicks on Hypertextuality. (This parenthesized matter, they agree, is stuff that might be left out of or cut from The Fred and Irma Story—see below—but that they've agreed to put or leave in, at least for the present.) (In the opinion of one of them, there could be much more of it.) (In the opinion of the other, much less—but never mind.)

No surprise, Fred's selection: Hypertextuality is that (sub)title's obvious topic word, modified by the innocuous-seeming article before it and the homely prepositional phrase after (containing its own unexotic substantive [Life] with adjectival modifier [Everyday]). The man of them, one infers correctly, is the sort who gets right down to business, to the meat of the matter. Everybody knows, after all (or believes that he/she knows), what "everyday life" is, different as may be the everyday lives of Kuwaiti oil sheiks and of American felons serving life sentences in maximum-security prisons without possibility of parole (different, for that matter, as may be the everyday lives of FWFs [Friends Who Fornicate] when they're at their separate businesses). The term "hypertextuality" itself may or may not interest our Fred; he's computer-knowledgeable, but not computer-addicted. The phrase "everyday life," however, most certainly doesn't, in itself. The fellow's too busy *leading* (perhaps being led by?) his everyday life to be attracted to it as a subject. With the woman it's another story (possibly to come). But precisely because he hasn't associated something as fancy-sounding as "hypertextuality" with something as ordinary as "everyday life," the juxtaposition of the two piques Fred's curiosity. Not impossibly, for the man's no ignoramus (nor is his companion), he hears in it an echo of Sigmund Freud's provocatively titled 1904 essay *The Psychopathology of Everyday Life*. Everyday life psychopathological? (Try asking Irma, Fred.) (He will—another time.) Everyday life hypertextual? How so? In what sense? To find out, Fred has clicked on the implied proposition's most prominent but least certain term.

There are those (the computer script now declares in effect, along with most of the paragraph above) who out of mere orneriness will select one of the phrase's apparently insignificant elements—the The, for example, or the of—as if to say, "Gotcha! You said 'Click on any word....'" The joke, however, if any, is on them: A good desk dictionary will list at least eight several senses of the homely word "the" in its adjectival function plus a ninth in its adverbial ("the sooner the better," etc.): twenty lines of fine-print definition in all, whereas the comparatively technical term just after it, "theanthropic," is nailed down in a mere three and a half. As for "of": no fewer than nineteen several definitions, in twenty-five lines of text, whereas the fancy word "oeuvre," just before it, is dispatched in a line and a half. Try "as," Fred, as in "As for 'of'"; try "for," Irm, or "or": The "simple" words you'll find hardest to define, while such technoglossy ones as "hypertextuality" . . .

Well. F and friend have just been shown an example of it, no? The further texts that lie behind any presenting text. Look up (that is, click on) the innocent word "of," and you get a couple hundred words of explanation. Click on any one of those or any one of their several phrases and clauses, such as "phrases and clauses," and get hundreds more. Click on any of *those*, etc. etc.—until, given time and clicks enough, you will have "accessed" virtually the sum of language, the entire expressible world. That's hypertext, guys, in the sense meant here (there are other senses; see Hypertext): not the literal menus-of-menus and texts-behind-texts that one finds on CD-ROMs and other computer applications, but rather the all-but-infinite array of potential explanations, illustrations, associations, glosses and exempla, even stories, that may be said to lie not only behind any verbal formulation but behind any real-world image, scene, action, interaction. Enough said?

(If so, click EXIT; otherwise select any one of the four foregoing—image, scene, etc.—for further amplification.)

Restless Fred moves to click on action but defers to Irma (their joint mood is, as mentioned, still tentative just now; he's being more deferential than is his wont), who clicks on scene and sees what the Author/Narrator sees as he pens this: a (white adult male right) hand moving a (black MontBlanc Meisterstück 146 fountain) pen (left to right) across the (blue) lines of (three-ring looseleaf) paper in a (battered old) binder on a (large wooden former grade-school) worktable all but covered with the implements and detritus of the writer's trade. (Parenthesized elements in this case = amplifications that might indeed be cut but might instead well be "hypertexted" behind the bare-bones description, to be accessed on demand, just as yet further amplifications [not given, but perhaps hypertexted] might lie behind "white" "adult male," "MontBlanc" "Meisterstück," etc.) For example, to mention only some of the more conspicuous items: miscellaneous printed and manuscript pages, (thermal) coffee mug (of a certain design) on (cork) coaster, (annotated) desk calendar (displaying MAY), notebooks and notepads, the aforeconsulted (*American Heritage*) desk dictionary open to the "the" page (1333) on its (intricately hand-carved Indian) table-stand, (Panasonic auto-stop electric) pencil sharpener (in need of emptying), (Sunbeam digital) clock (reading 9:47 A.M.), (AT&T 5500 cordless) telephone (in place on base unit), Kleenex box (Scott tissues, actually) half full (half empty?) . . . et cetera. Beyond the table one sees the workroom's farther wall: two (curtained and venetian-blinded double-hung) windows, between them a (three-shelf) bookcase (not quite filled with books, framed photos, and knickknacks and) topped by a wall mirror. The mirror (left of center) gives back a view not of the viewer—fortunately, or we'd never get out of the loop and on with the story—but of the workroom door (presently closed against interruption) in the wall behind. (The two windows are closed, their figured curtains tied back, their blinds raised. Through them one sees first the green tops of foundation shrubbery [from which Irm infers, correctly, that it's a ground-floor room], then assorted trees [L] and a sward of lawn [R] in the middle distance, beyond which lies a substantial body of water, currently gray. Two wooded points of land can be seen extending into this waterway from the right-hand window's right-hand side, the first perhaps half a mile distant, an uncamouflaged gooseblind at its outboard end, the second perhaps a mile distant and all but obscured now by a light drizzle that also blurs the yet-more-distant horizontal where [gray] water meets [gray] sky.)

(Click on any of these items, including those in brackets.)

But "Enough already," says nudgy Fred, and commandeers the mouse to click <u>action</u>, whereupon some of the leaves on some of those trees move slightly in some breeze from some direction, the water-surface ripples, and across it a large waterfowl flaps languidly left to right, just clearing some sort of orange marker-float out there on his/her way . . . upstream, one reasonably supposes, given that the stretch beyond that bird and those two points seems open water.

"That's action?" Fred scoffs, and moves to click again, but determined Irma stays his mouse-hand with her free right

(Irm's a southpaw) while she registers yet a few further details. Atop that bookcase, for example (and therefore doubled in the mirror), are (L to R:) a (ceramic-based) lamp, the carapace of a (medium-size horseshoe) crab, and a (Lucite-box-framed) photograph of three (well-dressed) people (L to R: an elderly man, a middle-aged man, and a younger woman) in (animated) conversation (at some sort of social function).

(Click on any detail, parenthesized or non-, in this scene.)

Irma springs for well-dressed—not nearly specific enough, by her lights, as a description of three people "at some sort of social function" in the photograph on the bookcase in the not-yet-fully-identified scene on their computer's video display terminal. With a really quite commendable effort of will, "Fred" restrains his impulse to utter some exasperated imprecation and snatch the freaking mouse from his freaking partner to freaking click Fast Freaking Forward, On with the Story, EXIT, QUIT, Whatever. Instead, he busses again his lover's (glossy) (auburn) hair, bids her "Have fun; I'll be futzing around outside, okay?," and (having slipped into jeans and T-shirt) clicks with his feet, so to speak, on the scene beyond his own workroom window.

Which twilit scene happens to be a small suburban back yard near the edge of the nation's troubled capital city, where this occasionally dysfunctional pair pursue their separate occupations: Mark the Expediter, as he has lately come to call himself; Valerie the Enhancer, ditto. Those are their "real" given names, if not really the real names of their jobs, and with the reader's permission (because all these digressions, suspensions, parentheses, and brackets are setting this Narrator's teeth on edge as well as Mark's) we'll just follow him out there for a bit while Val explores to her still-bruised heart's content the hypertextuality of everyday life.

Okay. How they got into that "Fred and Irma" business (Mark and I can reconstruct less distractedly now as he waves to a neighbor-lady and idly deadheads a few finished rhododendron blooms along their open side-porch) was as follows: They having pretty well burned out, through this late-May Sunday, their scorching quarrel of the day before—enough anyhow to make and eat together a weary but entirely civil dinner—after cleanup Mark had volunteered to show Valerie, as he had several times previously promised, some things he'd lately learned about accessing the Internet for purposes other than e-mail; more specifically, about navigating the World Wide Web, and in particular (Valerie being Valerie, Mark Mark) about the deployment of "bookmarks" as shortcuts through that electronic labyrinth, the black hole of leisure and very antidote to spare time. Mark is, as aforenoted, no computer freak; the PC in his Expediter's office, their Macintosh at home, are tools, not toys, more versatile than fax machine and phone but more time-expensive, too, and—like dictionaries, encyclopedias, and hardware stores (this last in Mark's case; substitute department stores and supermarkets in Val's)—easier to get into than out of. Tactfully, tactfully (by his lights, anyhow) (the only lights he can finally steer by)—for they really were and are still burned, and their armistice is as fragile as it is heartfelt—he led her through the flashy homepage of their Internet service provider's program, actually encouraging her to sidetrack here and there in the What's New? and What's Cool? departments (she trying just as determinedly to blind her peripheral vision, as it were, and walk straight down the aisles, as it were, of those enticing menus) and then sampling a curious Web site that he had "bookmarked" two days earlier, before their disastrous Saturday excursion to the National Aquarium in Baltimore.

http://www.epiphs.art, it was addressed: the homepage of an anonymous oddball (Net-named "CNG") who offered a shifting menu of what he/she called "electronic epiphanies," or "e-piphs." On the Friday, that menu had comprised three entrées: (1) Infinite Regression v. All-but-Interminable Digression, (2) "Flower in the Crannied Wall," and (3) The Hypertextuality of Everyday Life. Mark had clicked on the curious-sounding second option and downloaded a spiel that at first interested but soon bored him, having to do with the relation between a short poem by Tennyson—

> Flower in the crannied wall,
> I pluck you out of your crannies,
> I hold you here, root and all, in my hand,
> Little flower—but *if* I could understand
> What you are, root and all, and all in all,
> I should know what God and man is.

—and the virtually endless reticulations of the World Wide Web. This time (that is, on this post-meridianal, post-prandial, post-quarrel but ante-makeup-sexual Sunday) the menu read (1) The Coastline Measurement Problem and the Web, (2) "The Marquise went out at five" (CNG seemed to favor quotations as second entries; this one was familiar to neither of our characters), and (3) The Hypertextuality of Everyday Life. That third item being the only carryover, M suggested they see what was what. V clicked on it—the entire title, as no option was then offered to select from among its component terms—and they found themselves involved in a bit of interactive "e-fiction" called "Fred and Irma Go Shopping," of which I'll make the same short work that they did:

Onscreen, the underlined items were "hot": i.e., highlighted as hypertext links to be clicked on as the interacting reader chose. Methodical Mark would have started with Fred and worked his way L to R, but Valerie, left-handing the mouse, went straight for Irma:

> Irma V., 43, art-school graduate, divorced, no children, currently employed as enhancer by small but thriving graphics firm in Annapolis MD while preparing show of her own computer-inspired fractal art for small but well-regarded gallery in Baltimore. Commutes to work from modest but comfortable and well-appointed rowhouse in latter city's Bolton Hill neighborhood, 2 doors up from her latest lover, Fred M.

(more on Irma) (on with story)

"My turn?" Mark had asked at this point, and clicked on Fred M. before Valerie could choose from among divorced, no children, enhancer, latest, well-appointed rowhouse, and more.

Fred M., software expediter and current lover of Irma V.

(more on Fred) (on with story)

"That's the ticket," in Mark's opinion: "Who cares how old the stud is or where he majored in what? On with their story already."

"My friend the Expediter," Val had murmured warningly, having raised her free hand at his "Who cares?" Whereat her friend the Expediter (it was from here that they borrowed those job-titles for themselves: Valerie in fact does interior design and decoration for a suburban D.C. housing developer; Mark, a not-yet-successful novelist, does capsule texts on everything under the sun for a CD-ROM operation in College Park, distilling masses of info into style-free paragraphs of a couple hundred words), duly warned, had replied, "Sorry there: Enhance, enhance."

But she had humored him by clicking on on, whereupon the title reappeared with only its last term now highlighted: "Fred and Irma Go Shopping."

"Off we go," had invited M. But when the clicked link called up a three-option menu—Department Store, Supermarket, Other—V said "Uh-oh," and even Mark had recognized the too-perilous analogy to their debacle of the day before. Expediter and Enhancer in Supermarket, he with grocery list in one hand, pencil in other, and eye on watch, she already examining the (unlisted) radicchio and improvising new menu plans down the line. . . .

"Unh-unh," he had agreed, and kissed her mouse-hand, then her mouth, then her throat. By unspoken agreement, bedward they'd headed, leaving the Mac to its screen-saver program (tropical fish, with bubbly sound effects). Somewhere later

Valerie/Irma, re-undied, had returned to check for e-mail; the marine fauna dispersed into cyberspace; there floated CLICK in place of CNG's unpursued interactive e-tale—and here we all are.

Rather, here's Valerie at Mark's workstation in their (detached suburban) house (V's studio is across the hall; unlike those FWFs Irma and Fred, our couple are committed [though unsanctified and unlegalized] life-partners, each with half equity in their jointly owned [commodious, well-appointed, 1960s-vintage] split-level in Silver Spring [MD]), and here are Mark and I out on the dusky porch, deadheading the rhodos while thinking hard and more or less in synch about certain similarities among (1) the sore subject of their Saturday set-to, (2) a certain aspect of their recent makeup sex, (3) the so-called Coastline Measurement Problem afore-optioned by CNG, (4) an analogous problem or aspect of storytelling, and (5) how it is, after all, to be a Self, not on the World Wide Web but in the wide web of the world. Can M think hard about five things at once? He can, more or less expeditiously, when his attention's engaged, plus (6) Zeno's famous paradox of Achilles and the Tortoise, plus (7) the difference between Socrates's trances and the Buddha's. Our chap is nothing if not efficient—a phrase worth pondering—and I'm enhancing his efficiency as worst I can, by impeding it. Valerie, meanwhile (at my offscreen prodding), has reluctantly torn her attention away from that photograph on that bookshelf in that creekside workroom in that onscreen scene hypertexted behind the word "scene" in the definition hypertexted behind <u>Hypertextuality</u> in CNG's menu-option (3) <u>The Hypertextuality of Everyday Life</u>, itself hypertexted the second time up behind the word CLICK. Twenty-year-old wedding-reception photo, she has learned it is, of (present) Narrator with (present) wife and (late) father at (post-)wedding do for (now-divorced) daughter and (then-) new son-in-law—and nothing accessible therebeyond. Interactivity is one thing, restless Reader; prying's another. Having lingered briefly on the <u>shrub</u> outside the <u>RH window</u> (*Vibur-*

num burkwoodii: grows to 6 ft [but here cropped to 4 for the sake of view and ventilation], clusters 3 in. wide, blooms in spring, zone 4, and it's a lucky wonder her professional eye didn't fix on those figured curtains, or we'd never have gotten her outside) and then on that waterfowl (great blue heron [*Ardea herodias,* not *coerulea*]) flapping languidly up-creek (off Chesapeake Bay, on Maryland's Eastern Shore, where Narrator pens these words as he has penned many others), she's "progressing" unhurriedly toward those two intriguing points of land in the farther distance but can't resist clicking en route on that orange marker-float out yonder near the creek channel:

> Marks an eel pot, 1 of 50 deployed in this particular tidal creek at this particular season by waterman Travis Pritchett of nearby Rock Hall MD in pursuit, so to speak, of "elvers": young eels born thousands of miles hence in the Sargasso Sea and now thronging instinctively back to the very same freshwater tributaries of the Chesapeake from which their parents migrated several years earlier to spawn them in mid-ocean: one of nature's most mysterious and powerful reproductive phenomena. Pritchett's catch will be processed locally for marketing either as seafood in Europe and Japan or as crab bait for Chesapeake watermen later in the season.

Travel-loving Val goes for Sargasso Sea, and there we'll leave her to circulate indefinitely with the spawning eels and other denizens of the sargassum while we click on item (1) some distance above: the sore subject of their Saturday set-to:

They love and cherish each other, this pair. Although neither is a physical knockout, each regards the other and her- or himself as satisfactorily attractive in face and form. Although neither can be called outstanding in his or her profession, both are entirely competent, and neither is particularly career-ambitious in her or his salaried job. Both enjoy their work and take an interest in their partner's. Most important, perhaps, although neither has a history of successful long-term relations with significant others, both have enough experience, insight, and un-arrogance to have smoothed their rougher edges, tempered their temperaments, developed their reciprocal forbearance, and in general recognized that at their ages and stages neither is likely to do better than they've currently done in the mate-finding way; indeed, that despite their <u>sundry differences</u> (at least some of which they've learned to regard as compensations for each other's shortcomings: See below), they are fortunately well matched in disposition, taste, and values. Neither drinks more than an occasional glass of wine at dinner, or smokes tobacco, or sleeps around, or fancies house-pets; both are borderline vegetarian, environmentally concerned, morally serious but unsanctimonious secular unenthusiastic Democrats. Mark has perhaps the quicker intelligence, the duller sensibility, the more various knowledge; Valerie perhaps the deeper understanding, the readier human insight, the sounder education. They've never quarreled over sex or money. Both wish they had children, but neither finally wants them. (<u>Etc.</u>—though that's really enough <u>background</u> for <u>their Saturday set-to</u>, no?)

They do have differences, of course: M enjoys socializing with others more than V does; she enjoys traveling more than he. He's the more liberal (or less frugal) with money; she's the more generous in the good-works way. He's less ready to take offense but also slower to put their occasional tiffs behind him. She leaves closet and cabinet doors ajar and will not learn how to load their dishwasher properly (by *his* standards) (and the user's manual's); he wears his socks and underwear for two days before changing (turning his briefs inside out the second day!) and often makes no effort to stifle his burps and farts when it's just the two of them. (Etc., although [etc.]) These lapses or anyhow disharmonies they've learned to live with, by and large. The difference that really drives each up her or his wall is the one herein amply hinted at already, if scarcely yet demonstrated: at its mildest, a tease- or sigh-provoker, a prompter of rolled eyes and of fingertips drummed on dashboard, chair arm, desk- or thigh-top; at its sorest...

Saturday. Their week's official work done and essential house-chores attended to, they had planned a drive up to nearby Baltimore to tour that city's Inner Harbor development, which they hadn't done in a while, and in particular the National Aquarium, which they'd never. After a not unreasonable detour to an upscale dry-goods emporium in the vast shopping complex at Four Corners, a quick shot from their house—where Val really did need to check patterns and prices of a certain sort of figured drapery material for a job-in-the-works (and, having done so, pointed out to Mark that there across the mall was a Radio Shack outlet where he could conveniently pick up the whatchacallit-adapter that he, not she, insisted they needed for their sound system's FM antenna [while she popped into the next-door Hallmark place for just a sec to replenish their supply of oddball greeting cards, which was running low])—they zipped from the D.C. Beltway up I-95 to Baltimore and reached Harbor Place in time for a pickup lunch about an hour past noon (no matter, as they'd had a latish breakfast)—hour and a half past noon, more like, since the main parking lots were full by that time, as Mark had fretsomely predicted, and so they had to park (quite) a few blocks away, and it wouldn't've made sense not to take a quick looksee at the new Oriole Park at Camden Yards that was such a hit with baseball fans and civic-architecture buffs alike, inasmuch as there it stood between their parking garage and the harbor and since their objective, after all (she reminded him when he put on his Fidget Face), wasn't to grab a sandwich, see a fish, and bolt for home, but to *tour* Harbor Place, right? Which really meant the city's harbor area, which surely included the erstwhile haunts of Babe Ruth and Edgar Allan Poe. They were on no timetable, for pity's sake!

Agreed, agreed—but he *was* a touch hungry, was Mr. Mark, and therefore maybe a touch off his feed, as it were, especially after that unscheduled and extended stop at Four Corners; and it was to be expected that the ticket line at the Aquarium might well be considerable, the day being both so fine and so advanced. . . .

"So we'll catch the flight-flick at the IMAX theater in the Science Center instead," Val verbally shrugged; "or I'll stand in the Aquarium line while you fetch us something from the food pavilion, and then you stand while I do The Nature Company. What's the problem?"

The problem, in Mark's ever-warmer opinion, was—rather, the problems were—that (a) this constant sidetracking, this what's-the-rush digression, can take the edge off the main event by the time one gets to it, the way some restaurants lay on so many introductory courses and side dishes that one has no appetite for the entrée, or the way foreplay can sometimes be so protracted that (etc.). Having no timetable or deadlines doesn't mean having no agenda or priorities, wouldn't she agree? And (b) it wasn't as if this were just something that happened to happen today, or he'd have no grounds to grouse; it was the way certain people went at *everything*, from leaving for work in the morning to telling an anecdote. How often had he waited in their Volvo wagon to get going in time to drop her off at her Metro stop on the way to his office and finally gone back into the house and found her with one earring and one shoe on, making an impulsive last-minute phone call while simultaneously revising her DO list with one hand and rummaging in her purse with the other? (Valerie is a whiz at cradling the phone between ear and shoulder, a trick Mark can't manage even with one of those gizmos designed for the purpose.) How often had he been obliged to remind her, or to fight the urge to remind her, in mid-narrative in mid–dinner party, that the point of her story-in-regress was their little niece's *response* to what Val's sister's husband's mother had said when the tot had walked in on her in the guest-bath shower stall, not what that widow-lady's new Cuban-American boyfriend (whom she hadn't even met yet at the time of the incident) apparently does for a living? And (c) . . .

But he never reached (c) *(click on it if you're curious)*, because by this time V was giving as good as she got, right there on the promenade under the old USS *Constellation*'s bowsprit, where their progress toward the distant tail of the National Aquarium ticket line caesura'd for this exchange. As for (a), damn it to hell, if in his (wrongheaded) opinion she was a Gemini who preferred appetizers to entrées both at table and (as he had more than once intimated) in bed, then *he* was a bullheaded whambamthankyouma'amer of a Taurus whose idea of foreplay was three minutes of heavyweight humping to ejaculation instead of two; and (b) who, because he himself had his hands full thinking and breathing simultaneously, couldn't imagine anyone's doing five things at once better than he could manage one; for the reason that (c)...

But she never reached (c), for the reason that (b) (now [b1]) reminded her that (b2) *his* idea of a joke was the punchline, his idea of a whodunit the last page, revealing who done it (no wonder he couldn't place his Middle-less novels even with an agent, much less with a publisher); and (a2) if she might presume to back up a bit, now that it occurred to her, his idea of a full agenda was a single item, his top priority always and only the bottom line, his eternal (and infernal) *Let's get on with the story* in fact a *Let's get* done *with the story*, for the reason that— (b3), she guessed, or maybe (a3), who gave a damn?—his idea of living life was the same, *Let's get done with it*, and every time she saw him ready and fidgeting in the car a full ten minutes earlier than he knew as well as she they needed to leave for work, she was tempted to suggest that they drive straight to the funeral parlor instead and *get done with it* (etc., okay? On to the freaking fish already!).

But they never reached the FF ticket line, far less the marine exhibits themselves, and that's a pity, inasmuch as in the 2.5 million recirculating gallons of scrupulously monitored exhibit-water in the National Aquarium's 130-odd tanks and pools are to be found some 10,000 specimens (eels included), concerning every one of which much of natural-historical interest might be said. Under the volatile circumstances, however, it is no doubt as well they didn't, for how could they imaginably have moved and paused harmoniously through the exhibits (Valerie tranced at the very first of them, Mark glancing already to see what's next, and next after that) without re-opening their quarrel? Which quarrel, mind, was still in noisy progress, if that's the right word, there under the *Constellation*'s mighty bowsprit—which bowsprit, at the time I tell of, extended halfway across the promenade from the vessel's prow toward the second-floor Indian restaurant above the first-floor Greek one in Harbor Place's Pratt Street pavilion, but which at the time of this telling is alas no longer there, nor are those restaurants, nor is the formidable frigate-of-war (sister ship of Boston's legendary Old Ironsides) whose bow that bowsprit sprits, or spritted, said vessel having been removed indefinitely for much-needed, long-overdue, and staggeringly expensive major overhaul—to the glancing amusement of passersby (the lovers' spectacular, hang-it-all-out quarrel, I mean, of course, not the *Constellation*'s shifting to some marine-repair Limbo) including Yours Truly, who happened just then to be passing by and sympathetically so saw and heard them, or a couple not unlike them, toe-to-toeing it, and who then or subsequently was inspired to imagine (etc.).

Embarrassed, wasted, desperate, and sore, tearfaced Valerie anon turned her back on the dear, congenitally blinkered bastard whom she so loves and just then despised and stomped off back toward the Light Street food pavilion and their parking garage, no objective in mind except breathing space and weeping room. Mark was damned if he'd go chasing after the beloved, indispensable, impossible, darling bitch, but he did so after all, sort of; anyhow trudged off in the same general direction, but made himself pause—Valerie-like, though in part to spite her—to half attend a juggling act in progress at the promenade's central plaza. Although he was as aware as was V (and no less alarmed) that the heavy artillery just fired could never be unfired and that it had perilously, perhaps mortally, wounded their connection, he nonetheless registered with glum admiration the jugglers' so-skillful routine: their incremental accumulation of difficulties and complications at a pace adroitly timed to maximize dramatic effect without straining audience attention past the point of diminishing returns, a business as tricky in its way as the juggling itself—and now he couldn't refind Valerie among the promenaders. Well, there was The Nature Company yonder; she had mentioned that. And beyond it were the food concessions; she must have been as hungry by then as he, but probably as appetiteless, too, from their wring-out. And somewhere beyond or among those concessions were the public restrooms, whereto she might have retreated to collect herself (V's better than M at self-collection), and beyond them the parking ramp. Did she have her car keys? Probably, in her purse; anyhow there were spares in a magnetic holder under the rear bumper-brace. Would she drive off without him, for spite? He doubted it, although she seemed more hurt and angry than he'd ever known her to be; anyhow the ramp-ticket was in his wallet—not that she mightn't pay the hefty lost-ticket fee just to strand him or, more likely, just to get out of there, with no thought of him either way. Most probably, however, she would just collapse in furious tears in the Volvo's passenger seat, poor sweetheart, and then lay into him with more of her inexcusable even if not wholly off-the-mark insults when he tried to make peace with her, the bitch.

Well, she wasn't in The Nature Company, where among the coruscating geodes and "Save the Rain Forest" stuff his attention was caught by one of those illuminated flat-projection earth-map clocks that show which parts of the planet are currently daylit and which in darkness (the East Coast of North America was just then correctly mid-afternoonish; darkness was racing already across Asia Minor, dawn approaching Kamchatka and Polynesia). What (momentarily) arrested him in this instance was not that vertiginous reminder of on-streaming time and the world's all-at-onceness, but rather the profusion of continental coastlines, necessarily much stylized in so small-scale a rendering, but considerably articulated all the same. Chesapeake Bay, for example—180-some miles in straight-line length, but with upward of 9,600 miles of tidal shoreline in its forty major rivers and their all-but-innumerable creeks and coves—was a simple nick up there between Washington and Philadelphia, yet quite distinguishable in shape and position from Delaware Bay, just above it; even the Delmarva

Peninsula between them, no bigger here than a grain of rice, had overall its characteristic sand-flea shape. Framed nearby, as if to invite speculation on the contrast, was a large-scale, fine-grained aerial-photo map of Baltimore's Inner Harbor, every pier and building sharply resolved, including the no-longer-present-as-I-write-this *Constellation:* One could distinguish not only individual small watercraft paddling about or moored at the harbor bulkheads but their occupants as well, and strollers like varicolored sand-grains on the promenade.

One could not, however (Mark duly reflected, looking now for the exit to the food courts and/or for a glimpse of Valerie's ... yellow blouse, was it? Yes, he was almost certain: her yellow whatchacallit blouse with those thingamajigs on it and either a white skirt or white culottes; he couldn't recall which and saw no sign of either), even with so fine a resolution, distinguish male from female, for example, or black from white from Asian; much less identify himself and Valerie having it out under the frigate's bowsprit if they'd happened to be there doing that at that moment; much less yet see the thingumabobs on her whatchacallits and much less yet the individual whatsits on each thingumabob (etc.)—any more than the most finely drawn map of the Chesapeake could show every barnacle on every pile of every pier on every creeklet (etc.): the famous Coastline Measurement Problem afore-referred-to, in terms whereof the estuary's shore-length could as well be put at 96,000,000 miles as 9,600 (etc.). Which-all led him to, but not yet across, the verge of recognizing...

Yellow blouse? Yes, out there by the Polish-sausage stand, but minus thingumajiggies and blousing a red-faced matron whose steatopygous buttocks were hugely sheathed in pink cotton warm-up pants (though there might, to be sure, he reminded himself, be a truly saintly spirit under all that [maybe helplessly genetic] grossness). *No Middles to his novels,* V had told him! His eye ever on the destination, not the getting there! Already figuring the server's tip while she lingered over the appetizer! No greater evidence of the degree of Pal Val's present pissed-offness than that she had been sidetracked neither in

The Nature Company, as even he had briefly been, nor in the food court (where she would normally have been provisioning the pair of them, bless her, with goodies both for present consumption and for future relishment at home), nor on the pedestrian overpass to the parking ramp, where in other circumstances she was entirely capable of dawdling to contemplate at length the vehicular traffic below, the cumulus formations overhead, the observation elevators up-and-downing the Hyatt Regency façade nearby. Unless she had indeed withdrawn into a women's room (he had forgotten to locate the WCs; couldn't've done anything in that precinct anyhow except dumbly stand by), she must have beelined for the car, as did he now finally too.

No Valerie. Well, she was more liable than he to forgetting the level- and pillar-number of their parking slot. Not impossibly, in her present turbled state, she was wandering the ramps in a weepy rage. Plenty turbled himself, he walked up one level and down one, gave up the search as counterproductive, leaned against the Volvo's tailgate for some minutes, arms crossed, then trudged back, *faute de mieux*, toward the walkway/footbridge/overpass/whatever. Halfway across it he stopped, disconsolate, and simply stood—facing uptown, as it happened, but really seeing nothing beyond his distress.

Which let's consider himwith for just a paragraph. A physically healthy, mentally sound, well-educated, (usually) well-fed, comfortably housed and clothed, gainfully employed, not-unattractive early-fortyish middle-class male WASP American is at least temporarily on the outs with his housemate/girlfriend, a comparably advantaged and not-unattractive professional who has declared her opinion that he hasn't the talent to achieve his heart-of-hearts career aim and that this deficit is of a piece with one general characteristic of his that she finds objectionable. So Mr. Mark's pride is bruised, his self-respect ruffled, the future of his closest and most valued personal relationship uncertain indeed. *So what?* he has asked himself before any of us can ask him. The world comprises approximately 4.7 zillion more mattersome matters, from saving the tropical rain forests to finding money enough in the chaotic post-Soviet Russian economy to bring their fiscally stranded cosmonauts back to earth. Not that love and loss, or commitment and (potential) estrangement, aren't serious even among Volvo-driving yuppies, but really, what of real consequence is at stake here? If this were fiction (the wannabe writer asked himself), a made-up story, why should anyone give a damn?

Well, it *wasn't* fiction, from Mark's perspective, although out of aspirant-professional habit he couldn't help considering (as he resumed his troubled path-retracement back to and through the Light Street pavilion in search of his dear damned Valerie) how, if it were, it ought properly to end. Reconciliation? On what terms? Uneasy armistice? Virtual divorce? In each case, signifying what of interest to a reader who presumes the characters and situation to be imaginary?

From *our* point of view, of course, they *are* imaginary, and so these questions immediately apply (in a proper story they would never have come up; bear in mind that it was heart-hurt Mark who raised them) and shall be duly though not immediately addressed. Even their allegedly Middle-challenged poser understood, however—as he rescanned in vain the food concessions and monitored for a fruitless while the traffic to and from the women's room after availing himself of the men's— that more's at stake here than the ups and downs of early-middle-aged Baby-Boomer love. Not until "tomorrow" (the Sun. following this sore Sat.) will CNG's interactive e-fiction serendipitously supply them the terms "Expediter" and "Enhancer" to shorthand the characterological differences that erupted under the *Constellation*'s awesome bowsprit; but already back there on the footbridge Mark sensed that the conflict here is larger than any temperamental incompatibility between "Fred" and "Irma" or himself and Val: It's between fundamentally opposite views of and modes of dealing with the infinitely complex nature of reality.

Valerie sensed that, too; she was, indeed, already deep into the pondering thereof when, almost simultaneously, she espied him approaching from the second-level fooderies and he her at a railing-side table on the open deck out there overlooking the promenade. So far from roaming the ramps in a weepy blind rage or storming off alone in the Volvo (Val's better than Mark, we remember, at shrugging off their infrequent blowups; he himself tends to forget that and to project from his own distress), our yellow-bloused Enhancer, her chair tipped back and feet propped on balcony rail, was finishing off a chocolate-chocolate-chip frozen-yogurt waffle cone while simultaneously (a) teaching her sumbitch lover a lesson by neither fleeing nor chasing after him; (b) facilitating their reunion by staying put, as her mother had taught her to do in little-girlhood if "lost" in, say, a department store or supermarket; and (c) calming her still-roused adrenaline with a spot of yogurt while keeping an eye out for friend M and at the same time considering, in a preliminary way, his criticisms of her and the differences, as she saw them, between Socrates's famous occasional "trances," the Buddha's, and her own. They had in common, those trances, a self-forgetfulness, a putting of circumambient busyness on hold in favor of extraordinary concentration. But Buddha under the bo tree was transcendently *meditating*, thinking *about* nothing in particular while subsuming his ego-self into the cosmic "Buddha self"; Socrates, tranced in the agora or come upon by his protégés stock-still in some Athenian side street, was strenuously *contemplating*, presumably in finely honed logical terms, such uppercase concepts as Knowledge, Reality, Justice, and Virtue. Herself, however—beguiled indefinitely by ... by the hypertextuality of everyday life, we might as well say, as encountered in the very first fish tank in the National Aquarium, or in the book beside the book up-shelf from the book that she had gone to fetch from the library stacks, or on the counter across from the counter in the department en route to the department that she had been vectored toward in the Wal-Mart next door to the supermarket that she was finally aiming for—was not so much meditating or contemplating as *fascinating:* being bemused and fascinated by the contiguities, complexities, interscalar resonances, and virtually endless multifariousness of the world, while at the same time often doing pretty damned efficiently several things at once.

"*Damn*," said Mark, hands on hips on deck beside her. "Damn and damn."

"The same," came back his unfazed friend. "That said, is it on with our day or on with our spat?"

"Spat!" had all but spat more-than-ever-now-pissed-off M.

"Pity." Val gave her (glossy auburn) hair a toss and licked a drip from her (waffle) cone. "I thought *you* were the big mover-onner and I was the overdweller-on-things. Lick?"

"No, thank you. There's a difference between moving on and hit-and-run driving, Val."

"Shall we discuss that difference?" More a challenge than a cordial invitation.

"No, thank you. Because what happened back there was no accident."

"So let's discuss *that:* its non-accidentality."

"No, thank you very much," the fire gone out of him. "Because there'd be no bloody end to it. Let's go the hell home."

But "Not so fast, buster," had countered Ms. Valerie, and although they did in fact then go the hell home after all, they ventilated reciprocally all the way, each charging the other now with spoiling the day. Through that evening, too, they had kept scarifyingly at it, heartsick Mark from time to time declaring, "What it all comes down to . . . ," and tearful Valerie being damned if she'd let him shortcut to that bottom line before he'd had his nose thoroughly rubbed en route in this, that, and the other. Exhausted half-sleep, as far apart as manageable in their king-size bed; then a grumpy, burned-out Sunday, both parties by that time more saddened and alarmed than angry, each therapeutically pursuing her or his separate business till Happy Hour—which wasn't, but which at least brought them civilly together as was their custom for their (single) glass of wine with a bit of an hors d'oeuvre, over which they exchanged tentative, strained apologies, then apologies less strained and tentative. Through dinner prep, each guardedly conceded a measure of truth in the other's bill of complaints; through dinner itself (with, uncharacteristically, a second glass of wine, much diluted with club soda), a measure less guarded and more generous. Thereafter, by way of goodwill respite from the subject, M had offered to show V that business he'd mentioned sometime earlier about navigating the World Wide Web. She had welcomed the diversion; they had booted up Mark's Macintosh, shortcut to CNG's e-piphanies homepage with its e-tale of Expediter Fred and Enhancer Irma; had aborted it early in favor of makeup sex (etc.)—and here they are.

Mm-hm. And where is that, exactly?

That exactly is in separate rooms of their (jointly owned, jointly tenanted) Silver Spring house and likewise in their extraordinarily strained but by no means severed connection. More exactly yet, it is (a) in Mark's case, on their pleasant, now-dark side porch, where—having thought hard and efficiently about those five or seven interrelated matters aforelisted (Saturday set-to, makeup sex, Coastline Measurement Problem, analogous aspect of storytelling, selfhood in the world's wide web, etc.)—in a sudden access of loving appreciation of his companion and their indispensable differences he turns from his idle rhododendron-tending to hurry herward with the aim of embracing her and ardently reaffirming that she is not only to him indispensable but by him treasured, and that he is determined to temper his maddening get-on-with-itness with as much of her wait-let's-explore-the-associationsness as his nature permits. And (b) in Valerie's case, in Mark's workroom, where—having floated a fascinated while in the Sargasso Sea of everyday life's virtual hypertextuality (but at no time so bemused thereby as to lose sight of the subject of their Saturday set-to)—in a sudden access of loving etc. she bolts up from Mark's Mac to hurry himward with corresponding intent. The physical halfway point thembetween happens to be the fourth-from-bottom step of the staircase connecting their house's ground floor (living room, dining room, kitchen/breakfast room, lavatory, front and rear entry halls, side porch, attached garage) and its second (main bedroom and bath, V's and M's separate workrooms with hallway and #2 bath between, library-loft [accessible from main BR] over garage) (additionally, in basement and thus irrelevant to their projectable rendezvous: TV/guestroom, workshop, utility room). Where they'll actually meet is another matter, perhaps suspendable while Narrator tidies a few loose ends. To wit:

- Any reasonable reader's suspicions to the contrary notwithstanding, "CNG" stands in this context not for Compressed Natural Gas, but rather for Center of Narrative Gravity: in a made-up story, the author's narrative viewpoint; in real life-in-the-world, however, the self itself, of which more presently, unless it's clicked on now. . . .
- Presently, then. Meanwhile, as to the aforedemonstrated essential difference between Ms. Valerie's sensibility and Mr. Mark's, it is nowhere more manifest than in the way each, in the other's opinion, tells a story. "Anna train squish" is how Val claims Mark would render Leo Tolstoy's *Anna Karenina*; indeed, given the man's Middle-challengedness, she suspects he might skip the train. She, on the other hand (claims he, whether teasingly or in their Saturday Set-To mode), would never get beyond Count Tolstoy's famous opening sentence—"Happy families are all alike," etc.—indeed, would never get through, much less past it, inasmuch as she would need to pause to explore such counter-evidence as that her family and Mark's, for example, while both prevailingly quite "happy," are as different in nearly every other respect as aardvarks and zebras; and once having clicked on Mark's family, or equally on hers (or, for that matter, on aardvarks or zebras), she would most likely never get *back* to Tolstoy's proposition, not to mention on to its second half and the eight-part novel therebeyond.
- Myself, I'm on both their sides in this matter, not only because M and V seem equally reasonable, decent, harmless souls, but also because their tendencies represent contrary narrative impulses of equal validity and importance. A sat-

isfyingly told story requires enough "Valerie"—that is, enough detail, amplification, and analysis—to give it clarity, texture, solidity, verisimilitude, and empathetic effect. It requires equally enough "Mark"—i.e., efficiently directed forward motion, "profluence," on-with-the-storyness—for coherence, anti-tedium, and dramatic effect. In successful instances, a right balance is found for the purpose (and adjusted for alternative purposes). In unsuccessful instances . . .

Friend of Valerie and Mark's: So, how'd your vacation go, guys?

M: Cool: Spain in ten days.

V: Really terrific, what little we got to see. The very first morning, for example, in Ávila—Do you know Ávila? Saint Teresa and all that?—we were in a Parador Nacional, just outside the old city wall. You've stayed in the Spanish *paradores*, right? So, anyhow, the one in Ávila's this fifteenth-century palace called Piedras Albas ('cause that's what it's made of, white stones from [etc., *never getting past the breakfast churros, inasmuch as "hypertexted" behind them, for Valerie, lies all of Spanish history, culture, geography, and the rest, inseparable from the rest of Europe's and the world's. Mark had had practically to drag the rapt, protesting woman out of that stern and splendid place, to get on with their itinerary*]) . . .

- So what? you ask, unless one happens to take some professional interest in storytelling, which you, for one, do not? Thanks for clicking on that Frequently Asked Question, reply CNG and I: The "so what" is that that same right-balance-for-the-purpose finding applies to the measurement of coastlines, the appropriate scaling of maps, and— hold that clicker—not only interpersonal relations, Q.E.D., but *intra*personal ones as well.

Intrapersonal relations?
Thanks again, and yes indeed. For what is Valerie, finally,

what is Mark, what are you and what am I—in short, what is the self itself, if not what has been aptly called a "posited center of narrative gravity" that, in order to function in and not be overwhelmed by the chaotically instreaming flood of sense-data, continuously notices, ignores, associates, distinguishes, categorizes, prioritizes, hypothesizes, and selectively remembers and forgets; that continuously spins trial scenarios, telling itself stories about who it is and what it's up to, who others are and what they're up to; that finally *is*, if it is anything, those continuously revised, continuously edited stories. In sum, what we're dealing with here is no trifling or merely academic matter, friends: Finding, maintaining, and forever adjusting from occasion to occasion an appropriate balance between the "Mark" in each of us and the "Valerie" ditto is of the very essence of our selfhood, our being in the world. We warmly therefore hope, do CNG & I (click on that & and see it turn into an =, + much more on intrapersonal relations), that that couple work things out, whenever and wherever they recouple.

When. One short paragraph from now, it will turn out, although given the infinite subdivisibility of time, space, and narrative (not to mention The Hypertextuality of Everyday Life), it could as readily be ten novels hence or never. See Zeno's paradoxes of time and motion; see swift Achilles close forever upon the tortoise; see Spot run. . . .

Where. Not on that fourth-step-from-the-bottom *Mittelpunkt*, it turns out, but back where this story of them started. Mark (inescapably himself even when determined to be more Val-ish) is off the porch and through the dining room and up the staircase and into the upstairs hallway by the time Valerie (who, decidedly herself even after deciding to be more Mark-like, has stepped from M's workroom first into the #2 bathroom to do a thing to her hair or face before hurrying porchward, then into their bedroom to slip a thigh-length T-shirt over her undies in case the neighbor-lady's out there gardening by streetlight, then back into M's workroom to exit the Internet so that their access-meter won't run on while they finish making up, which could take a happy while), hearing him hurrying herward, re-rises from Mark's Macintosh to meet its open-armed owner with open arms.

To her (glossy) (auburn) hair he groans, "I love you so damned much!"

To his (right) collarbone she murmurs, "I love you more."

They then vow (<u>etc.</u>), and one thing sweetly segues to another right there on the workroom's (Berber) wall-to-wall, while the screen saver's <u>tropical fish</u> and <u>seahorses</u> burble soothingly per program themabove.

- *The Marquise Went Out at Five* (*La Marquise Sortit à Cinq Heures*) is the title of a 1961 novel by the French writer Claude Mauriac and a refrain in the Chilean novelist José Donoso's 1984 opus *Casa de Campo* (*A House in the Country*). The line comes from the French poet and critic Paul Valéry, who remarked in effect that he could never write a novel because of the *arbitrariness*, the vertiginous *contingency*, of such a "prosaic" but inescapable opening line as, say, "The Marquise went out at five"—for the rigorous M. Valéry, a paralyzing toe-dip into what might be called the hypertextuality of everyday life.

Not too fast there, Mark. Not too slow there, Val. That's got it, guys; that's got it . . . (so "CNG" [= I/you/eachandallofus] encourages them from the hyperspatial wings, until agile Valerie lifts one [long] [lithe] [cinnamon-tan] leg up and with her [left] [great] toe gives the Mac's master switch a

Works Cited

Abbott, H. Porter. *The Cambridge Introduction to Narrative*. New York: Cambridge University Press, 2002.
Achebe, Chinua. *Things Fall Apart*. New York: Anchor, 1994.
Ahmad, Aijaz. *In Theory: Class, Nations, Literatures*. New York: Verso, 1992.
Alighieri, Dante. *Dante's Convivio* [Banquet]. Trans. William Walrond Jackson. Oxford: Clarendon, 1909.
——. *De Vulgari Eloquentia*. Trans. Steven Botterill. Cambridge Medieval Classics. New York: Cambridge University Press, 1996.
——. *The Divine Comedy*. Trans. John Ciardi. New York: Penguin, 2003.
——. *Vita Nuova* [New Life]. Trans. Dino Cervigni and Edward Vasta. Notre Dame: University of Notre Dame Press, 1995.
Alter, Robert. "One Man's Kafka." *New Republic*, April 2005. 31–35.
Amory, Frederik. "The Classical Style of 'Death in Venice.'" *Modern Language Review* 59 (1964): 399–409.
Ast, Friedrich. "Hermeneutics." Trans. Dora Van Vranken. In *Grundlinien der Grammatik, Hermeneutik und Kritik*. Landshut, 1808. 165–212. Rpt. in *The Hermeneutic Tradition: From Ast to Ricoeur*, eds. Gayle L. Ormiston and Alan D. Schrift. SUNY series Intersections: Philosophy and Critical Theory. Albany: State University of New York Press, 1990. 39–56.
Attridge, Derek. *J. M. Coetzee and the Ethics of Reading: Literature in the Event*. Chicago: University of Chicago Press, 2004.
Barney, Stephen A. *Allegories of History, Allegories of Love*. Hamden, CT: Archon, 1979.
Barth, John. "Ad Lib Libraries and the Coastline Measurement Problem: A Reminiscence." In *Further Fridays: Essays, Lectures, and Other Nonfiction, 1984–1994*. New York: Little, Brown, 1995. 238–53.
——. "Click." In *The Book of Ten Nights and a Night: Eleven Stories*. New York: Houghton Mifflin, 2004. 234–60.

———. *The Floating Opera and The End of the Road.* New York: Anchor, 1988. 255–442.
———. "Lost in the Funhouse." In *Lost in the Funhouse: Fiction for Print, Tape, Live Voice.* Garden City, NY: Doubleday, 1968. 72–97.
———. "Tales Within Tales Within Tales." *Antaeus* 43 (1981): 45–63.
Barthes, Roland. *S/Z.* Trans. Richard Miller. New York: Hill and Wang, 1974.
Battersby, James, and James Phelan. "Meaning as Concept and Extension: Some Problems." *Critical Inquiry* 12 (1986): 605–15.
Beissner, Friedrich. *Der Erzähler Franz Kafka: ein Vortrag.* Stuttgart: W. Kohlhammer, 1959.
Ben-Ephraim, Gavriel. "Making and Breaking Meaning: Deconstruction, Four-Level Allegory and *The Metamorphosis.*" *Midwest Quarterly* 35 (1994): 450–67.
Benjamin, Walter. *Illumination.* Trans. Harry Zohn. New York: Schocken Books, 1968.
———. *The Origin of German Tragic Drama.* Trans. John Osborne. New York: Verso, 1998.
Berek, Peter. "Interpretation, Allegory, and Allegoresis." *College English* 40 (1978): 117–32.
Bitzer, Lloyd. "The Rhetorical Situation." In *Contemporary Theories of Rhetoric: Selected Readings,* ed. Richard L. Johannesen. New York: Harper and Row, 1971. 381–93.
Bloom, Harold. *The Western Canon: The Books and Schools of the Ages.* New York: Riverhead, 1994.
Bloomfield, Morton. "Allegory as Interpretation." *New Literary History* 3 (1972): 301–17.
Booth, Wayne C. *A Rhetoric of Fiction.* 2nd ed. Chicago: University of Chicago Press, 1983.
———. *A Rhetoric of Irony.* Chicago: University of Chicago Press, 1974.
Brinkley, Edward S. "Fear of Form: Thomas Mann's *Death in Venice.*" *Monatshefte* 91 (1999): 2–27.
Bunyan, John. *The Pilgrim's Progress: From this World to That Which is to Come.* Ed. James Blanton Wharey. New York: Oxford University Press, 1960.
Butler, Judith. "Desire." In *Critical Terms for Literary Study.* 2nd ed. Ed. Frank Lentricchia and Thomas McLaughlin. Chicago: University of Chicago Press, 1995. 369–86.
Caserio, Robert L. "'A Pathos of Uncertain Agency': Paul de Man and Narrative." *Journal of Narrative Technique* 20 (1990): 195–209.
Cervo, Nathan. "Jackson's 'The Lottery.'" *Explicator* 50 (1992): 183–85. Retrieved from EBSCOhost database (accessed July 20, 2010).
Chambers, Aiden. "The Reader in the Book." In *Booktalk: Occasional Writing on Literature and Children.* London: Bodley Head, 1985. Rpt. in *Children's Literature: The Development of Criticism,* ed. Peter Hunt. New York: Routledge, 1990. 91–114.
Clarke, Bruce. *Allegories of Writing: The Subject of Metamorphosis.* Albany: State University of New York Press, 1995.
Clifford, Gay. *The Transformations of Allegory.* Boston: Routledge and Kegan Paul, 1974.
Cocks, Neil. "The Implied Reader. Response and Responsibility: Theories of the Implied Reader in Children's Literature Criticism." In *Children's Literature: New Approaches,* ed. Karín Lesnik-Oberstein. New York: Palgrave, 2004. 93–117.
Coetzee, J. M. *Elizabeth Costello.* New York: Viking Penguin, 2003.
———. *Slow Man.* New York: Viking Penguin, 2005.
———. *Stranger Shores: Literary Essays, 1986–1999.* New York: Viking Penguin, 2001.

———. *Waiting for the Barbarians*. New York: Viking Penguin, 1982.
Cohn, Dorrit. *The Distinction of Fiction*. Baltimore: Johns Hopkins University Press, 1999.
Collins, Billy. "The Death of Allegory." In *Sailing Alone Around the Room: New and Selected Poems*. New York: Random House, 2001. 27–28.
———. "The Lesson." In *Sailing Alone Around the Room: New and Selected Poems*. New York: Random House, 2001. 6.
Consigny, Scott. "Aschenbach's 'Page and a Half of Choicest Prose': Mann's Rhetoric of Irony." *Studies in Short Fiction* 14 (1977): 359–67.
Copeland, Rita, and Stephen Melville. "Allegory and Allegoresis, Rhetoric and Hermeneutics." *Exemplaria* 3 (1991): 159–87.
Corngold, Stanley. *The Commentators' Despair: The Interpretation of Kafka's Metamorphosis*. Port Washington, NY: Kennikat, 1973.
Crews, Frederick, C. "Kafka Up Close." *New York Review of Books,* February 10, 2005, 4–7.
Dällenbach, Lucien. *The Mirror in the Text*. Trans. Jeremy Whiteley and Emma Hughes. Chicago: University of Chicago Press, 1989.
de Man, Paul. *Allegories of Reading: Figural Language in Rousseau, Nietzsche, Rilke, and Proust*. New Haven, CT: Yale University Press, 1979.
———. *Blindness and Insight: Essays in the Rhetoric of Contemporary Criticism*. Minneapolis: University of Minnesota Press, 1983.
Dentan, Michel. *Humour et Création Littéraire Dans L'Oeuvre de Kafka*. Paris: Librairie Minard, 1961.
Derrida, Jacques. "Devant la Loi." Trans. Avital Ronell. In *Kafka and the Contemporary Critical Performance: Centenary Readings,* ed. Alan Udoff. Bloomington: Indiana University Press, 1987. 128–49.
Edmundson, Mark. "Against Readings." In *Profession 2009,* ed. Rosemary G. Feal. New York: Modern Language Association of America, 2009. 56–65.
Elder, Arlene. "The Paradoxical Characterization of Okonkwo." In *Approaches to Teaching Achebe's "Things Fall Apart,"* ed. Bernth Lindfors. Approaches to Teaching World Literature 37. New York: Modern Language Association of America, 1991. 58–64.
Eliot, T. S. *Selected Essays*. New York: Harcourt, Brace, 1950.
Else, Gerald. *Aristotle's Poetics: The Argument*. Cambridge, MA: Harvard University Press, 1963.
Emrich, Wilhelm. *Franz Kafka: A Critical Study of His Writings*. Trans. Sheema Zeben Buehne. New York: Fredrick Ungar, 1968.
"*Everyman.*" In *Medieval Drama: An Anthology,* ed. Greg Walker. Malden, MA: Blackwell, 2000. 282–97.
Falk, Eugene. *Types of Thematic Structure: The Nature and Function of Motifs in Gide, Camus, and Sartre*. Chicago: University of Chicago Press, 1967.
Fickert, Kurt. *Kafka's Doubles*. Utah Studies in Literature and Linguistics 15. Las Vegas: Peter Lang, 1979.
Fineman, Joel. "The Structure of Allegorical Desire." In *Allegory and Representation,* ed. Stephen J. Greenblatt. Baltimore: Johns Hopkins University Press, 1981. 26–60.
Fletcher, Angus. *Allegory: The Theory of a Symbolic Mode*. Ithaca, NY: Cornell University Press, 1964.
Flores, Ralph. *A Study of Allegory in Its Historical Context and Relationship to Contemporary Theory*. Lewiston, NY: Edwin Mellon, 1996.

Forster, E. M. *Aspects of the Novel*. New York: Harcourt, Brace, 1927.
Frye, Northrop. *Anatomy of Criticism: Four Essays*. Princeton, NJ: Princeton University Press, 1957.
Gadamer, Hans-Georg. *Truth and Method*. 2nd, rev. ed. Trans. Joel Weinsheimer and Donald G. Marshall. New York: Continuum, 1997.
Genette, Gérard. *Narrative Discourse: An Essay in Method*. Trans. Jane E. Lewin. Ithaca, NY: Cornell University Press, 1980.
Gray, Richard T., Ruth V. Gross, Rolf J. Goebel, and Clayton Koelb. "Allegory." In *A Franz Kafka Encyclopedia*. Westport, CT: Greenwood, 2005. 7–8.
Gray, Ronald. *Franz Kafka*. Cambridge: Cambridge University Press, 1973.
———, ed. *Kafka: A Collection of Critical Essays*. Englewood Cliffs, NJ: Prentice-Hall, 1962.
Greenberg, Martin. *The Terror of Art: Kafka and Modern Literature*. New York: Basic Books, 1968.
Greenfield, Sayre. *The Ends of Allegory*. Newark: University of Delaware Press, 1998.
Hansen, Jim. "Formalism and Its Malcontents: Benjamin and de Man on the Function of Allegory." *New Literary History* 35 (2005): 663–83.
Harlow, Barbara. "'The Tortoise and the Birds': Strategies of Resistance in *Things Fall Apart*." In *Approaches to Teaching Achebe's "Things Fall Apart,"* ed. Bernth Lindfors. Approaches to Teaching World Literature 37. New York: Modern Language Association of America, 1991. 74–79.
Harrison, Robert Pogue. *The Body of Beatrice*. Baltimore: Johns Hopkins University Press, 1988.
Henel, Ingeborg. "The Legend of the Doorkeeper and Its Significance for Kafka's *Trial*." Trans. James Rolleston. In *Twentieth-Century Interpretations of The Trial: A Collection of Critical Essays*, ed. James Rolleston. Englewood Cliffs, NJ: Prentice-Hall, 1976. 40–55.
Hirsch, E. D. Jr. *The Aims of Interpretation*. Chicago: University of Chicago Press, 1976.
———. "Meaning and Significance Reinterpreted." *Critical Inquiry* 11 (1984): 202–25.
———. "Transhistorical Intentions and the Persistence of Allegory." *New Literary History* 25 (1994): 549–67.
———. *Validity in Interpretation*. New Haven, CT: Yale University Press, 1967.
Holman, C. Hugh, and William Harmon. *A Handbook to Literature*. 6th ed. New York: Macmillan, 1992.
Honig, Edwin. *Dark Conceit: The Making of Allegory*. 1959. New York: Oxford University Press, 1966.
Hoy, David Couzens. *The Critical Circle: Literature, History, and Philosophical Hermeneutics*. Berkeley: University of California Press, 1978.
Irr, Caren, and Ian Buchanan, eds. *On Jameson: From Postmodernism to Globalization*. Albany: State University of New York Press, 2006.
Jackson, Shirley. "Biography of a Story." In *Shirley Jackson: A Study of the Short Fiction*, by Joan Wylie Hall. New York: Twayne, 1993. 125–29.
———. "The Lottery." In *The Lottery: or, The Adventures of James Harris*. New York: Farrar, Straus and Company, 1949. 291–302.
Jameson, Fredric. *The Political Unconscious: Narrative as a Socially Symbolic Act*. Ithaca, NY: Cornell University Press, 1981.
———. "Third-World Literature in the Era of Multinational Capitalism." *Social Text* 15 (1986): 65–88.

Jauss, Hans Robert. *Toward an Aesthetic of Reception.* Trans. Timothy Bahti. Minneapolis: University of Minnesota Press, 1982.
Kafka, Franz. *The Metamorphosis, In the Penal Colony, and Other Stories.* Trans. Willa and Edwin Muir. New York: Schocken, 1975.
———. "A Report to an Academy." In *The Metamorphosis, In the Penal Colony, and Other Stories,* trans. Willa and Edwin Muir. New York: Schocken, 1975. 173–84.
———. *The Trial.* Trans. Willa and Edwin Muir. New York: Schocken, 1984.
Kegley, Jacquelyn. "*The End of the Road:* The Death of Individualism." In *Philosophy and Literature,* ed. A. Phillips Griffiths. New York: Cambridge University Press, 1984. 115–34.
Kelley, Alice van Buren. "Von Aschenbach's Phaedrus: Platonic Allusion in 'Death in Venice.'" *Journal of English and Germanic Philology* 75 (1973): 228–40.
Kelley, Theresa. *Reinventing Allegory.* Cambridge Studies in Romanticism. New York: Cambridge University Press, 1997.
Kirchberger, Lida. "'Death in Venice' and the Eighteenth Century." *Monatshefte* 58 (1966): 321–34.
Koelb, Clayton. "Kafka Imagines His Readers: The Rhetoric of 'Josephine die Sängerin' and 'Der Bau.'" In *A Companion to the Works of Franz Kafka,* ed. James Rolleston. New York: Camden House, 2002. 347–59.
———. *Kafka's Rhetoric: The Passion of Reading.* Ithaca, NY: Cornell University Press, 1989.
La Fontaine, Jean de. "The Fox and the Grapes." Trans. James Michie. In *The Norton Anthology of Western Literature.* 2nd ed. Vol. 2. Ed. Sarah Lawall. New York: Norton, 2006. 205.
Lamberton, Robert. *Homer the Theologian: Neoplatonist Allegorical Reading and the Growth of the Epic Tradition.* Berkeley: University of California Press, 1986.
Lanser, Susan S. "(Im)plying the Author." *Narrative* 9 (2001): 153–60.
Lessing, Gotthold Ephraim. *Laocoön: An Essay on the Limits of Painting and Poetry.* Trans. Edward Allen McCormick. Baltimore: Johns Hopkins University Press, 1984.
Lewis, C. S. *The Allegory of Love: A Study in Medieval Tradition.* London: Oxford University Press, 1936.
Madsen, Deborah L. *Rereading Allegory: A Narrative Approach to Genre.* New York: St. Martin's, 1994.
Mann, Thomas. *Death in Venice.* Trans. Clayton Koelb. New York: Norton, 1994.
McHale, Brian. "*En Abyme:* Internal Models and Cognitive Mapping." In *A Sense of the World: Essays on Fiction, Narrative, and Knowledge,* ed. John Gibson, Wolfgang Huemer, and Luca Pocci. New York: Routledge, 2007. 189–205.
———. "Weak Narrativity: The Case of Avant-Garde Narrative Poetry." *Narrative* 9 (2001): 161–67.
Muir, Edwin. "Franz Kafka." In *Kafka: A Collection of Critical Essays,* ed. Ronald Gray. Englewood Cliffs, NJ: Prentice-Hall, 1962. 33–44.
Nelles, William. *Frameworks: Narrative Levels and Embedded Narrative.* New York: Peter Lang, 1997.
Nietzsche, Friedrich. *The Birth of Tragedy and The Genealogy of Morals.* Trans. Francis Golffing. New York: Doubleday, 1956.
Niranjana, Tejaswini. *Siting Translation: History, Post-Structuralism, and the Colonial Context.* Berkeley: University of California Press, 1992.

Nugent, S. Georgia. *Allegory and Poetics: The Structure and Imagery of Prudentius' "Psychomachia."* New York: Verlag Peter Lang, 1985.
Oppenheimer, Judy. *Private Demons: The Life of Shirley Jackson.* New York: Putnam, 1988.
Orwell, George. *Animal Farm.* New York: Harcourt, Brace and World, 1946.
———. *The Collected Essays, Journalism, and Letters of George Orwell, Volume 3: As I Please 1943–1945.* Ed. Sonia Orwell and Ian Angus. New York: Harcourt, Brace and World, 1968.
Osborne, Charles. *Kafka.* New York: Barnes and Noble, 1967.
Paris, Bernard J. *Imagined Human Beings: A Psychological Approach to Character and Conflict in Literature.* New York: New York University Press, 1997.
Parker, Kevin. "Winckelmann, Historical Difference and the Problem of the Boy." *Eighteenth-Century Studies* 25 (1992): 523–44.
Paxon, James. *The Poetics of Personification.* Cambridge: Cambridge University Press, 1994.
Phelan, James. "Editor's Column: Voice, He Wrote." *Narrative* 13 (2005): 1–10.
———. *Experiencing Fiction: Judgments, Progressions, and the Rhetorical Theory of Narrative.* Theory and Interpretation of Narrative Series. Columbus: The Ohio State University Press, 2007.
———. *Living to Tell about It: A Rhetoric and Ethics of Character Narration.* Ithaca, NY: Cornell University Press, 2005.
———. *Narrative as Rhetoric: Technique, Audiences, Ethics, Ideology.* Theory and Interpretation of Narrative Series. Columbus: The Ohio State University Press, 1996.
———. *Reading People, Reading Plots: Character, Progression, and the Interpretation of Narrative.* Chicago: University of Chicago Press, 1989.
———. *Worlds from Words: A Theory of Language in Fiction.* Chicago: University of Chicago Press, 1981.
Politzer, Heinz. *Franz Kafka: Parable and Paradox.* Ithaca, NY: Cornell University Press, 1962.
Prince, Gerald. *A Dictionary of Narratology.* Lincoln: University of Nebraska Press, 1989.
———. *Narrative as Theme: Studies in French Fiction.* Lincoln: University of Nebraska Press, 1992.
Prudentuis. *The Poems of Prudentius, Volume 2: Apologetic and Didactic Poems.* Trans. Sister M. Clement Eagan. The Fathers of the Church Series 52. Washington, DC: Catholic University of America Press, 1965.
Quilligan, Maureen. *The Language of Allegory: Defining the Genre.* Ithaca, NY: Cornell University Press, 1979.
Quintilian. *The Orator's Education: Books 6–8.* Ed. and trans. Donald A. Russell. The Loeb Classical Library 126. Cambridge, MA: Harvard University Press, 2001.
Rabinowitz, Peter. *Before Reading: Narrative Conventions and the Politics of Interpretation.* Ithaca, NY: Cornell University Press, 1987.
Reed, T. J. *"Death in Venice": Making and Unmaking a Master.* New York: Twayne, 1994.
———. *Thomas Mann: The Uses of Tradition.* New York: Oxford University Press, 1974.
Ritter, Naomi. "*Death in Venice* and the Tradition of European Decadence." In *Approaches to Teaching Mann's "Death in Venice" and Other Short Fiction*, ed. Jeffrey B. Berlin. New York: Modern Language Association of America, 1992. 86–92.
Rolleston, James, ed. *Twentieth-Century Interpretations of "The Trial."* Englewood Cliffs, NJ: Prentice-Hall, 1976.

Ron, Moshe. "The Restricted Abyss: Nine Problems in the Theory of *Mise-en-Abyme*." *Poetics Today* 8 (1987): 417–38.

Rorty, Richard. *Contingency, Irony, and Solidarity.* New York: Cambridge University Press, 1989.

———. "The Last Intellectual in Europe." In *George Orwell,* ed. Graham Holderness, Bryan Loughrey, and Nahem Yousaf. New Casebooks. New York: Saint Martin's, 1998. 139–60.

Roth, Philip. *American Pastoral.* New York: Vintage, 1997.

———. *Everyman.* Boston: Houghton Mifflin, 2006.

Salerno, Steven. *Coco the Carrot.* Delray Beach, FL: Marshall Cavendish, 2002.

Schiller, Friedrich. "Naive and Sentimental Poetry" and "On the Sublime." Trans. Julius A. Elias. New York: Frederick Ungar, 1966.

Schless, Howard H. "The Backgrounds of Allegory: Langland and Dante." *Yearbook of Langland Studies* 5 (1991): 129–42.

Scholes, Robert, and Robert Kellog. *The Nature of Narrative.* New York: Oxford University Press, 1996.

Shackleford, Laura. "Narrative Subjects Meet Their Limits: John Barth's 'Click' and the Remediation of Hypertext." *Contemporary Literature* 46 (2005): 275–310.

Shakespeare, William. *Hamlet.* Oxford World's Classics. New York: Oxford University Press, 1998.

———. *Romeo and Juliet.* Oxford World's Classics. New York: Oxford University Press, 2000.

Singleton, Charles S. *An Essay on the "Vita Nuova."* Cambridge, MA: Harvard University Press, 1958.

Spenser, Edmund. *Edmund Spenser's Poetry.* 2nd ed. Ed. Hugh Maclean. New York: Norton, 1982.

Stach, Reiner. *Kafka: The Decisive Years,* trans. Shelley Frisch. New York: Harcourt, 2005.

Teskey, Gordon. *Allegory and Violence.* Ithaca, NY: Cornell University Press, 1996.

Thiher, Allen. *Franz Kafka: A Study of the Short Fiction.* Twayne's Studies in Short Fiction 12. Boston: Twayne, 1990.

Tobin, Robert. "The Life and Work of Thomas Mann: A Gay Perspective." In *Thomas Mann: Death in Venice,* ed. Naomi Ritter. Case Studies in Contemporary Criticism. New York: Bedford Books, 1998. 225–44.

Wasserman, Julian N. "The Sphinx and the Rough Beast: Linguistic Struggle in Chinua Achebe's *Things Fall Apart*." In *Understanding "Things Fall Apart": Selected Essays and Criticism,* ed. Solomon O. Iyasere. Troy, NY: Whitson, 1998. 77–85.

Weinstein, Philip. *Unknowing: The Work of Modernist Fiction.* Ithaca, NY: Cornell University Press, 2005.

White, Hayden. *The Content of the Form: Narrative Discourse and Historical Representation.* Baltimore: Johns Hopkins University Press, 1987.

Whitman, Jon. *Allegory: The Dynamics of an Ancient and Medieval Technique.* Oxford: Clarendon, 1987.

Wimsatt, W. K., and Monroe Beardsley. *The Verbal Icon: Studies in the Meaning of Poetry.* Lexington: University of Kentucky Press, 1954.

Winckelmann, Johann Joachim. *Reflections on the Imitation of Greek Works in Painting and Sculpture.* Trans. Elfriede Heyer and Roger C. Norton. La Salle, IL: Open Court, 1987.

Wood, James. "Letting Go." *The New Republic,* May 22, 2006, 28–32.

Worthington, Marjorie. "Done with Mirrors: Restoring the Authority Lost in John Barth's *Funhouse*." *Twentieth-Century Literature* 47 (2001): 114–36.
Yarmove, Jay A. "Jackson's 'The Lottery.'" *Explicator* 52 (1994): 242–45. Retrieved from EBSCOhost database (accessed July 20, 2010).
Zamir, Tzachi. *Double Vision: Moral Philosophy and Shakespearean Drama*. Princeton, NJ: Princeton University Press, 2007.
Zola, Émile. Preface to the second edition of *Thérèse Raquin*, by Émile Zola. Trans. Leonard Tancock. New York: Penguin, 1962. 21–27.

Index

Abbott, H. Porter, 92–93
Achebe, Chinua. See *Things Fall Apart*
Aeneid (Virgil), 172n17, 176
Aesthetics. *See* allegory; *Death in Venice*
aesthetic correlative, 163–64, 169, 179
Aesop. *See* "The Fox and the Grapes"
"Affective Fallacy, The" (Wimsatt and Beardsley), 164
Ahmad, Aijaz, 22n13
Alice in Wonderland (Carrol), 120
Alighieri, Dante, 65n11, 189; and allegoresis, 26–27; and allegory, 150–51. See also *The New Life*; *Divine Comedy*
allegoresis, 27–28, 27n18, 36n1, 93, 111, 131, 137, 140–44, 147, 159. *See also* Dante
allegory: and aesthetic judgments, 20–21, 28, 34–35, 137; attitudes toward, 33–36, 149; and character names, 48–49, 104–6; and characterization, 25–26, 168–81; and children's literature, 30n20, 50–55; death of, 1–3, 20, 33–34, 129; definition of, 8–15, 19, 37; and figuration, 12–13; and formalism, 24–26; and genetic concerns, 17–24; and genre, 3–4, 7, 16, 19, 33, 80, 141; and historical context, 21; levels of, 150, 157, 182, 189–92; metaphor, compared to, 4–7; narrative structure of, 5–8, 10, 11n6, 13–15, 130–33, 148; in non-allegorical narratives, 48, 79–128, 197; and parable, 6–7, 92–99; rhetorical approach to, 9, 21, 193–98; rhetorical origins, 4, 14–15; symbol, compared to, 13–15, 34, 72–74, 90; theme, relationship to, 130; and third-world literature, 21–24; and transformation, 5–6, 8, 10–12, 29, 133–35, 157–58, 168, 190. *See also* allegoresis; embedded allegory; ironic allegory; strong allegory; phenomenon; thematic allegory; theme; weak allegory
Allegory: The Theory of a Symbolic Mode (Fletcher), 34–36, 152–53
Alter, Robert, 78
American Pastoral (Roth), 130, 137–48, 149; Swede as allegory, 138–48; Swede as symbol, 138; narrative voice, 145–46. *See also* irony;

236 · Index

rhetorical purpose; thematic allegory; theme; voice
Amory, Frederic, 161n12
Anatomy of Criticism: Four Essays (Frye), 15, 27, 35, 56–57, 70, 93, 131–32, 141, 148
Animal Farm (Orwell), 11, 17–32, 42, 52, 70, 186, 195; aesthetic judgments of, 20–21; and character, 25; and intrinsic genre 30; language of 25; readers' initial reactions to, 29–30; and rhetorical situation, 24, 31; as strong allegory, 36–38; and theme, 133–34. *See also* personification; phenomenon transformed; rhetorical purpose; textual phenomena; theme
Aristotle, 113
Ast, Friedrich, 195–96
Attridge, Derek, 136–37
Atwell, David, 136n5
authorial audience, 28, 40–43, 45, 49, 150, 197; in children's literature, 52; in *The Metamorphosis,* 64; narrative audience, compared to, 37–40, 162. *See also* "The Lottery"; Rabinowitz; strong allegory

Barney, Stephen, 111
Barth, John, 106–7, 107n20; *Lost in the Funhouse,* 192. *See also* "Click"; *The End of the Road*
Barthes, Roland, 72n19, 73
Battersby, James, 194n1
Beardsley, Monroe. *See* "The Affective Fallacy"
"Before the Law" (Kafka), 94–99, 104, 109, 114; and *Elizabeth Costello,* 117–28. See also *The Trial*
Beissner, Friedrich, 67
Benjamin, Walter, 3n3, 55n6, 71, 73–74, 78
Berek, Peter, 27n18
Bitzer, Lloyd, 24, 55. *See also* rhetorical situation
Blindness and Insight (de Man), 14, 71–73, 74n18, 74n19
Bloomfield, Morton, 24–25

Boccaccio, Giovanni, 189
Booth, Wayne, 25, 38–39, 69
Brinkley, Edward S., 168n15
Brod, Max, 55n6, 67
Bruner, Jerome, 183
Buchanan, Ian, 22n13
Bunyan, John. See *Pilgrim's Progress*
Butler, Judith, 11

Calasso, Roberto, 78
Caserio, Robert L., 14n8
Cervo, Nathan, 48–49
Chambers, Aiden, 52
Christ, Jesus, 5, 7, 48–49
Chronicle, San Francisco, 43
Clarke, Bruce, 58n8, 135n4
"Click" (Barth), 9, 113n23, 149n1, 182–92, 196; and embedded allegory, 182–90; as postmodern allegory, 182–83, 189–91, 196; and strong allegory, 189–92; and thematic allegory, 186–89; and theme, 183. *See also* implied author; phenomenon transformed; rhetorical purpose; theme; voice
Clifford, Gay, 13, 28, 93, 94n14
Cocks, Neil, 52
Coco the Carrot (Salerno), 50–55, 63, 135. *See also* feedback loop; rhetorical purpose; textual phenomena; theme; weak allegory
Coetzee, J. M. See *Elizabeth Costello*
Cohn, Dorrit, 166n14, 180
Coleridge, Samuel, 3; and allegory/symbol distinction, 34
Collins, Billy, 189; *see also* "The Death of Allegory"
Consigny, Scott, 180n22
Copeland, Rita, 36n1
Corngold, Stanley, 73–78
Crews, Frederick, 67
Curious George (Rey), 53–54

Dällenbach, Lucien, 81–82
Dante. *See* Alighieri, Dante
Darwin, Charles, 62
Davidson, Donald, 136

Death in Venice (Mann), 150, 158–81; and aesthetics, 160–81; and decadence, 168n15; and Eros, 158–59, 171; as gay novel, 159–61; and ironic allegory, 149–81; narrator of, 160, 162, 166–68, 170–71, 174, 176–77, 180–81; and *The New Life*, 158–60, 162–64, 171–73, 175, 177, 180–81. *See also* implied author; irony; phenomenon transformed; rhetorical purpose; theme
"Death of Allegory, The" (Collins), 1–2, 129–30. *See also* irony
de Man, Paul, 3n3, 36n1, 71–73, 77. *See also Blindness and Insight*
Dentan, Michel, 67
dependent embedded allegory, 99–106; definition of, 99; effect of, 104–6. See also *The End of the Road*
Derrida, Jacques, 86n8
Dichter. See *Schriftsteller*
Dionysus, 179, 179n21
Divine Comedy, The (Dante), 3, 56, 153, 156–59
Dovey, Teresa, 136n5

Edmundson, Mark, 115n25
Elder, Arlene, 83
Eliot, T. S. *See* objective correlative
Elizabeth Costello (Coetzee), 114–28, 136–37, 197–98; allegory of the frogs, 122–24; and animal rights, 124–28; and "A Report to an Academy," 116–18, 126–27; sympathetic imagination, 125–27; and *The Trial*, 117–28. *See also* implied author; irony; mimesis; phenomenon transformed; rhetorical purpose; theme
embedded allegory, 8, 79–128; definition of, 79–80; *mise-en-abyme*, compared to, 81–82, 89, 95, 98, 100; types of, 81. *See also* "Click"; dependent embedded allegory; independent embedded allegory; interdependent embedded allegory
Emrich, Wilhelm, 62
End of the Road, The (Barth), 100–114;

characters and character names, 104–5; and dependent embedded allegory, 100–106; identity, theme of 102–3, 106; and interdependent embedded allegory, 109–14; Manichaean narrative in, 109–14; and Pygmalion, 108. *See also* implied author; irony; phenomenon transformed; theme; voice
Everyman, 39, 64, 92–93, 105, 191; Roth's *Everyman*, 135–36

Faerie Queene (Spencer), 18n10, 153
Falk, Eugene, 40–41
feedback loop, 16, 28–30, 88; and *Coco the Carrot*, 52; and embedded allegory, 80; and interdependent embedded allegory, 114; and "The Lottery," 47–49; and *The Metamorphosis*, 61; and strong allegory, 32, 40; and weak allegory, 194. *See also* Phelan
Fickert, Kurt, 92
Fineman, Joel, 72n16
Flaubert, Gustave, 21
Fletcher, Angus. *See Allegory: The Theory of a Symbolic Mode*
Flores, Ralph, 3n3
focalization. *See* perspective
Ford, Richard, 10
Forster, E. M., 110
"Fox and the Grapes, The": Aesop, 6–8, 11–12; La Fontaine, 12
Frankenstein: or, The Modern Prometheus (Shelley), 153
Frederick the Great, 168, 169n16
Freud, Sigmund, 78; and uncanny 120
Frye, Northrop. See *Anatomy of Criticism*

Gadamer, Hans-Georg, 33–34
Genette, Gérard, 80n1, 87
genre. *See* allegory
genre, intrinsic. *See* Hirsch
Gide, André, 81
Goethe, Johann, 169
Gray, Richard, 55n6

Gray, Ronald, 91–92
Greenberg, Martin, 62
Greenfield, Sayre, 27

Haeckel, Ernst, 62
Handbook to Literature (Holman and Harmon), 13
Hanson, Jim, 15, 72
Harlow, Barbara, 85–89, 110
Harmon, William. See *Handbook to Literature*
Head, Dominic, 136n5
Heidegger, Martin, 59
Heller, Erich, 55n6
Henel, Ingeborg, 90, 97–98
hermeneutic circle, 169, 195–96
hermeneutics, 7, 10–12, 16, 21, 27–30, 32, 38–39, 41, 48–49, 55–56, 62, 65, 70n14, 74n18, 82, 89, 99, 104, 110, 116, 131, 135, 161–62, 186, 189, 191. *See also* feedback loop; hermeneutic circle
Hirsch, E. D., 1, 19, 27, 194–95; and intrinsic genre, 30, 37, 42, 51; and meaning 39
Holman, C. Hugh. See *Handbook to Literature*
Holz, Arno, 62
Homer, 6n4, 26, 89; *Iliad,* 133
Honig, Edwin, 1, 3, 8, 34–35, 77, 79–80, 82, 88, 95–97, 119
Hoy, David Couzens, 195
Hughes, Ted, 124–26, 128

implied author: and "Click," 192; and *Death in Venice,* 180–81; and *Elizabeth Costello,* 128; and *The End of the Road,* 110, 112, 114; and *The Metamorphosis,* 63–64, 67n13, 69–70; and strong allegory, 41; and theme, 135; and *Things Fall Apart,* 87. *See also* Phelan
implied reader, 52, 52n2, 53
independent embedded allegory, 8, 82–89, 100; compared to interdependent embedded allegory, 114; definition of, 81. *See also Things Fall Apart; The Trial*
intention, authorial. *See* rhetorical purpose
interdependent embedded allegory, 106–27; relationship to host narrative, 109–10, 114, 127–28; compared to independent embedded allegory, 121, 121n28; and *Elizabeth Costello,* 114–27; and *The End of the Road,* 109–14
interpretation, concordant, 40–41, 49
ironic allegory, 159, 180, 193, 196; definition of, 9, 150; 149–81. *See also Death in Venice*
irony: allegory, compared to 38; and *American Pastoral,* 138; and de Man, 14, 72; and *Death in Venice,* 160, 162, 176, 180–81; and "The Death of Allegory," 130; and *Elizabeth Costello,* 116, 119; and *The End of the Road;* liberal irony, 123; and "The Lottery," 48
Irr, Caren, 22n13

Jackson, Shirley: "Biography of a Story," 41–43, 47–48, 189. *See also* "The Lottery"
Jakobson, Roman, 72n16
Jameson, Fredric, 21–22, 26, 32, 36, 88, 130–31
Jauss, Hans-Robert, 161
Johnson, Samuel, 65–66, 143–144
Joyce, James, 115

Kafka, Franz: and allegory, 55–56, 84, 194, 197; "A Country Doctor," 94n13; and embedded allegory, 110, 114–15; "A Dream," 61; and naturalism, 60–63; relationship with father, 60; and vermin, 60, 75–76. *See also The Metamorphosis;* metaphor; "A Report to an Academy"; *The Trial*
Kant, Immanuel, 167
Kegley, Jacquelyn, 104–5, 110, 114

Kelley, Alice van Buren, 161n11
Kelley, Theresa, 1
Kellogg, Robert. See *The Nature of Narrative*
Kirchberger, Lida, 169n16
Koelb, Clayton, 55–56, 68
Köhler, Wolfgang, 126–27
Kossew, Sue, 136n5

Lacan, Jacques, 72n16
La Fontaine, Jean. See "The Fox and the Grapes"
Lamberton, Robert, 26n16
Lanser, Susan, 112
Laocoön, 172, 174–76, 178
Lessing, Gotthold, 169–70, 175–78
Lévi-Strauss, Claude, 72n16
"Lottery, The" (Jackson), 41–49, 52, 195; and authorial audience, 42–43, 45–46; characters, names of, 48–49; and Holocaust, 46; and narrative audience, 46; narrator, 43–44, 46–47; reader response to, 41–42; and scapegoating, 41, 45, 48. See also feedback loop; *The New Yorker*; rhetorical purpose; textual phenomena; theme; voice

Mann, Thomas. See *Death in Venice*
McDonald, Peter, 136n5
McHale, Brian, 54, 81–82, 100
Melville, Stephen, 36n1
Metamorphosis, The (Kafka), 56–78, 92–93, 98, 121, 158; compared to strong allegory, 58–59, 70–71, 77–78; and perspective, 67–69; and theme, 158; and voice, 67–70. See also authorial audience; feedback loop; implied author; mimesis; personification; phenomenon transformed; rhetorical purpose; textual phenomena; voice
metaphor, 4–7, 89, 104; and Kafka, 60, 74–77; paralogical, 6, 13. See also allegory

metonymy, 4–5, 127–28
Milosz, Czeslaw, 126n30
mimesis, 13, 25, 40, 84, 89, 92, 104–5, 129–30, 137, 144, 146, 160; in *Elizabeth Costello*, 112–118, 122, 128–30; in *The Metamorphosis*, 60, 62–66, 78
mise-en-abyme. See embedded allegory
motif, 40–41, 49, 80, 95, 133, 160. See also theme
Muir, Edwin, 90

Nabokov, Vladimir, 20
narrative audience, 52, 153, 197; compared to authorial audience, 37–40
narrative progression, 14, 45, 51, 93, 111, 113, 141–42, 147, 175, 190, 196. See also Phelan
Nature of Narrative, The (Scholes and Kellogg), 13
Nelles, William, 81n3
New Life, The (Dante), 150–59; Beatrice, 151, 153–58; death of Beatrice, 156–57; love, Christian, 151–59. See also *Death in Venice*; phenomenon transformed; theme
New Yorker, The: and "The Lottery," 41–43, 49
Nietzsche, Friedrich, 179n21
Nugent, Georgia S., 105–6

objective correlative, 163–64. See also aesthetic correlative
Oppenheimer, Judy, 41–43 49
Orwell, George, 18, 66n12, 134n3, 189–90; "Shooting the Elephant," 23–24. See also *Animal Farm*
Osborne, Charles, 91

Paris, Bernard J., 105n17, 114
Parker, Kevin, 174n18
Paxon, James, 152n7
personification, 2, 49, 65n11, 151; in *Animal Farm*, 30–31; in *The Metamorphosis*, 58, 65–66, 92; and nar-

rative, 66; and plot, 143. See also *prosopopeia*
perspective, 18, 26, 30, 65, 67–70, 87, 96, 108, 119–20, 131, 143–48, 164, 166n14, 167, 179
Phelan, James, 15–16, 21, 28–30, 63n10, 69–70, 194n1, 196. See also feedback loop; implied author; rhetorical purpose; rhetorical theory of narrative
phenomenon transformed, 5, 8–13, 19, 141–42, 195–96, 198; and *Animal Farm*, 20, 29, 133, 186; and "Click," 182–86; and *Death in Venice*, 169; and *Elizabeth Costello*, 123; and *The End of the Road*, 103; and ironic allegory, 150; and *The Metamorphosis*, 58–61, 63; and *The New Life*, 157–58; and strong allegory, 37, 40; and theme, 134–36; and *Things Fall Apart*, 85; and *The Trial*, 91n11, 93–94; and weak allegory, 53–54, 90.
Piers Plowman (Langland), 68, 134
Pilgrim's Progress, The (Bunyan), 3, 33, 64, 68, 92, 105, 153
Plato, 161, 177n19
point of view. *See* perspective
Politzer, Heinz, 55n6, 91, 95n15
Prince, Gerald, 133–35, 133n2, 142
prosopagnosia, 152n6
prosopopeia, 151–53. See also voice
Prudentius. See *Psychomachia*
Psychomachia, The (Prudentius), 33, 105–6
Pygmalion, 108, 170

Quilligan, Maureen, 27, 106n19
Quintilian, 4–7, 13

Rabinowitz, Peter J., 37, 40, 42, 52, 59, 99, 197. See also authorial audience
reader. See authorial audience; narrative audience
readerly concerns, 26–32. See also Phelan

Reed, T. J., 160, 163, 165n13
"Report to an Academy, A" (Kafka), 61. See also *Elizabeth Costello*
rhetorical purpose, 7–13, 16, 21, 38, 194–95; *American Pastoral*, 141; *Animal Farm*, 17–19, 27, 38; "Click," 182, 186; *Coco the Carrot*, 50–52, 54; *Death in Venice*, 159, 162, 181; *Elizabeth Costello*, 114; "The Lottery," 43, 48–49; *The Metamorphosis*, 59–78; *The Trial*, 59
rhetorical situation, 17, 24, 31, 46, 55, 87n9, 99. See also Bitzer
rhetorical theory of narrative, 15–17, 28, 52n3, 53, 79–82, 158, 194, 196.
Ritter, Naomi, 168n15
Rockwell, Norman, 44
Ron, Moshe, 81n4, 82n6
Rorty, Richard, 20, 24, 123–24
Roth, Philip, 189. See also *American Pastoral*; *Everyman*
Rousseau, Jean-Jacques, 72

Sacks, Oliver, 183
Saint Sebastian, 174
Salerno, Steven. See *Coco the Carrot*
Saussure, Ferdinand, 72n16
Scheherazade, 189
Schiller, Friedrich, 165–66, 168, 169–71, 177
Schless, Howard, 65n11
Scholes, Robert. See *The Nature of Narrative*
Schriftsteller; compared to *Dichter*, 163, 165
Shakespeare, William, 80, 88, 155, 163–64
simile, 4–5; Homeric, 6n4, 89
Singleton, Charles S., 157
Socrates, 107
Sontag, Susan, 136
Spencer, Edmund. See *The Faerie Queene*
SpongeBob SquarePants, 54
Stach, Reiner, 60, 99
Steig, William, 52n4

strong allegory, 8–9, 29–32, 33–49, 52–54, 56–60, 63, 66, 70–71, 77–79, 85, 91, 93–95, 104–5, 131, 134–35, 142, 146n10, 149n1, 157–58, 193–97; and audience, 37–40; and character, 104–5; and theme, 40–41, 135. *See also* feedback loop; *Animal Farm*; "The Lottery"
synecdoche, 4–5, 98, 152
Szeman, Imre, 22n13

Teskey, Gordon, 65–66, 123, 143
textual phenomena, 16, 24–26, 39; and *Animal Farm*, 28–30, 31, 36; and *Coco the Carrot*, 50, 52; and embedded allegory, 80, 106, 114; and "The Lottery," 49; and *The Metamorphosis*, 78; and *Things Fall Apart*, 88; and *The Trial*, 98–99
thematic allegory, 8, 129–48, 186–89; definition of, 141
theme: and *American Pastoral*, 149; and *Animal Farm*, 25, 31; and "Click," 182–83, 189–91; and *Coco the Carrot*, 52; and *Death in Venice*, 168n15; definitions of, 40–41, 142; and *Elizabeth Costello*, 116; and *The End of the Road*, 110n22; and Kafka, 67; and "The Lottery," 49; in mimetic narratives, 13; and *The New Life*, 156; as textual phenomenon, 8, 26, 197; and *Things Fall Apart*, 86. *See also* thematic allegory
Thiher, Allen, 65
Things Fall Apart (Achebe), 83–89, 110; Okonkwo's suicide, 87–88; "Tortoise and the Birds" fable, 84–89, 104, 109; and tragedy, 83–84. *See also* implied author; independent embedded allegory; phenomenon transformed; rhetorical purpose; textual phenomena; theme

Tobin, Robert, 160–61
tone. *See* voice
Trial, The (Kafka), 59, 61, 70n14, 83, 86n8, 104, 109, 114; and embedded allegory, 89–99; in *Elizabeth Costello*, 115–28. *See also* "Before the Law"; phenomenon transformed; rhetorical purpose; textual phenomena; theme
trope, 4–8. *See also* allegory; metaphor; metonymy; simile; synecdoche

voice, 35; and *American Pastoral*, 145; and "Click," 192; and *The End of the Road*, 112; and "The Lottery," 47; and *The Metamorphosis*, 63–70; and *prosopopeia*, 152

Wagenbach, Klaus, 62
Wasserman, Julian, 88
weak allegory, 8, 50–78, 157–58, 194; definition of, 54; and poststructuralism, 71–78; and theme, 134–35. *See also* feedback loop; *Coco the Carrot*; *The Metamorphosis*
weak narrativity. *See* McHale
Weinstein, Philip, 70n14
White, Hayden, 10
Whitman, Jon, 36
Whitman, Walt, 25n15
Wimsatt, W. K. *See* "The Affective Fallacy"
Winckelmann, Johann, 169–70, 172–77, 179
Wordsworth, William, 14, 72, 74
Worthington, Marjorie, 191

Yarmove, Jay A., 46, 49

Zola, Émile, 46, 49

www.ingramcontent.com/pod-product-compliance
Lightning Source LLC
Chambersburg PA
CBHW030134240426
43672CB00005B/130